SPECIAL ARTIST'S
HANDBOOK

ENGAGING ART ACTIVITIES FOR ALL STUDENTS • ART HEROES IN ART HISTORY & EVERYDAY HEROES
ADAPTATIONS FOR SPECIAL NEEDS INCLUDING AUTISTIC SPECTRUM DISORDER

SUSAN RODRIGUEZ

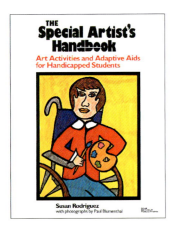

ABOUT THE COVER

The original cover (left) was designed by Dante Swinton, a student in the Philadelphia School District's Overbrook Educational Center for Students with Visual Impairments in Philadelphia, Pennsylvania.

Front cover: Enthusiasm in the author's art room at the Overbrook Educational Center—which offered the only program for Students with Visual Impairment within the Philadelphia School District. They attend a Magnet Program for Art and Music, developed by the principal, Dr.Marilyn A. Moller, who employed the arts to sucessfully teach a wide spectrum of special needs in addition to visual impairment. Dr. Moller is presently the Dean of Students at Rosemont College in Rosemont, PA.

Back cover: Students display their creations, encouraged by art teacher Ellen Cohan, who sparks creativity at ChathamPark Elementary School in Havertown,PA.

The "Instant Art Show!" concept was created by author Susan Rodriguez, who taught in many spaces where a full critique and exhibition might not be available. The "Instant Art Show" closure to an art lesson caught on with the students, who were free to show their works, as well as see those of their classmates. It became a very popular "show stopper" and a handy inclusionary device.

Library of Congress Cataloging-in-Publication Data

Rodriguez, Susan, 1944-
 The special artist's handbook : engaging art activities for special needs including autism spectrum disorder / Susan Rodriguez. — Second [edition].
    pages cm
 ISBN 978-1-56290-708-2
 1. Children with disabilities—Education. 2. Art—Study and teaching. I. Title.

 LC4025.R63 2014
 371.9—dc23

                              2013043253

ISBN 978-1-56290-708-2

Printed in Hong Kong

Crystal Productions

THIS BOOK IS DEDICATED TO THE MEMORY OF TOM HUBBARD,
a man OF SPIRIT and VISION....

ACKNOWLEDGMENTS
PHOTOGRAPHIC and major contributions:

Bruce Lewis
May Sam
Krissy Krygiel-Evans
Amy Jared
Ellen Cohan
Paul Blumenthal

Heartfelt Gratitude...

The author extends her thanks to the many friends, colleagues, school districts, agencies, and students who have contributed to the production of *The Special Artist's Handbook*, 2014. Foremost, the generous assistance of May Sam, artist and educator, who represents the best of the Upper Darby School District in Pennsylvania, and truly allowed this book to be realized through her constant support and assistance...and thank you, dear Bruce! The dynamic Amy Jared, art educator of The Russell Byers Charter School in Philadelphia, Pennsylvania is deeply thanked, as are Ellen Cohan, art teacher extraordinaire, of Chatham Park Elementary School, Havertown School District. Thanks go to the assistance of Brian Elstein; dedicated art educator Argie Fafalios of Springfield High School District, Delaware County is further recognized.

Krissy Krygiel-Evans, the amazing art teacher of Uwchlan Hills Elementary School in Downingtown, Pennsylvania... Laura, Mark, Andrew and Scott Evans — how can we ever thank you! Further thanks to Emily Barthomew, A.J.Goepfert, Danielle Alvisi, Laura and Liam McDowell, as well as Mathew and Stephanie Tutterice. Esther Chwalow, consultant for deaf education, Tel Aviv, Israel is remembered. Paul, Ilana and Dena Blumenthal are greatly thanked — along with Leora Chwalow. Rande Blank, Karyn Tufarolo, Stacy Zellner, Margot Livingston, Stephanie Struse, Benjamin De Meo, Adres Lora, Mel Charkowski, Magan Truempy, Jordan White, Asdrey Irizarry, Hye Min Kim, Caitlan Renna, Christian Davidson and his talented nephew Stephen Davidson...of The University of the Arts in Philadelphia, Pennsylvania. Thanks go to Rande Blank for her support...and Rob Smith for photographic assistance. Hugs to precious friends Bette Star Simons, Helene Walsey and Rose Skolnick, always there for endless encouragement. Appreciation to The Philadelphia Museum of Art, thank you Barbara Bassett, Steve Wills, Street Thoma, Judy Wise and Marla Shoemaker for your friendship and inspiration! Understandably, the most profound appreciation goes to the many wonderful young artists — far too numerous to name — whose talented work lives within the pages of the new book. Please knoe that as many names as could be are included here — please forgive me if you don't see your name...you are appreciated just the same!

Further thanks to publisher Amy Woodworth, Lorry Hubbard, and Kelly Badeau of Crystal Productions. The kind contribution of June Murray James — professional interpreter of ASL for students who are deaf — we love you!

A special note of gratitude is extended to Marilyn Moller of Rosemont College, former principal of the Philadelphia School District's Overbrook Educational Center for visual impairment and blind education — whose belief in art in special needs, and the author, made the first edition of *The Special Artist's Handbook* possible.

Credit is given to the mouth and foot painters by the courtesy of the Association of Mouth and Foot Painting Artists Worldwide; The National Center on Workforce and Disability (NCWD), U.S. Department of Labor, Mid-Hudson Library System, Poughkeepsie, NY; Lifeprint.com; and to United Cerebral Palsy for permissions.

ABOUT THE AUTHOR: SUSAN RODRIGUEZ

Susan Rodriguez is an art educator, author, artist, and an accomplished teacher of students with special needs — as well as a recognized proponent for cultural understanding through the arts. She has taught children who are blind, visually impaired — and sighted — within the Philadelphia School District for three decades and is the repeated recipient of grants and honors for her work with special as well as non-disabled and bilingual students. Susan received **The National Presidential Honor of Pennsylvania Teacher of the Year** in 1996, and captured **numerous awards and commendations** as a classroom art teacher. She was further awarded the distinctive **Disney American Teacher of Visual Arts of the Year**, as well as the prestigious **Milken Family Foundation Outstanding Educator Award** in 1995 for her methods and leadership in teaching of art to all children. Susan is further a professional speaker on the topics presented here and more.

Inspired by her own students with visual impairments, Susan wrote her first book, *The Special Artist's Handbook*, for teachers of students with diverse exceptionalities. The revised edition of this popular book was published in 2014 by Crystal Productions. Susan credits her experience with her remarkable young artists with helping her to rethink the creative process. "It was my blind students who have taught me how to see — not with my eyes, but with my whole being, especially my heart."

As an exhibiting studio artist, Susan is devoted to teaching art — as well as enjoying, creating, and appreciating art. She is an Adjunct Full Professor at The University of the Arts + Design in Philadelphia, Pennsylvania where she collaborates programs between The Philadelphia Museum of Art and her Art Education university students. She is also active in professional development, primarily on the topics which her books represent. They are: *Art Smart!* (Museum and Art History for the Art Classroom); *Portfolios I and II*; *Culture Smart!* (Multicultural Learning through World Art); and *Travels with Monet*, published by Crystal Productions in 2011, representing the influential Claude Monet, as he traveled — both literally and figuratively — through Impressionism, Post-Impressionism, Early Modern Art, and Japanese Art.

Susan is an active member of the National Art Education Association (NAEA) and Pennsylvania Art Education Association (PAEA). She is a consultant — as well as a member — of many art advisory boards and panels, such as the U.S. Department of Education: The National Board for Professional Standards: Elementary to Middle School Art. She holds a B.F.A. and M.Ed. from Tyler School of Art, Temple University, and completed The Barnes Foundation Program of Appreciation and Philosophy of Art, in Merion, Pennsylvania. For her work in the art and education field, Rodriguez received an *Honorary Doctorate of the Fine Arts* from The Moore College of Art and Design. She is an advocate for the arts in education in an inclusive society. Susan is the wife of Costa, and mother of lovely daughter Nicole and son Rennie, who is married to Kelley. They have blessed her with grandbaby Tomas — a radiant promise of the future.

THAT WAS THEN...

You are an art teacher meeting a new class. One child, who is deaf, arrives with an interpreter. A young boy follows the tapping of his white cane as he enters the art room. A little girl, seated, rocks back and forth in her chair. Is she autistic? Good question. Another child refuses to sit down...all have disabilities. Some disabilities are apparent, while others are not visible.

Perhaps you have years of experience as an art educator, or maybe you are beginning your career. Whatever the extent of your background, you will likely be teaching students with exceptionalities similar to those just described. Either now — or in the near future — your role as an art teacher will be shaped by this reality.

Since Public Law 94-142, in 1973, granted "the right to education in the least restrictive environment" to students with disabilities, special needs students are very much a part of school populations.

Are art teachers prepared to respond to this challenge as sensitive and effective educators?

University art education programs cannot always be relied upon to fully train pre-service teachers for teaching art to exceptional students. Not until recently have courses been offered that attempt to fill the gap between special education and art education. While special education degrees may or may not be expected of art educators, the teaching of special students most definitely IS expected — by law. This clearly leaves the art teacher with a need for information and guidance. It is in response to this need that *The Special Artist's Handbook* was published....then and now! As a matter of fact, the educational direction for special needs today is a growing demographic.

In recognizing your special students, you will be accepting them and assisting them with art experiences. You do this when you set goals, with margins for interpretation. The art teacher should be aware that students may be more capable than they may appear. So while you adjust your expectations to include modest results, you may also be surprised by considerable accomplishments. Working with students who are disabled often produces the unexpected — which is why your lessons should be structured with room for individual creative growth.

In turn, art therapists understand modest results. The emphasis in art therapy is usually placed on the "process" — all that occurs within the art experience. The "product" or final outcome is secondary to the process itself, which holds the real therapeutic aspect. The sensory qualities of art materials are indeed a joy for any artist, while their manipulation can teach cognitive skills as well. Even if a final product is not of a recognizable nature, learning and enjoyment are occurring.

All this is important to remember because we as art educators look forward to a final product that communicates an idea. When that does not happen, professional frustration can set in. Keep in mind that development may be uneven in many special students, but it is still taking place.

As a creative teacher, no one has to convince you of the importance of art. You teach it because you believe in it, and you fully understand the extent of the value of art. Your students' work touches you. When that stops happening, file for retirement or put in for a transfer. Although the business of teaching may have its trying moments, you manage to keep finding new sources of strength, renewal, and inspiration — and everyone benefits.

...THIS IS NOW

It's been more than three decades since Public Law 94-142 was established — a law that was viewed by many as akin to Civil Rights for people with disabilities. In the eighties, along came the **Americans with Disabilities Act (ADA)**. The educational arm of this law is **IDEA**...the **Individuals with Disabilities Education Act,** which was revised in 2004. Among other aspects that grant an education in the least restrictive environment (LRE), the **language** of special education has changed. Most importantly, today it's ***people first***! What do we mean? Instead of saying "That handicapped student needs to board the bus," try, "That student is orthopedically impaired, so he'll need accommodation to board the bus." It may take some getting used to, but it is a more considerate, respectful way to treat anyone with a disability. There are many other terms that are no longer in use.

The goal of special education remains the same today as it did in the 1970s: prepare the student — as best as one is able — to participate as a contributing member in society, with the ability to "pursue happiness"... the same as anyone! Within the realm of educational terminologies, students are *included* in school and classroom activities. The word *inclusion* replaces "mainstreaming," which is no longer used.

What is important to keep in mind is that education...and special education particularly... is ever-evolving. Terms and descriptions change over time. The demographics of certain conditions shift as well. At this time, autistic spectrum disorder is growing exponentially. In our quest to recognize and help to remediate through identification of exceptionalities, we are simply making our best assessment of the situation — with or without an Individual Educational Plan (IEP). What may best explain why sometimes our best efforts fall short is this: There is simply no one-size-fits-all answer for any group or individual. While we have tons of information on Special Education at large, finding the most successful solution for a specific problem with a student with disabilities requires innovation, patience, and improvisation. Art teachers are at an advantage in this regard, for these elements are intrinsic to the creative process. As the great Albert Einstein once stated, "*Imagination is more important than knowledge.*" As you may know, Einstein, a true genius who advanced our world through discovery, was a person with learning disabilities.

Philosophically speaking, we are all in this together. Disabilities and conditions may be temporary or permanent...they may be congenital... or acquired through accident, injury, or disease. They may be emotional, cognitive, or physical, or present as a combination. The disability may be invisible or apparent. Few, if any conditions are fixed in time. Compassion — not pity — goes a long way. If you've ever broken a leg, for example, and needed a wheelchair for a while, you may have found yourself resenting a handicapped parking space occupied by a non-handicapped driver. Some nerve, right? There's nothing like firsthand experience to drive a point home.

On the other side of this equation is making assumptions. Students may appear disabled to the extent that one might make assumptions about their well-being or quality of life. There is no scientific basis to support the notion that a person who is blind and uses a seeing eye dog is any more or less well-adjusted or content than a star athlete or a fashion model. We can't superficially judge others nor generalize about their circumstances.

We do know that communication is a key factor in knowing more about ourselves and others. That's where *The Special Artist's Handbook* comes into play. The purpose of this book is to expand meaning...and not limit any one group to a particular activity based on a definition. Although specific adaptations are clearly needed and provided, consider other adaptations beyond the individuals you are teaching. Remember you are teaching students, not disabilities. Let your students show you what they can do.

HOW TO USE THIS BOOK

The Special Artist's Handbook is an art activities reference manual for art teachers, special education teachers, art teachers, classroom teachers, recreational therapists, parents, and anyone who is involved with the education of exceptional children. Art is an area of abundance for the special student. The book is divided into six major sections. The Art Activities section represents the heart of the book. The other sections support and expand upon the successful implementation of the art activities.

It is important to become familiar with the characteristic traits of the exceptionalities and to help select appropriate projects and approaches. The more you know about your students, the more likely you are to both meet their needs and be satisfied with the outcome.

RAINBOW SPECTRUM: AN OVERVIEW offers explanations of the more commonly occurring conditions seen in school settings. Along with this information, you'll find **ETIQUETTE... TIPS FOR INTERACTION WITH STUDENTS WITH DISABILITIES**...and **ART CHARTS**, a quick reference for art and disability information.

The **SIGN LANGUAGE GUIDE** is helpful for use with students who are deaf or hard of hearing...or with students on the autistic spectrum who are non-verbal.

ART ACTIVITIES. The activities are presented in an uncomplicated, step-by-step format. Each activity is designed as a core lesson unit that would be appropriate for any student, whether disabled or non-disabled. Specific adaptations and recommendations for each exceptionality appear with each lesson.

The activities are meant to foster student independence. Many times the interaction is placed with and between students, rather than between student and teacher. This encourages students to find their own style.

The Special Artists Handbook acknowledges every student's need for self-esteem, particularly students who may already have many difficulties to overcome. The projects build confidence. Lessons are meant to improve concepts and overall awareness. Activities are also "imagination tickling," which will captivate attention. The point is to get the student engaged in his or her work. A satisfied student means a satisfied teacher, so all are winners.

ADAPTIVE AIDS. Section Three will make teachers aware of the many easy-to-construct devices that can be made from ordinary materials. These will enable students to fully participate in lessons from which they might otherwise be overlooked. Commercial aids are also widely available that will help students with physical disabilities.

The real value of the adaptive aids is that they give students independence. When teachers do not have to intervene in a technical process, it puts students in charge of their own work.

THE ART CLASSROOM. Section Four looks at the environment in which art is taking place. The removal of possible barriers — and making art activities more accessible — are important concerns for teachers. Room arrangements will be considered. This section also points out ways to maintain a healthier and safer art room.

THE SPECIAL MUSEUM OF ART. Eye-pleasing and idea-inducing images, created by our students. We are also reminded of the importance of museum education for all students... with suggestions and examples of museum accommodations for special programs and visits.

ART HEROES! Meet other artists with great spirit! Famous artists such as Frida Kahlo, Vincent van Gogh, and Henri Matisse remind us that sometimes, as Matisse said, "Creativity takes courage." Along with the famous notables, we'll meet artists who are orthopedically impaired — and paint by mouth or foot — or by touch, as is the case of sculptor Carol Saylor, who is deaf/blind. Art activity suggestions accompany this distinctive section.

contents

SECTION ONE: THE EXCEPTIONALITIES

SECTION TWO: ART ACTIVITIES

SECTION THREE: ADAPTIVE AIDS

SECTION FOUR: THE ART CLASSROOM

SECTION FIVE: THE SPECIAL ART MUSEUM

SECTION SIX: ART HEROES!

GLOSSARY

section one
THE EXCEPTIONALITIES

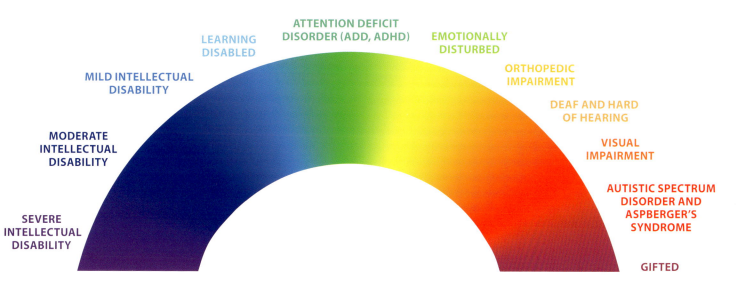

LEARNING DISABLED

ATTENTION DEFICIT DISORDER (ADD, ADHD)

EMOTIONALLY DISTURBED

MILD INTELLECTUAL DISABILITY

ORTHOPEDIC IMPAIRMENT

DEAF AND HARD OF HEARING

MODERATE INTELLECTUAL DISABILITY

VISUAL IMPAIRMENT

AUTISTIC SPECTRUM DISORDER AND ASPBERGER'S SYNDROME

SEVERE INTELLECTUAL DISABILITY

GIFTED

RAINBOW SPECTRUM: An overview to indentify special needs. The following categories are presented for your referral. Remember, all conditions exist on a spectrum, ranging from mild to severe.

INTELLECTUAL DISABILITY. The *medical* term Mental Retardation does cover the categories known as Severe, Profound, Trainable and Mild Intellectual Disability — all are spectrum disorders — but Mental Retardation is no longer accepted as an educational term! The term Mental Retardation is being discontinued by the medical community as well. Students with intellectual disabilities are on a spectrum that is principally determined by their cognitive function or IQ (the terminology has changed; the condition has not.) This is a cognitive impairment.

EMOTIONAL DISTURBANCE. This category refers to a student's difficulty in maintaining impulse control. Other aspects may include lack of appropriate interaction, general authority oppositional behavior and aggressiveness. Also, in this category are students who are socially withdrawn, and may be depressed. Often, refusal to adhere to classroom decorum is exhibited. The acronym ODD means oppositional defiance disorder. AOD represents authority oppositional disorder. This is an emotional disorder associated with maladaptive social interaction.

LEARNING DISABILITIES. Essentially, learning disability is a "brain processing" condition in which information is often misinterpreted. This includes **dyslexia**, which is the inability to make sense out of the printed page   reading and writing with accuracy and understanding is problematic. Other aspects may include organizational challenges, as well as forms of graphic mispresentation (dysgrafia). Note: Attention Deficit Disorder (ADD) and Attention Deficit Hyperactive Disorder (ADHD) are disruptive patterns that affect learning. Although ADD and ADHD are arguably "learning disabilities," they should not be strictly categorized as such. ADHD typically presents with distracted behaviors that physically and cognitively interfere with focus on a task and learning overall. (Art activities that are adapted for students with emotional disturbance are often successful for use with students diagnosed as ADHD, although this does not imply emotional disturbance in ADHD.) This is an area impacted directly by neurological misinterpretation and should not be confused with intellectual disability.

ORTHOPEDIC IMPAIRMENT. A physical disability, such as multiple sclerosis or cerebral palsy, would appear in this category. Adaptive methods and materials in the art room are very helpful. It is important to remember that a wide variety of conditions would affect the locomotion and motor function of any particular student with orthopedic impairment. This is a physical disability associated with motor impairment and, in some cases, partial or full paralysis.

DEAF AND HARD OF HEARING. Deafness is a disability which affects the student's capacity to decipher certain words and sounds within a specific frequency range. Hearing loss can be measured and is quantified in a range from mild to severe. Communication can include lip reading, sign language and the spoken word. Appliances such as hearing aids or cochlear implants may be indicated for use. Decisions are made on the basis of individual evaluations. This is a sensory impairment.

VISUAL IMPAIRMENT. Sight loss is defined by the student's ability to visually identify objects, light sources, and details. Visual acuity, which is primarily determined through ophthalmological examinations, can vary dramatically. For example, what is commonly considered blindness is, by definition, called severe visual impairment. Contrary to conventional belief, blindness is rarely a complete lack of vision, as one might imagine total blackness. Conversely, the diagnosis of Legal Blindness does not define the extent of what a student sees. This is a sensory impairment.

GIFTED. Students who exhibit academic and intellectual abilities that exceed their developmental levels are typically considered gifted. While giftedness may be disputed as a special educational area in some districts, the fact remains that students who are mentally gifted require specially designed support services to appropriately meet their exceptionalities. Features of mentally gifted students may include demonstrated advance performance and higher level thinking skills, which would be evidenced in the creative arts as well as other subject areas. The social skill area may present difficulties for many gifted students. This is an advanced cognitive function by definition.

AUTISTIC SPECTRUM DISORDER AND ASPERGER'S SYNDROME. The category of Autism specifically refers to a set of behaviors that commonly appear early in the child's life. Children with Autistic Spectrum Disorder typically avoid eye contact — sometimes physical contact as well — and show little interest in conversation. Other characteristics include lack of peer interaction, inability to follow directions, and difficulty with creative expression. Additionally, some students may be unable to recognize the meaning of facial expressions ("mind blindness"). Repetitive behaviors, also known as "stimmies" (self-stimulation) involve perseveration (repetitive) movements, rocking, hand rolling, and hand flapping. Students with autism respond well to pictorial supports, sensory materials, and gross motor techniques. Repetitive behaviors are not exclusive to the Autistic spectrum.

Asperger's Syndrome is arguably viewed as an autistic condition that falls to the higher end of the autistic spectrum. Note: The term sometimes used to describe the group of these and other complex autistic disorders is Pervasive Developmental Disorder (PDD).

Unlike the previously described features of Autism, students with Asberger's typically have no speech or cognitive delays. A student with Asperger's Syndrome may initially appear as "normal" (neurologically typical). Students with Asperger's soon demonstrate that their focus is on self-initiated ideas, a behavior that is unlike that of their peers. For instance, they may become "experts" on trains while the teacher is presenting another topic. Other distinguishing features are the desire to socialize, although students with Asperger's may be unable to understand the subtleties of language, such as irony or humor — even the use of everday gestures. Also, there may be difficulty with abstract concepts, yet memory skills are good. Younger students with Asperger's Syndrome have been referred to as "little professors," consistent with their knowledge in select areas.

Generally, Autism Spectrum Disorder is considered a communication disorder with complexities and remains medically uncertain as to cause and origin.

A WORD TO THE READER: The conditions outlined and selected for this book are the ones most commonly seen in the classroom. Please keep in mind that there are many more conditions than addressed in this resource guide, especially when you realize that just about every diagnosis an adult might receive, a child may receive as well. Without creating a long, daunting list, know that students may be diagnosed with rheumatoid arthritis, multiple sclerosis, bipolar disorder...just to name a few. Of course, these conditions may categorically fit into Orthopedic Disabilities, or Emotional Disturbance. Other considerations to note are students who present with the conditions listed on the following page.

TOURETTE SYNDROME is most frequently recognized by facial tics, and some vocalization as well. Blinking, coughing, throat-clearing, and sometimes uncontrolled body movement, such as twitching limbs, define Tourette Syndrome. The student has little or no control over these behaviors. Sometimes teachers work out classroom "signals" — if a student with Tourette Syndrome is having a bad day, a pre-understood "break time," negotiated between teacher and student — may then be strategically used, so that a student can regroup in a less restricted way, in a pre-designated space. Tourette Syndrome cannot be "hidden," although symptoms can sometimes be suppressed. Coprolalia — identified when the student repeatedly shouts out obscenities — represents only a small number of those with this disorder. Tourette Syndrome is sometimes considered a cousin of Obsessive Compulsive Disorder.

OBSESSIVE COMPULSIVE DISORDER (OCD). OCD is an anxiety disorder; however, not everyone with an anxiety disorder has OCD. Obsessive Compulsive Disorder is a condition with a very specific set of behaviors and is sometimes misdiagnosed, as well as misunderstood. There is nothing funny about OCD, although popular culture often uses the condition for comical derision or the brunt of bad jokes. Contrary to the exaggeration of the "neatness" myth (although the need for perfection may occur in OCD in various ways) students with OCD typically experience the repetition of disturbing, negative thoughts. There is also a drive to engage in ritualistic actions. One such compulsion is "checking/rechecking" — for instance, the need to be sure a door is locked properly. So-called "magical" numbers, phrases, or words may be involved in these and other actions as an illogical attempt to control events. If a particular, self-imposed number is not met, the student may feel that terrible consequences will result. OCD can be secretive, embarrassing, and excessively time-consuming. However, the most defining and dominant feature of the disorder is the fear of contamination, which may be quite severe. The good news is that OCD can be successfully treated through proper behavioral therapy. Exposure techniques, conducted by the behavioral therapist with patient cooperation, will help to gradually release even the most extreme fears. Talk therapy alone has been found to be of limited use when compared to the exacting methods of behavioral therapy.

BODY DYSMORPHIC DISORDER (BDD) is a disorder (or a part of other disorders) in which the individual regards his or her own appearance in a highly distorted way. For example, a student with everyday looks may truly believe he/she is ugly or repulsive — or a dangerously underweight person may regard herself as fat. BDD certainly plays a big part in anorexia, bulimia, and other eating disorders. All of these conditions share a false mirror of self-image, along with obsessive preoccupations. Because it is commonly the adolescent who comprises a large portion of the eating disorder population, we as teachers (particularly art teachers) can try to help our students gain a better sense of confidence through acceptance, by examples of physical diversity. Images of various body types can be incorporated into activities, journals, and discussions. Also, beware of how you define a student's appearance. For instance, remarks such as "Wow, Tiffany, you look great... did you lose weight?" can actually feed into the wrong-minded idealism that backs up unrealistic expectations. Even when weight loss does equal better health, recognition might come with a more well-placed remark, such as "Tiffany, you are looking fit." As non-medical professionals, there is still much we can do — with the hope students with BDD and eating disorders are concurrently in treatment! These are very serious conditions that can be difficult to resolve and are life-threatening, often causing irreversible, chronic diseases. It certainly does not help that the media continues to barrage young people with constant, unachievable images — often with photograghic alteration. Is there a fashion or general audience magazine that does not feature a fabulous new diet monthly, supported by constant internet messages? It could be easily argued that we have become a nation obsessed by endless, unreasonable diets, and extreme weight control measures — strictly based on appearance, without real health issues in mind. In a smarter world, perhaps the "new normal" will begin by our openly accepting variety.

EPILEPSY. Many believe epilepsy no longer exists, much like the disappearance of polio. This is entirely incorrect. According to The Epilepsy Foundation, there are larger numbers of individuals diagnosed with epilepsy than those diagnosed with autistic spectrum disorder, cerebral palsy, multiple sclerosis, and Parkinson's disease — all combined! Epilepsy is a neurological disorder that requires public awareness. To identify the disorder... an individual with two unprovoked seizures per year typically indicates epilepsy. As a teacher, it is critically important to know what to do when a student has a seizure. For more information on seizure disorder, please see page 131.

ART CHART: A REFERENCE GUIDE FOR ART AND EXCEPTIONALITIES
SHORT DEFINITIONS OF TYPICAL CONDITIONS AND EXCEPTIONALITIES

INTELLECTUAL DISABILITY
(FORMERLY KNOWN AS MENTAL RETARDATION — A TERM NO LONGER ACCEPTABLE IN EDUCATION)

INTELLECTUAL DISABILITY: SEVERE (FORMERLY SEVERELY AND PROFOUNDLY IMPAIRED)

The student has limited experience with his or her environment. Art activities that focus on sensory interaction between the student and the materials is often the most satisfying. There is usually a response to the physical movement and textural qualities that are intrinsic to art experiences

STUDENT MAY NOT EXHIBIT:

1. **ABILITY TO UNDERSTAND DIRECTIONS.** Attention span is short.

2. **BASIC CONCEPTS.** May not understand simple concepts like in/out, up/down, etc.

3. **SENSORY DEVELOPMENT AND DISCRIMINATION.** May be tactilely defensive — repelled by certain textures.

4. **MOBILITY AND KINESTHETIC ABILITY.** Poor coordination. Not able to move one or more parts of the body in a functional way. Has difficulty walking, running, jumping, etc.

5. **AWARENESS OF BODY PARTS, SPATIAL RELATIONSHIPS.** May lack bilateral movement (two hands together). May be spastic or athetoid, or lack ability to cross arms past "midline" of body to opposite side.

6. **FINER GRASPING TECHNIQUE, FINE MOTOR SKILL.** May lack pincer grasp.

7. **APPROPRIATE GROUP BEHAVIORS AND SELF AWARENESS.** May "rock," make noises and gestures that are incongruous in the classroom. May exhibit "stimmies" — rocking, flicking fingers in front of face, banging, etc. May keep head down.

MAY REQUIRE:

One-step directions. Student needs steps broken down — he or she may not understand more than one direction at a time.

When instructing, gently turn student's head (if feasible)in the direction of the task. Student will need lots of time on an activity. Keep it simple. Give physical and verbal prompting. Reinforce repeatedly.

Demonstrate with concentrate objects and movement: i.e., produce both a big object and small object when showing size differences.

Concrete experience to point out differences, as in rough/smooth (i.e., providing sample of sandpaper and of satin.) Use desensitizing techniques for tactual aversions to paint, clay, etc. For example, introduce clay to student in small amounts, and allow student to get acquainted with the material. If student appears to be repelled by the clay, don't force him or her to continue. Remove the material and present it again at a later time.

Use student's "functional" body parts and try to incorporate lesser functioning body parts. Projects should be adapted so that student can carry them out. Teacher can help student to physically understand larger movements. Work with students and guide them through motions. Use physical prompting and verbal cues, i.e., "We are pounding the clay." Assist in activity and "fade out" as student learns the motion.

Gently ease students into movements by hand-over-hand method. Place student's hands in directions desired for activity, having student use one hand.

Work into smaller movements progressively from larger movements. Use adaptive techniques if possible.

Use student's name frequently: i.e., "Ms. Jones is helping Billy make a building." Use touch and eye contact to back up verbal communication. Attempt to limit socially unacceptable behavior by placing hand on student's upper arm, reminding him or her not to bang the desk, etc. Redirect attention.

Inappropriate behavior is often due to a lack of outside stimulation. Offer alternatives to unacceptable behavior — bring student's attention into activity. Recognize positive behavior with praise!

ART CHART: A REFERENCE GUIDE FOR ART AND EXCEPTIONALITIES
SHORT DEFINITIONS OF TYPICAL CONDITIONS AND EXCEPTIONALITIES

INTELLECTUAL DISABILITY: MODERATE (FORMERLY TRAINABLE MENTALLY RETARDED)

Generally should be able to do matching, sorting, random brush and crayon work, clay, paper tearing, building parts, and replication of simple forms. Many students with Down Syndrome are part of this group.

STUDENT MAY NOT EXHIBIT:	MAY REQUIRE:
1. **DEDUCTIVE REASONING, ABSTRACT THINKING.** Cannot usually form own conclusions based on information given by teacher.	No more than two to three steps at a time. Care should be taken not to overload with information, as it will overwhelm the student.
2. **CONCEPT DEVELOPMENT.**	Concrete examples, i.e., "stop/go," "in/out," "over/under" can be demonstrated to students. These are useful concepts for daily living.
3. **REFINED GROSS MOVEMENT.** May appear awkward, have difficulty navigating body spatially. May not handle art materials with ease.	Art lessons that involve gross movement (such as *Faces and Traces*, page 48) will create greater body awareness. Offer simple art materials and methods (clay, paint, crayons) until student seems ready for more complex projects. Teach proper materials usage.
4. **SOCIALIZATION SKILLS.** Often unwilling to participate. May display stubbornness, refusal to join group. May be tactually defensive.	Group activities that allow for positive "teamwork." Sharing experiences (such as the tactile explorations, page 34) help to improve class interaction. Desensitization may be used for tactual defensiveness — patience, this may take time.
5. **INDEPENDENCE, SELF-HELP.**	Give student work at his or her skill level so he or she will succeed. For example, if a student can sort objects well, let him or her sort out crayons. Give praise and support for a job well done.
6. **ABILITY TO COMMUNICATE IDEAS IN A DIRECT WAY.**	Listen to students' ideas with interest. Give them a chance to express themselves, without judging "correctness" of expression.

INTELLECTUAL DISABILITY: MILD (FORMERLY EDUCABLE MENTALLY RETARDED)

Often capable of some abstract thinking, and can sometimes do problem solving. Ability to follow and understand more complex directions varies with age levels and life experiences.

STUDENT MAY NOT EXHIBIT:	MAY REQUIRE:
1. **ABILITY TO FOLLOW COMPOUNDED DIRECTIONS.**	Break down multifaceted lessons into manageable chunks. Student can usually handle three or four steps, but attending to instruction depends on how many variables exist (motivation, interest, age, etc.) Repetition of instruction is often needed. Reminders and reinforcements are helpful.
2. **SELF-ESTEEM.** Easily frustrated. Students have greater awareness of perceived shortcomings, making self-acceptance difficult. Display of anger is not uncommon. Note: Bad behavior is often an expression of frustration and embarrassment.	Make sure student understands what a job requires in order to be done successfully. Goals should be clear and reasonable; offer praise and encouragement whenever it is indicated.
3. **LIFE EXPERIENCES.** Information and enrichment gathered through travel, general participation. May have limited opportunities to learn about world outside their immediate environment.	Bring in outside reference materials frequently. Share travel images, talk about events of interest. Neighborhood walks, museum visits are helpful. Use media to expand awareness. Holiday and seasonal lessons complement student's own experiences and are usually pleasant to recall.

ART CHART: A REFERENCE GUIDE FOR ART AND EXCEPTIONALITIES
short definitions of typical conditions and exceptionalities

learning disabilities [ADHD/ADD]

Dysfunction in the student's ability to process information, which affects basic learning skills. The student may be very successful in one academic area but very deficient in another.

Learning disabled students should typically have normal or above-normal intelligence.

STUDENT MAY NOT EXHIBIT:

MAY REQUIRE:

1. **TYPICAL PERCEPTION.** Can't seem to "make sense" out of information and directions. Has difficulty interpreting material. Because of difficulties with thought processes, ability to organize and plan may be affected.

Clear explanations. This doesn't mean "talking down"; It means using simple and straightforward language. Make sure that student understands one step before proceeding to the next. Do not bombard student with information; it tends to be overwhelming. Review requirements and directions whenever necessary.

2. **DIRECTIONALITY.** May have spatial orientation problems, be poorly coordinated. May confuse left and right, up and down, etc.

A starting point or reference point. This can be a line, a mark, or a physical demonstration. Teacher may need to guide student at certain times, but not at all times. Questions like "Where does it start? What comes first?" can be helpful.

3. **BASIC SKILLS.** Very common problem is dyslexia – problems with the ability to read. Words appear scrambled or in reverse ("d" for "b," "saw" becomes "was").

Demonstrate steps in lesson or process. Teacher cannot assume that students can read directions from chalkboard or print material. Allow extra time to complete task, if indicated.

4. **MEMORY** (visual, auditory). May lack short or long-term recall.

Reinforce directions. Ask students to feed back information. Repeat whenever necessary.

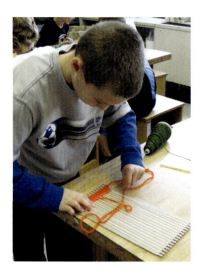

ART CHART: A REFERENCE GUIDE FOR ART AND EXCEPTIONALITIES
SHORT DEFINITIONS OF TYPICAL CONDITIONS AND EXCEPTIONALITIES

EMOTIONAL DISTURBANCE

Repeated, aggressive behavior that interferes with learning. Inappropriate behaviors may range from withdrawn and depressed to outright defiance.

The student can come from any social-economic background. Often the life and events outside of school contribute to the difficulties the student is undergoing. NOTE: Students whose behavior is extreme enough to threaten their own safety of the safety of others suggests a clinical and/or residential placement outside of the school and are cause for immediate action. Specific conditions inappropriate for the classroom include symptoms of psychiatric conduct disorder, such as harmful psychotic episodes or violent, threatening behaviors.

STUDENT MAY NOT EXHIBIT:	MAY REQUIRE:
1. **ABILITY TO CONCENTRATE.** May not be able to focus on the task- may be restless or appear uninterested. May refuse to work, often getting out of seat and wandering around the room.	High interest material. Projects that elicit personal involvement. Learning new techniques can provide challenges and force students to get involved with their work. Students need to experience concrete accomplishments to appreciate using their skills. Students should be encouraged to carry out all steps of an activity and complete it.
2. **SELF-ESTEEM.** May be withdrawn into own world and be isolated, with lack of interest in self and others. On the other side, may be attention-seeking, over reactive and ill-tempered. Mood swings are common.	Building better self-image. Projects that "accent the positive" help. Studio experiences often create opportunities for self-expression and self-exploration without placing rigid expectations on students. Reassurance and praise should be given whenever indicated.
3. **TYPICAL INTERPERSONAL RELATIONSHIPS.** May be distrustful, negative, and rebellious. Often unresponsive or hostile toward authority (parents, teachers, etc.) Poor attitudes may range from uncooperative to spiteful.	Providing opportunities for productive interaction. Group projects and "buddy" projects are excellent. Encourage group discussion, sharing ideas and thoughts in a nonjudgmental atmosphere. Teacher needs to be accessible and approachable — it's not necessary to be the ultimate disciplinarian at all times (just when it seems needed.)
4. **SELF-CONTROL.** Unable to manage own behavior. May be poorly motivated with no confidence in ability to make decisions. May disregard classroom order with disruptive, challenging behaviors.	Firm guidelines. Make expectations clear and stick to them. Avoid confrontations that go nowhere, i.e., let reaction to unacceptable behavior be known, but leave the student room to change it and improve. Be consistent.
5. **POSITIVE LIFE EXPERIENCES.** May be cynical and lack a "working philosophy." Personal values may be confused or deficient.	Widening student's world. Discussions, presentations, classroom guests, and trips can help. Teacher can affect student's life with own positive attitude. Let student gain from teacher's own experience (i.e. if teacher has special interests, likes sports, playing an instrument, etc., share it!).

ART CHART: A REFERENCE GUIDE FOR ART AND EXCEPTIONALITIES
SHORT DEFINITIONS OF TYPICAL CONDITIONS AND EXCEPTIONALITIES

Orthopedic Impairment

Orthopedic, physical, or central nervous system impairment that interferes with learning.

When a function is diminished or absent, other more functional physical parts are engaged to help. Adaptive aids can be especially useful to students with orthopedic impairment. See Adaptive Aids, page 122

STUDENT MAY NOT EXHIBIT:	MAY REQUIRE:
1. **FULL MOBILITY AND KINESTHETIC AWARENESS.** May be unable to get around without braces, wheelchair, crutches, etc. Movement is restricted.	Activities and materials that are tailored to student's needs. For example, if activity asks for gross movement and student is in a wheelchair, activity will need modification (see page 126). Engage the kinesthetic sense whenever feasible.
2. **POSITIVE SELF-IMAGE.** If the disability is "new" (accident, trauma), there may be more emotional difficulty in accepting it. Congenital conditions may or may not support self-acceptance — depending on attitudes of family, friends, etc.	Offer activities through which student can acquire a sense of accomplishment. Projects should be adapted so that student can function as independently as possible. Provide opportunities for achievement and success, such as pre-cut portrait forms .
3. **STAMINA, PHYSICAL STRENGTH.** Often, conditions (and medications) are energy draining. Student's condition may weaken him or her, leaving student low on physical drive.	Assistance from teacher — beware of student over-reliance on classroom assistants. Teacher should be sensitive to signs of strain, yet motivate and encourage whenever possible. Offer activities that students can manage by themselves, in order to build independence.
4. **CONTROL OF BODY.** May lack full use of hands, arms, legs, etc. May not have typical head movement. May be spastic, athethoid, or contracted. May have partial or complete paralysis.	Activities that engage and exercise the body such as manipulative skills (tearing paper, pounding clay), kinesthetics (large drawing movement), etc. If hand/arm movement is absent, head movement can be substituted. Adaptive aids are very useful (see pages 122-126).

Deaf and Hard of Hearing

Partial to complete deafness. Communication, speech, and language disorders may be involved. Hearing aids and cochlear implants may or may not assist all conditions (Deafness is an example of an invisible handicap — it must be first indentified.)

Art is an important avenue of self-expression. It is a visual language for those who may have limited skills in the spoken language — a boundless form of pictorial or dimensional communication.

NOTE: There are deaf students who feel that hearing is a matter of choice — and that sign language is the only language they need. This is just to say that not every deaf individual is interested in learning to communicate with non-deaf people. Learning sign language is still highly recommended! (See Sign Language Guide, pages 24-28)

STUDENT MAY NOT EXHIBIT:	MAY REQUIRE:
1. **COMPENSATORY LANGUAGE SKILLS.** May have difficulty in communicating – cannot always understand others or express self clearly. May lack vocabulary.	Greater teacher awareness of student communication problems. Movement should be tolerated in the classroom so that student can get proper attention and can "read" facial expressions, etc.
2. **ABILITY TO FOCUS ATTENTION.** Not always sure of what is expected. Does not always understand what is happening.	Make sure student sees teacher's face and can read teacher's lips. Light should be on teacher's face. Do not exaggerate or shout. Flick lights on and off to get student's attention. Eye contact is important. Use concrete examples when giving explanations.
3. **SELF-ASSURANCE.** Diminished confidence in self and own decisions.	More freedom in making own choices. Hearing impaired students are constantly being "directed" because of their lack of communication skill. Accept the physical nature of the hearing impaired — touching, moving around, etc. That is how they can get their messages across.
4. **A SENSE OF BELONGING.** There is a feeling of isolation attached to hearing loss.	Offer opportunities for positive interplay. Group and "buddy" projects are recommended.

ART CHART: A REFERENCE GUIDE FOR ART AND EXCEPTIONALITIES
SHORT DEFINITIONS OF TYPICAL CONDITIONS AND EXCEPTIONALITIES

VISUAL IMPAIRMENT AND BLINDNESS

A partial to complete sight loss that interferes with learning and cannot be corrected by lenses (glasses). Visual conditions involve varying degrees of acuity and/or field loss.

Student with "residual vision"(small amount) will respond to bright and highly contrasted colors, illuminated and fluorescent materials with increased enthusiasm. Students with visual impairments can create dynamic artworks of all kinds... not just three-dimensional art. Students who have severe visual impairment (blind) can develop visual images, although development is slower and adaptive aids are often required (see screenboards, etc., page 124). Students are receptive all art materials, regardless of the degree of sight loss.

STUDENT MAY NOT EXHIBIT:	MAY REQUIRE:
1. **CONCEPTS.** Real-world objects and ideas may not be understood. May have poor comprehension of "parts-to-whole" relationship, particularly when student is unable to see the complete "picture."	Basic information. Simple pointers, like where facial features are located, may need to be taught. Provide 3-D models and tactual reference material whenever possible, particularly for students who are blind.
2. **ABILITY TO UNDERSTAND VISUAL CUES.** May not be able to read regular print, see from a distance or from all angles. If blind, cannot see facial expressions or body language — but usually has "light perception."	Be "extra" verbal with student. Describe what you are doing to student who is blind. If you want his or her attention, knock on desk (this is helpful for seating student). Use touch (i.e., a hand on student's upper arm) to communicate your presence. Students with some vision require adjustment of visual material — bringing it closer to student, allowing student to find the right position. Feel free to ask if student needs to change seats, can see material okay, etc.
3. **AWARENESS OF SELF IN THE PHYSICAL ENVIRONMENT.** Unsure of placement of objects and spatial boundaries. May be awkward and exhibit poor body postures. Students, understandably, often lack a sense of mobility. Some students may be tactilely defensive towards art materials (clay, paste, etc.) and display "blindisms" (rocking, flicking fingers, etc.). These actions may convey their anxiety.	**NOTE:** Art activities can engage other senses; smell, touch, etc. can be both stimulating and informative for the visually handicapped student (see pages 124-125 for suggestions).

Guidance through a mobility trainer. (If asked, offer your loosely bent arm.) Help student to become more self-aware through activities that emphasize this concept. Provide concrete experiences for student, using tactual references. Allow student to become familiar with classroom; never move the furniture without first telling students. For tactually defensive students, use desensitization techniques as best you can. Discourage "blindisms"(aka "stimmies") — they only separate the student more from his or her peers. Substitute with positive activities, but don't force it.

To help student understand where materials are located and to recognize the perimeters of work space, guide student's hand. Student uses free hand as a "marker" to establish where work is taking place. |

GIFTED

The National Association of Gifted Children regard level of intellectual functioning that exceeds the intellectual average. Gifted refers to students who exhibit outstanding aptitude in one or more domains. Gifted or Talented students further show exceptional ability to learn or reason, as well as exhibit high achievement and competence in performance.

The gifted student has the ability to understand complex, abstract problems and has deductive reasoning powers that allow them to hypothesize. Gifted students often display the empirical, scientific approach to problem solving. In most states, students who are identified as gifted require an IEP — which helps explain why they are still considered for special needs education.

STUDENT MAY NOT EXHIBIT:	MAY REQUIRE:
1. **SOCIAL SKILLS.** May be set apart from peers by his or her exceptional knowledge or intelligence. May not be well accepted by the group.	Group activities. Opportunities created for positive exchange between students to help socialization process.
2. **CONCENTRATION.** Might be "distracted" by mental preoccupations. Daydreaming and fantasizing are recognized characteristics of gifted thinkers.	Bringing attention back to task. Remind student to focus. Whenever possible, provide lessons that utilize imagination.
3. **INTEREST.** May already know topic details. Straightforward or predictable assignments may be boring for the gifted student.	Challenges! Present activities that have the problem-solving element built into them. (See adaptations throughout the activities — under "Gifted" — reinforce these points.)

ETIQUETTE FOR INTERACTION WITH STUDENTS WITH DISABILITIES

ETIQUETTE FOR ALL AGES: GENERAL TIPS

- Assistive devices (cane, wheelchairs, crutches, communication boards, etc.) should be respected as personal property
- Always direct communication to the individual with the disability. If they are accompanied, do not direct your comments to the companion.
- Use the same level of formality with everyone present.
- Relax. Do not be embarrassed if you happen to use common expressions like "See you later" or "Got to be running along" that seem to relate to the person's disability.
- It is appropriate to shake hands when introduced to a person with a disability. People who have limited use of their hand or who wear an artificial limb can usually shake hands. Shaking with the left hand is acceptable. For people who cannot shake hands, touch the person on the shoulder or arm to welcome and acknowledge their presence.
- Focus on the individual and the issue at hand, not the disability.
- People with disabilities are interested in the same topics of conversation as people without disabilities.
- If someone needs you to speak more loudly, they will ask.
- People with disabilities, like all people, are experts on themselves. They know what they like, what they do not like, and what they can and cannot do. If you are uncertain what to do, ask. Most people would rather answer a question about protocol than be in an uncomfortable situation.
- Offer assistance in a dignified manner with sensitivity and respect. Be prepared to have the offer declined. If the offer is accepted, listen to and accept instructions.
- When mistakes are made, apologize, correct the problem, learn from the mistake, and move on.
- Let people provide information about their disability on their own initiative. They are not responsible for educating the public by sharing their story.

INTELLECTUAL DISABILITY

- When speaking to someone who has an intellectual disability, try to be alert to their responses so that you can adjust your method of communication if necessary.
- Use language that is concrete rather than abstract. Be specific, without being too simplistic.
- People with brain injuries may have short-term memory deficits and may repeat themselves or require information to be repeated.
- People with auditory perceptual problems may need to have directions repeated, and may take notes to help them remember directions or sequence of task.
- People with perceptual or "sensory overload" problems may become disoriented or confused if there is too much to absorb at once. Provide information gradually and clearly. Reduce background noise if possible.
- Repeat information using different wording or different communication approach. Allow time for the information to be fully understood.
- Don't pretend to understand if you don't; ask the person to repeat what was said.
- In conversation, people may respond slowly, so give them time. Be patient, flexible, and supportive.
- Some people who have a cognitive disability may be easily distracted. Try not to interpret distraction as rudeness. Instead, try to redirect politely.
- Do not expect all people to be able to read well. Some people may not read at all.

ORTHOPEDIC IMPAIRMENT

- Do not make assumptions about what a person can and cannot do. A person with an orthopedic impairment is the best judge of his or her own capabilities.
- Do not push a person's wheelchair, or grab the arm of someone walking with difficulty, without asking if you can be of assistance. Personal space includes a person's wheelchair, crutches, or other mobility aid. Never move someone's crutches, walker, cane, or other mobility aid without permission.
- When speaking with someone using a wheelchair for more than a few minutes, try to find a seat for yourself so the two of you are at eye level.

VISUAL IMPAIRMENT

- Identify yourself when you approach a person who is blind. If a new person approaches, introduce him or her.
- Face the person and speak directly to him or her. Use a normal tone of voice.
- Don't leave without saying you are leaving.
- If you are offering directions, be as specific as possible, and point out obstacles in the path of travel. Use clock cues ("the door is at two o'clock")
- Alert people who are blind or visually impaired to posted information.
- **NEVER** pet or otherwise distract a guide dog unless the owner has given you permission.
- You may offer assistance if it seems needed, but if your offer is declined, do not insist. If your offer is accepted, ask the person how you best can help.

DEAF AND HARD OF HEARING

- Ask the person how he or she prefers to communicate (writing notes, lip reading, or need for an interpreter).
- If you are speaking through an interpreter, remember that the interpreter may lag a few words behind — especially if there are names, numbers, or technical terms that need to be finger spelled. Pause occasionally to allow him or her time to translate completely and accurately.
- Talk directly to the person who is deaf or hard of hearing.
- Before you start to speak, make sure you have the attention of the person you are addressing. A wave, light touch on the shoulder, or other visual or tactile signals are appropriate ways of getting the person's attention.
- Speak in a clear, expressive manner. Do not over-enunciate or exaggerate words.
- Unless you are specifically requested to do so, do not raise your voice. Speak in a normal tone; do not shout.
- To facilitate lip reading, face the person directly and maintain eye contact. Don't turn your back or walk around while talking. If you look or move away, the person might assume the conversation is over.
- While you are writing a message for someone who is deaf or hard of hearing, don't talk, since the person cannot read your note and your lips at the same time.
- If you do not understand something that is said, ask the person to repeat it or write it down. The goal is communication; do not pretend to understand if you do not.
- If you know any sign language, try using it. It may help you communicate, and it will at least demonstrate your interest in communicating and your willingness to try.

WATCH YOUR LANGUAGE: PEOPLE FIRST!

The blind *The* disabled *The* autistic; etc.	Views people in terms of their disability; Condescending; does not reflect the individuality, equality, or dignity of people with disabilities.	People who are blind People with disabilities People with autism; etc.
Handicapped	Outdated; disabilities don't handicap; attitudes and architecture handicap.	People with disabilities
The Disabled	An individual is a person before one is disabled. People with disabilities are individuals who share a common condition.	People with disabilities
Normal, healthy, whole (when speaking about people without disabilities)	People with disabilities may also be normal, healthy, and whole. Implies that a person with a disability isn't normal.	Non-disabled Person without a disability
Deaf and Dumb Dumb Deaf-mute	Implies mental incapacitation; Simply because someone is deaf does not mean that they cannot speak.	Deaf; Hard of hearing; Non-verbal Person who does not speak Unable to speak Uses synthetic speech
Hearing impaired Hearing disability Suffers a hearing loss	Negative connotation of "impaired," "sufferers."	Deaf Hard of hearing
Confined to a wheelchair Wheelchair-bound	Wheelchairs don't confine; they make people mobile	Uses a wheelchair Wheelchair user Person who uses a wheelchair
Cripple Crippled	From Old English meaning "to creep;" was also used to mean "inferior." Dehumanizing.	Has a disability/physical disability Physically disabled
Deformed Freak	Connotes repulsiveness, oddness Dehumanizing	Multiple disabilities Severe disabilities
Crazy Insane Psycho Maniac	Stigmatizing Considered offensive Reinforces negative stereotypes	Behavior disorder Emotional disability Person with mental illness Person with a psychiatric disability
Retarded/Retard Mentally Defective Slow/Simple Moron/Idiot	Stigmatizing Implies that a person cannot learn	Cognitive disability Developmental disability (the term mental retardation is not acceptable)
Mongoloid	Considered offensive	Person with Down Syndrome
Stricken/Afflicted by MS	Negative connotation of "afflicted," "stricken."	Person who has Multiple Sclerosis
Cerebral Palsy Victim	Cerebral palsy does not make a person a "victim."	Person with Cerebral Palsy
Epileptic	Stigmatizing; not "person first" language	Person with Epilepsy Person with Seizure Disorder
Fit/Throw a Fit	Reinforces negative stereotypes.	Seizure
Birth Defect	Implies there was something wrong with the birth.	Congenital disability
Midget	Outdated term; considered offensive.	Person of short stature

SIGN LANGUAGE IN THE ART CLASSROOM

The following words are important in any art classroom, but for students who cannot hear these spoken words, the visual signs are essential.

AND: Move hand from left to right.

BEGIN: Make half-turn with index finger of right hand.

BIG: Move palms away from each other.

BLACK: Draw finger across forehead.

BLUE: Shake hand a little.

BOTTOM: Lower the left hand twice.

BROWN: Move down.

CHALK: "Mime" writing.

CLAY: Cup hands, move slightly.

CLEAN: Brush right fingers across left palm.

COLOR: Flutter fingers.

CRAYON: Move "C" shape of hand across fingers.

CUT: Scissors motion!

DARK: Open both hands, palms in, cross in front of face.

DECORATE: Touch fingertips, turn hands, touch tips again.

DRAW: Draw little finger down opposite palm in wavy motion.

EASEL: The little finger makes a tracing motion in the air, followed by the index fingers tracing the outline of a rectangle.

FACE: Circle face with index finger.

GREEN: Rock hand back and forth.

HARD: Strike the fist with knuckles of other hand.

HELP: Raise hands together.

LATER: Rotate right hand forward.

LESS: Lower top hand slightly.

LIGHT: Move the hand downward a bit as it opens up. (As if representing the direction and travel of the light.)

LINE: Draw little fingers apart in straight line.

MESS: Stir claw-shaped right hand over left hand.

MIX: Stir right hand over left hand.

MORE: Tap fingertips together twice.

MUSEUM: "M" shaped fingers, both hands, tips touching. Draw apart and down, closing fingers over thumb.

NOW: Lower both hands slightly.

ORANGE: Squeeze!

OVER: Place the fingertips of the bent right hand into the palm of the left hand.

PAINT: Sweep fingers of right hand up and down on left palm.

PAPER: Slap base of right palm across base of left palm twice.

PASTE: Place middle finger on palm, draw back. Turn over middle finger, move in opposite direction.

PICTURE: Make "C" shape with hand against eye; move down to opposite open palm.

PINK: Brush chin down once.

PRACTICE: Brush fist over index finger.

PURPLE: Shake back and forth.

RED: Brush chin down twice.

ROUGH: Push claw hand out.

RUB: Rub back and forth.

SMALL: Draw palms close together.

SMOOTH (a): Cup hands.

SMOOTH (b): Move hands forward; thumbs slide along fingertips.

SOFT: Close and lower hands.

SPACE: Circle fists around to touch each other.

STOP: Chop right hand into left hand.

TOP: Form the letter "T."

UNDER: Pass right hand thumb under left palm.

USE: Move in circular motion.

WATER: Tap lips twice.

WHITE: Draw fingers together away from chest.

YELLOW: Shake Twice.

APPLAUSE (also YAY or KUDOS): Hold your hands in the air and twist them a couple of times.
For more American Sign Language (ASL) resources check out Lifeprint.com. © www.Lifeprint.com. Used by permission.

SECTION TWO
ART ACTIVITIES

"I LOVE PAINTING. IT'S DELICIOUS." – OVERHEARD BY AN ART TEACHER
WHEN A STUDENT SPONTANEOUSLY EXPRESSED HIS ENTHUSIASM

TEACHERS PLEASE NOTE: CORE ART ACTIVITIES ARE DESIGNED
FOR ALL STUDENTS. THE ADAPTATIONS ASSIST WITH SPECIFIC
EXCEPTIONALITIES, YET MAY BE WIDELY APPLICABLE.

APPLES AND ORANGES — AND BANANAS, TOO

MATERIALS

- Modeling clay or plasticine (wet clay may be substituted.)
- Tongue depressors or wooden ceramic tools
- Bag of fruit
- Bowl or basket
- Paper to cover desk or work table (optional)

TEACHER PREPARATION

Brightly colored modeling clay is recommended. If you have self-hardening clay that can be painted, that is also acceptable. Water-based clay can be used as well (if you have no kiln access, the results will be fragile), but the experience itself of using the "real" clay has its own value. Objects acquired through air-dried wet clay, as well as plasticine, will have a natural or earthy appearance. One fact about plasticine — it never dries and will retain its shape, unless it is manipulated. If you are using plasticine (oil-based clay), make sure that it is soft enough to use. Place the plasticine in a sunny spot for at least an hour before students use it. Students can break it down and rub it between their hands to get it into working order. Water-based clay should be moist, neither dry and hard nor too wet. If your clay is in a block, you can slice a good chunk out of it (like slicing a loaf of bread). Bring fruit to class and ask students to bring fruit.

DIRECTIONS

1. Carry the bag of fruit around the class. Ask students to reach in, feel fruit, and identify it without looking.
2. Give students clay and ask them to roll and pound it until it feels "right."
3. Set up a still life of the fruit in the bowl.
4. Ask students to create their own still life with the clay, making sure to include fruits that they have handled.
5. Be sure to repeat the term still-life and at the end when admiring their work.

SUGGESTIONS FOR FURTHER DEVELOPMENT

A fun way to make students observe the different qualities of the fruit is to try mixing wax or plastic fruits in with the natural fruit. Ask students to differentiate between the real and the artificial — and make them explain their choices. You can even mix in tennis balls, which usually gets a great reaction. Why wouldn't you confuse a tennis ball with an apple? When lessons are over, to the last group goes the spoils — give the fruit to the artists. Nothing brings home the quality of an apple like biting into it!

ADAPTATIONS

INTELLECTUAL DISABILITY

Often students with developmental disabilities are tactually (tactile) defensive — rejecting the clay entirely. These students need to be "exposed" to the offending material. Introduce clay in a ball or chunk and run students' hands over it. If students pull away or verbalize objections, wait awhile and try again. This might take some time. When students demonstrate readiness for materials, start with a simple shape that requires one motion to create, i.e., rolling a ball. Hand-over-hand method should be used.

Some students might "pick" at clay, creating a pile of tiny clay pieces. Help them to reshape the "parts" into a more meaningful "whole."

EMOTIONAL DISTURBANCE

Pounding of clay has long been considered a healthy emotional release for students. Give students the freedom to pound, but have some idea as to the noise factor — what is reasonable for the working classroom without total disruption? Boundaries can be established. Ask students to think about a character for their fruit, like "Banana Man" or "Apple Face," etc. They can create a fruit "family," using the still life as a model. When all are completed, allow time for them to verbalize about their creations.

Learning Disabilities

One area of difficulty for the students with learning disabilities is spatial perception. If you ask the group to interpret the still life in front of them, you might see pressed and flattened clay shapes on the working tables. To teach the concept, have students walk around the still life. Talk about what 3-D (three-dimensional) means. Make sure they roll their clay around. Spatial placement is another illusive concept. Have students observe the still life, thinking about questions like "What fruit is in front of the other? What's closest? What's farthest away?"

Orthopedic Impairment

Clay and plasticene (in good working order) are excellent materials for students with orthopedic impairments. Allow plenty of time for the exploration of the materials. Squeezing the clay is a valuable exercise for strengthening grip. Rolling the clay can involve the body in large, gross movement. Let the movement carry into the creation of the fruit shapes — go from a big, round movement to the smaller movement needed to create a ball or apple. All movements, including the rolling of clay circularly or in back and forth motions, will add to the development of a kinesthetic sense.

Note that a learned movement can be carried forward, i.e., rolling motions become the stirring motions needed in other activities. Movement, when repeated, enters "muscle memory" in the brain.

Deaf and Hard of Hearing

Teachers may want to seize this opportunity for social interaction between students. The teacher (or students) will prepare 3-by-5-inch cards with different pictures of fruit on them. Distribute cards that represent the fruits that will next be selected to assemble the still life. Using the buddy system, students will work together to create. Prior to clay use, students will plan their still life by trading cards. Once the partners decide on their shared idea for their still life, begin making clay fruits together. Proceed with clay still life.

Visual Impairment

Talk about shapes and textures of fruit. What do their skins feel like? (Smooth, fuzzy, bumpy, etc.) Give them ample opportunity to examine and compare the fruits as they go along.

While clay is regarded as "the" material for the blind, don't be shocked if some of your blind students don't like it. They are probably displaying tactile defensiveness — and you will need to let them ease into the medium. However, many more students who have visual impairments and are blind will respond with enthusiasm to clay. Note: "Fruit scented" Play-Doh is commercially available (See Play-Doh in Adaptive Aids, page 125). Teachers are encouraged to use the fruit-scented variety with students who are severely impaired or blind. This will enforce the associations between scent and object. Food is a perfect stimulant for developing this sensory aptitude. Teachers may need to prompt students... even though a purple banana sounds creative, it is best to match the clay's smell/color with the actual fruit.

Gifted

The gifted learner is challenged by problem solving and enjoys abstract thinking. Hold up a fruit and ask about the many ways that a fruit can change its shape. Using a paring knife, alter some fruit shapes by peeling and removing slices. Place in a still life.

Autistic Spectrum Disorder and Aspberger's Syndrome

The oily texture of plasticene might not be well received by students who are on the autistic spectrum. Softer alternatives are the *play dough* kinds of products — even water-based clay will do. Keep in mind that some youngsters may display a lack of muscle tone and weakness in their hands...all the more reason to conduct this activity. Manipulating clay is a therapeutic exercise. Note: Because some students may confuse the real fruit with the clay-produced counterparts, teacher awareness of this issue should be keenly considered! Students who tend to put non-food items in their mouths should be monitored.

BAGS BEAUTIFUL

MATERIALS

- Unbleached muslin
- Acrylic paints
- Brushes
- Felt
- Manila paper
- Sewing supplies — thread, needles, pins, safety pins
- Thimbles (optional)

TEACHER PREPARATION

Precut lengths of fabric for bags and felt strips for the straps, for students lacking in scissors skills. Stiff fabric brushes or oil painting brushes work best for painting on fabric.

DIRECTIONS

1. Use a practice paper to create the design. Consider using a strong pattern.

2. Cut fabric to twice the length you want for your bag.

3. Paint. Let dry. Fold, wrong side out.

4. Turn top down about 1 to 2 inches to create a channel for bag strap. For a finished look, turn *edge* of fold under ¼ inch, then pin the channel down under. Stitch, leaving an opening to insert strap.

5. Sew sides closed. Turn right side out.

6. Cut felt straps to fit into channel, making it about ¼ inch smaller than the channel size. (Ribbon and macramé cord may also be used for the strap.)

7. To push through, secure safety pin to one end of the strap and attach straight pin sideways to other end (to prevent the strap from "getting lost" in the channel). Ease through, straightening out the fabric as you go.

8. Even up ends and tie (see examples of finished bags.)

SUGGESTIONS FOR FURTHER DEVELOPMENT

The drawstring pouch presented here is just one bag shape that you can make. Other simple bag designs include clutch bags make with wooden dowels, and "envelope" purses.

ADAPTATIONS

INTELLECTUAL DISABILITY

For the students who are on the severe end of the autistic spectrum, you will want to familiarize students with the purpose of a bag. You might want to start by guiding students' hands into a sample bag, allowing them to explore the inside of it. Appropriate objects, such as combs, keys, brushes, can be put in and out of bags by students for a better understanding of the bag's utilitarian function.

If you do fabric bags with the student population just described, you will have to spend time by preparing the sewn bag in advance for the students to paint. Should the construction of bags be too time-consuming or impractical, consider the cigar box. Cigar boxes can be easily made into carry-alls. They can be painted by students. Yarn can be knotted into perforated holes in the box to create the straps for carrying.

EMOTIONAL DISTURBANCE

Some male students may object to making "girls' stuff." Remind them that many designers are men, that they can give the bags as gifts, and that football stars have been known to carry bags (and who dares to ask them why?). However an alternative to the purse is the book bag, which is the same basic style as the purse, only many times larger. Football and other sports insignias can be used as design motifs. Note: Students might want to create these items so they can give them as gifts — a generous gesture that warrants teacher endorsement!

LEARNING DISABILITIES

Create a "sewing line" for the students with a marker. They will sew along the edge in a basting stitch, following the marks as indicated. Eye-hand coordination is exercised with this activity. It's great for focus! The repetition of pattern that alternates in motif is further suggested.

ORTHOPEDIC IMPAIRMENT

You might want to use the burlap to make the sewing of the bags easier for the student with less physical control. Burlap is loosely woven and is therefore simple to penetrate with a large plastic needle. Once the bag has been finished, it can be painted decoratively.

DEAF AND HARD OF HEARING

Show a finished bag. If there are other bags available to show to students, point them out. To personalize students' work — as well as help with language development — ask students to design their names into bag's decoration, e.g., Danny's Bag, Barbara's Bag, Jamal's Bag, etc.

VISUAL IMPAIRMENT

Masking tape can be used as a guide for the stitching of the bag. Needles with large eyes (embroidering or tapestry type) and yarn should be used for sewing the bag together. Glue a variety of fabrics for the decoration, such as fake fur, corduroy, lace, etc. for sensory development.

GIFTED

Students might want to create their own "designer labels." Many students are aware of designer brands and will find this approach intriguing. They can look through fashion magazines and department store catalogues for idea generation. Teacher may want to use paper instead of cloth... designer bags may then be represented by their design qualities. Attention will be given to detail. When finished, cut out, display, and compare. Don't forget the personalized designer label or logo!

AUTISTIC SPECTRUM DISORDER AND ASPERGER'S SYNDROME

Students — depending on their demonstrated abilities — may require assistance at various levels of art production. This is a great teaching opportunity for students to learn basic stitching. The teacher can apply a row of dot symbols on the edge of the fabric so that students better understand where the threaded needle should go. Simple stitches are fine to create fabric closure. You can bring sewing to the next level with a wrap-around, running stitch if so desired.

Monitor activities as needed.

© Richard Griffin - Fotolia.com

THE BROWN BAG

MATERIALS

- Textural objects collected by students at home or on a nature walk (shells, buttons, postcards, clips — any assortment)

- White glue

- Lightweight paperboards

- Brown lunch bags

- Scissors

TEACHER PREPARATION

Students will need to know what they should bring to class in their brown bag (which you may want to provide). Another way to get material collected is to take the group on a nature walk — and you can add in other textural details.

DIRECTIONS

Students gather textural materials in a brown bag. Roll tops of bags closed.

Each student takes turns shaking the filled bag for the rest of the group (or a partner) who will guess its contents.

Students then open bags and allow others to reach into bag with eyes closed and further identify objects within it.

After all the guessing takes place, distribute the paperboards.

Students empty the bags onto their desks and reveal their secrets. Glue and scissors are distributed.

Students then compose their collage by arranging the contents in composition that makes sense to them.

NOTE: This lesson has both mystery and the element of surprise — but the best part is that almost any arrangement of the elements is pleasing to the student and the viewer!

ADAPTATIONS

INTELLECTUAL DISABILITY

Have two bags available for students to reach into, with teacher assistance. One bag will contain rough objects, such as pinecones, stones, wood bark, etc. The other bag will contain smooth objects, such as leaves, grass, and flower petals. If you are consistent with nature objects, then the students will get a fuller understanding of the immediate environment. An alternative to the nature concept is man-made objects. Combs, sandpaper, keys, clips, string, etc., can be provided. If students display tactual defensiveness toward any materials, respect their concerns. Arrange chosen objects on paper and glue down. For the youngsters with mild disabilities, follow core lesson. Be sure to engage students in discussion about the objects: Where are they from? What do we use them for? Talk about the concepts of hard, soft, rough, smooth, etc.

EMOTIONAL DISTURBANCE

Ask students to put their names on their bags in a decorative way to personalize them — or you can do it. Ask them to put at least one special or personally meaningful item into their bags, i.e., photo, letter, souvenir. The collage can be built around their personal experiences — a trip, a birthday, etc. Students should be encouraged to share the meanings of their collages with the rest of the group.

LEARNING DISABILITIES

Students should be made aware of the size of the page and think about how they will compose their space. Questions such as "Does this area look empty? What can be put over here?" helps the student to make informed spatial decisions.

The use of a variety of textures will be both visually and tactilely stimulating

Orthopedic Impairment

Students should have the experience of gathering materials from the environment for their collage themselves. Go on a "hunt," either on school grounds or in the neighborhood, for collage objects. Let students identify objects that they want — you can help with obtaining them for students with orthopedic support. Encourage students to make independent decisions and later to explain their choices.

Follow the directions of the core lesson for sharing bags. When collages are worked on by students, secure boards to desks with tape if needed.

Deaf and Hard of Hearing

Make sure that students understand the brown-bag lesson in its entirety. Demonstrate the steps if necessary. Show sample of finished product at the outset of lesson.

As a supplement to the core lesson, students would enjoy an old-fashioned "nature walk." Observing and exploring the environment creates greater general awareness and will add to the sensory experience of the brown-bag activity. This suggestion would also benefit students with visual impairment.

Visual Impairment

Clearly, the exploration of texture is perfectly suited to students with visual impairment and blindness. It is of significant importance for students to identify the qualities of the objects involved. Naming differences — smooth, rough, fuzzy, scratchy and so forth aid students in the development of discrimination skills. This is of particular importance when sight loss is involved. For students with vision loss, hands often perform the task of eyesight...and there is tactile stimulation offered by following the steps of the lesson.

Orthopedic Impairment

Textural aspects of the activity are important. Discuss similarities and differences between materials. Make sure students verbally identify the materials as they pull them out of the brown bag. Help make students aware of the perimeters of the page on which they are mounting their collages by leading their hands around the edge of the paper if appropriate. Also make sure when pasting elements that the "glue side" goes down on the paper.

Gifted

The focus of this lesson could be the creation of a "theme" collage. Ask students to gather a collection of objects in advance of the activity that add up to a specific subject. Some suggestions agree: "About Me" (photos, souvenirs, postcards, etc.), "Tools of the Trade" (objects that represent an occupation, such as nails, screws, sandpaper, ruler for carpenter), or "The Seasons" (pick one).

After students have gathered their "theme kit" a brown bag, they will close them at the top and switch with fellow classmates — without revealing the theme or contents.

The fun and challenge will be to construct the unknown theme into a collage reflecting the intended meaning!

Autism Spectrum Disorder and Asperger's Syndrome

Often students with Autism have tactile issues — certain textures, surfaces or art products can be upsetting. Since this lesson is of an unpredictable nature, the teacher may want to take it slowly, as children may be tentative about "the unknown." If a particular student has already demonstrated tactile defensive behavior, the teacher may want to allow contact with items outside of the bag. This is far less threatening to the learner. Note: under no circumstances, should the student's hand be forced into the bag, as explosive behavior would likely be the outcome of that action. Let's just enjoy this experience!

CHALK IT UP

MATERIALS

- 11-by-18-inch sheets of construction paper (black suggested)

- Colored chalks

- Cups or containers for water

- Paper towels

TEACHER PREPARATION

Fill water cups in advance and have them ready for distribution.

DIRECTIONS

Demonstrate technique. Dip the working end of the chalk into water. Remind students not to "float" the chalk in the water.

Dispense materials. Tell students to roll up their sleeves and to try to keep their arms away from their papers.

Draw. Encourage students to use chalk to build up areas of color. HINT: Avoid rubbing chalk-covered papers against each other when you collect work (to keep work from smearing).

SUGGESTIONS FOR FURTHER DEVELOPMENT

Wet chalk has the advantage of eliminating the unhealthy dust that dry chalk produces. The results of wet chalk resemble paintings in their rich surfaces.

Black paper used with colored chalk creates dramatic contrast. Designs have a strong impact, but here are some subject ideas: the city at night, stormy seas, fireworks, snowscapes, the sunset, and winter wonderlands.

ADAPTATIONS

INTELLECTUAL DISABILITY

Students will likely enjoy using jumbo colored chalk — the type sometimes used for the chalkboard emphasis or the sidewalk — with supervision. They should also like dipping the chalk in water, which presents a kind of water play activity in itself. Of course, hand-over-hand assistance may be required, and water containers should be stabilized. A bit of rolled masking tape under the watercolor cup on desks will help to keep it in place.

Students could try a fold-over print of their names. Fold paper lengthwise and open. Have students write their names on top of the folded line (assist as needed), then fold paper over and rub the back. Open. The students have a design made of their names. The printed side will be light to read, so go over letters with chalk. When designs are held in various positions, they begin to resemble different entities — trees, monsters, insects, and so forth. Students might want to develop the suggested image. NOTE: If students can't write, they should print their names. If they can't do either, you can help them. Using students' names should not be overlooked for its impact on self-recognition. Personalizing the lesson engages the student, while identifying him or her as a special and important person!

Responding to one's name may appear simplistic, but it is an integral part of social and individual development.

EMOTIONAL DISTURBANCE

Seat students so that they are close to each other's papers. Explain how important it is that they work as a team, because they will be "passing" a line from one to another. They will need the line to do their own drawing, yet the line will connect everybody together. Here's how it works: The student at the end of the table draws a curvy line over her paper and ends it on the edge of her paper next to her neighbor's paper. The end of her line becomes the starting point for her neighbor's line. The neighbor then draws a line and repeats process. Lines need to end where neighbor's papers begin — which might mean at different edges, depending on location of the next student.

Once all students have "the line," they create a picture based on what the line suggests to them — anything from a mountain scene to a "dreamscape". When all work is completed, match it and discuss individual interpretations. Display with corresponding elements intact, if possible.

Learning Disabilities

Students with learning disabilities could also benefit from the folded paper print method (please see Intellectual Disabilities). However, students may want to try a design motif. Fold blank paper in half (horizontally or vertically). On one side only of the paper, draw a geometrical design with a bold outline. Fold paper and rub the back with closed hand (fist). Open...a perfectly symmetrical design will appear! The printed side will have a weak replication of the drawn side. Students will need to refer to the original drawing when they chalk in the printed half. This bilateral exercise encourages concentration and makes students aware of relationships of parts, as it occurs in the balance of two halves.

Orthopedic Impairment

Students with grip issues may want to use a single chalk holder (see Adaptive Aids, page 122) in order to adjust their grasp on the chalk. The paper surface should be at a comfortable angle so that the students can build chalked surface on paper with ease.

If students have real problems dipping the chalk into the water, you as the teacher can pre-dip the chalk into the water — it should remain wet for hours.

Deaf and Hard of Hearing

Chalk murals are an exciting form for this activity to take. To add interest to the presentation of the chalk mural lesson, try this: peruse appropriate magazines in search of possible mural themes, i.e., towns, resorts, outdoor expanses, crowds of people. Remove from magazine, and for additional language development, print the name of the theme on the picture. Place all pictures in a hat (box or bag will substitute). Divide students into groups of three or four. One student, who represents the small group, will pick from the hat. This is the theme that group will carry out.

Be certain that students understand the "game" and its relationship to the activity. Demonstrate all phases of project to avoid confusion.

Visual Impairment

Visually impaired students might want to use fluorescent chalk with black paper. The effect is visually powerful and actually stimulates the retina. The combination of ultra-bright colors on black paper will make the images "pop!"

Fine sandpaper works nicely with chalk, and it is a surface that sight-impaired and blind students will appreciate. It is tactually interesting and has "tooth" for receiving chalk application.

Students who are blind will need to build up the surface considerably to feel their work. Decisions on composition will be made with students' fingers, so remind them to wash their hands when finished! Students might also need to be shown with helping hands where the water cups are located. A little rolled tape on the bottom of the cups should keep them from toppling over.

Gifted

Gifted students may be interested to see reproductions of work done by masters of pastel, such as Edgar Degas, Mary Cassatt, and Pierre-Auguste Renoir, and study the effects that they achieved. Students should experiment with techniques of rubbing and blending chalk with gum eraser and chamois cloth (tissue or clean rag will substitute). Work should represent a variety of suggested textures, from dappled to satin smooth.

Autism Spectrum Disorder and Asperger's Syndrome

Identification of one's self is a major feature encountered in students who are on the Autistic Spectrum. If students are functioning on an instructively receptive level, ask them to choose their favorite colors — three colors they really like. Ask students to draw a picture of themselves using these colors. (Use your own judgment about who should dip the chalk in water — you know your students best!)

CLAY POTS: PINCH & COIL

MATERIALS

- Wet clay
- Tongue depressors
- Clay tools
- Revolving clay stands or "lazy susans" (optional)
- Toothbrushes
- Manicure sticks
- Containers for water
- Slip
- Forks
- Small natural sponges
- Old shirts (smocks)
- Old pens

TEACHER PREPARATION

Wet, red clay that comes ready to use in plastic bags is recommended. Clay should be moist and malleable. Slice clay into individual portions using a wire. Have water, sponges, paper towels, etc. available for cleanup. Plastic tablecloths can be used to cover surfaces, but wooden tables and wooden boards work even better.

DIRECTIONS: PINCH POTS

Push, pound, and manipulate clay to get used to it and to make it workable.

Roll clay into a baseball-sized ball. Press the thumb of your working hand into the center of the ball of clay. Ease into bowl shape by pressing outside edge between thumb and fingers of one hand, and turning pot with the other hand.

Make walls of the pot as even in thickness as you can by smoothing and pressing. If you have a revolving stand and clay tools, you can refine the shape. Smooth outside wall with wet fingers. Remember, not too much water — it weakens the pot. Let pots dry thoroughly.

COIL POTS

Divide clay into strips with side of the tongue depressor. Roll out strips until they become coils, feeling for evenness.

With a toothbrush, fork, or tongue depressor, create grooves around inside perimeter of base and around the first coil that you will place on bottom. This is called "scoring." Repeat this process on coils until you have built your pot to desired height. Press coils together gently as you build the pot. NOTE: A wet mixture of clay and water can be stored in a plastic container. This mixture is called "slip" and can be applied between coils as they are joined. Slip acts as a binder in clay construction and helps strengthen clay joints.

SUGGESTIONS FOR FURTHER DEVELOPMENT

Here's a suggestion for changing the pinch pot into a completely different object: by turning it upside down, you will have a clay bell! While clay is wet, pierce a hole through the center. Using a leather shoestring or cord, attach a small "jingle" bell. Knot the cord where it meets the hole in the bell's dome, leaving enough string below to tie the bell and enough above for hanging the bell.

ADAPTATIONS

INTELLECTUAL DISABILITY

Students can benefit greatly by clay manipulation. It is both a rich sensory experience and an exercise in kinesthetic movement. However, students might respond to clay adversely at first, displaying tactile defensiveness (see *Apples and Oranges*, p. 30 for suggestions). Once any resistance has been worked through, assist students in a hand-over-hand manner with making a ball for the pinch pot and squeezing out the shape.

Students will also need physical and verbal prompting in rolling out clay "snakes," which require the motion of an open hand to create. You will need to provide the clay base and guide students in joining the coils to make the walls of the pot. A few coils should do it (don't worry too much about "scoring"). Students often delight in working with clay. Remember, the pinch and coil techniques are two different methods and should be presented separately. The pinch pot is rarely a frustration for students. Be prepared to assist with construction of coil pots until students get the basic idea.

EMOTIONAL DISTURBANCE

Pinch pots are simple to make, offering immediate success to students. Since the technical part of it is easy to manage, it is an ideal lesson to build upon. Ask students to give their pots another "purpose." How can they change them or add to them to make them into other objects? Have students pair up to solve the problem. Two possible answers: candle holders and planters. Encourage students to plan their ideas with their partners and carry them out to the fullest extent.

Seeing their cooperative efforts turning a lump of clay into a usable finished product teaches students interactive social skills and how to follow through creatively on their projects.

Learning Disabilities

Pinch and coil pots are great for demonstrating how things are made, because they "happen" right before your eyes. The dimensional nature of clay work also makes objects more concrete and imparts knowledge on how they arrived at that state. Understanding the process is important for learning disabled students. If you want to add to the experience, ask students to use a clay tool, manicure stick, or old pen to create patterns on the surface of their pot. Patterns should be continuous. This adds the elements of eye-hand coordination and closure to the activity.

Orthopedic Impairment

Pinching a pot involves some pincer grasp. If a student is limited in this area, you may want to get the pot "started" for him or her with your thumb — or experiment with some of your clay tools in creating the center hole. Rotating trays can be helpful. Also, check that the level of the work surface allows the student proper leverage. Clay manipulation is a great exercise for the hands and fingers. NOTE: You might consider a pottery wheel. Inquire about wheels that are adapted to be used with the students in wheelchairs.

Deaf and Hard of Hearing

The strong quality of clay usually makes it a hit among students with sensory losses. You can direct it easily, and new ideas occur to students as they work.

After a simple demonstration, let hearing impaired students develop their own ideas for clay works. Put materials forward that will help them — clay tools, objects that create texture (old kitchen tools, nuts and bolts, twine, etc.) Some freedom of choice is not only a pleasure but helps with decision-making skills. Deaf students are so often given directions from others because of their lack of communicative understanding. It is important that they have opportunities to develop their own ideas in an unrestricted manner.

Visual Impairment

Students with less severe sight loss should be able to follow the core as directed. However, as mentioned previously students who are blind are sometimes tactilely defensive toward clay. Once you have resolved that through recommended techniques, your students should enjoy the medium. Pinch pots should be no problem once demonstrated with physical and verbal cueing. Coil pots need a little more control to get coils "even" — sometimes they get so skinny at the middle and the ends that they break apart. Students should practice making coils until they get them into shape; you will assist with coil pot's base. Be sure students know how to "score" coils. Show them with your hand over their working hand where the container of water is. You might want to secure it with tape on the bottom.

Gifted

Gifted students can be challenged to build multilevel pots after basic methods have been presented. Pinch pots can be given slab bases and can be built in pinch pot multiples (shapes coming out of the sides, spouts, bottle necks, etc.). Students may also want to create lids for their pots.

In building coils, students can incorporate open space as well as curled and curvilinear coils. This becomes a design problem — the trick is using the right number of clay coil bands so that the pot walls do not collapse.

Students may also want to study the period of art history in Greece that produced black figureware pots. Students could actually draw similar figures on the dry pinch pot (try out your black markers and ink), taking the round surface of the pot into their design consideration. Scenes like people chasing animals, balls being thrown, and people dancing are all suitable subjects. If geometric designs are preferred, American Indian and Pueblo pottery should be researched.

Autistic Spectrum Disorder and Asperger's Syndrome

It is suggested that students on the Autistic Spectrum make thick, fat coils. According to our classroom experience, these coils can be more easily managed, particularly in the process of stacking. If the moisture of the clay is just right, the coils should adhere to each other, without the use of slip. For pinch pots, pre-formed into baseball-sized balls, the lesson may be followed as stated.

COWBOY STOCKING

MATERIALS

- Paper
- Staples
- Crayons
- String
- Markers

TEACHER PREPARATION

Precut boots for students lacking scissor skills.

DIRECTION

Talk about the shape and curvy stitching of cowboy boots. (Some students may even be wearing reasonable facsimiles, which work well for observation and discussion!)

Distribute paper that is large enough to fold and will provide a good-sized stocking. (Otherwise, give two sheets of paper (the same size) to each student.)

Offer drawing tools. Some students may want to incorporate Christmas motifs into their designs.

Cut boots and staple together front to back. Insert string at the top for hanging.

SUGGESTIONS FOR FURTHER DEVELOPMENT

A cowboy's or cowgirl's Christmas stocking is just one of the many other-than-ordinary Christmas stockings that you can make. Consider these: ballet slipper/tights; tap-shoe/mesh stockings; saddle shoes/patterned socks; and, of course, jogging shoes — to name a few. NOTE: Although "Cowboy's Holiday Stocking" is presented here in paper, this lesson could easily lend itself to felt. That would, of course, become a sewing project, but the design aspects are almost interchangeable between the paper and felt stockings.

ADAPTATIONS

INTELLECTUAL DISABILITY

If students are unlikely to grasp the lesson's core concept, you might want to stay with a traditional stocking shape. This will reinforce the stocking contour. To further create a sense of shape by emphasizing the boundary, cut yarn to go around the edge. Help students to glue entire outside shape of stocking. When yarn is dry, student will decorate within the shape with crayon and make curvy patterns (this step may precede the yarn application if desired). You will assist students in carrying out the motion required to make the design. Put students' names on stockings, add fluffy cotton on top, and display where students can see them.

Students along the spectrum should be able to handle precut cowboy boots and enjoy designing them. You can offer a starting point by drawing the first line on the boot. Students can repeat the linear pattern and develop into a design.

EMOTIONAL DISTURBANCE

"If you could design a cowboy boot that would be made into a real boot, what would you put into it? Zippers, bold patterns, buttons, different materials?" Try this as an opener. When students have finished their boot designs, have them use a "Western" design element to incorporate their names into their boots. Some suggestions are lasso rope, stars, studs, stitches. Encourage Internet search if appropriate.

LEARNING DISABILITIES

Remind students that they are designing two sides of the stocking — front and back. Make sure that when students are working, they are decorating the matching sides. Students may be capable of tracing a precut boot on paper and cutting it out, but they still need to coordinate the pieces.

To reinforce closure of the shape while adding an appealing touch, have students draw a stitch all along the edge.

ORTHOPEDIC IMPAIRMENT

It may be that students are capable of decorating the boot, yet they do not have the motor control to cut it out. Encourage students to do whatever they can manage. If they are able to outline the boot pattern, assist with the cutting. If they cannot decorate the boot with markers or crayons, offer sponges to apply patterns in paint. These materials do not require a fine grasp, which students may lack. Bingo markers are perfect!

Deaf and Hard of Hearing

Show students a completed cowboy stocking, a real cowboy boot, or both. It would be useful to have some "Western" reference material on hand. Again, the Internet can help. Make sure students understand activity. Follow core lesson.

Visual Impairment

Did you ever think about the sound that cowboy boots make when worn? If you or a student could introduce the lesson with a series of resounding "clacks" of boot heels walking across the floor, students could better understand the "character" of the boot. This is a sensory way to give the lesson more meaning. Of course, allowing students to tactually explore boots will provide tactile enrichment and "visual" information. Follow up introduction with precut cowboy boots, crayons, and screenboards for students who are blind. Remember, work with one side of the stocking at a time on the screenboard. If you want to give the stocking textural dimension, glue yarn in curvy lines.

Gifted

Cowboy boots are the arena for brilliant, contrasting colors and swirling patterns. Stars, snakes, cacti — whatever suitable motifs students choose — all can have a delightful "handmade boot" quality on these stockings. Students can produce studded effects with paper fasteners and a "flashy" style with the application of silver sticker stars.

Gifted students might try "wraparound" designs, to include design ideas that lend themselves to a continuous visual flow. Some suggestions are chase scenes, towering staircases, or boa constrictors.

Autistic Spectrum Disorder and Asperger's Syndrome

Students who have been diagnosed with Asperger's Syndrome are typically of normal intelligence — often above average. The most common feature of the disorder is an inability to initiate and maintain appropriate social interaction. Have students "buddy up" to design cowboy boots for one another! Make sure they understand what their partner wants in terms of style, motif, and design. When completed, allow time for each pair of students to discuss their process.

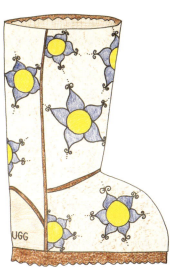

41

THE DANCING PAINTBRUSH

MATERIALS

- Watercolors
- White paper
- Paper towels
- Brushes
- Containers
- A source for playing music

TEACHER PREPARATION

You will need a player and selections with different rhythms: fast, slow, soft, strong, etc. Some suggestions: blues; acoustic guitar; vocalists; Irish jigs; country and western; rock; R & B; classical; and jazz, for sure!

Before the painting begins, make sure that students know how to use watercolors properly.

DIRECTIONS

You can either give students several 9 by 12-inch papers (or photocopy paper works well) to start a new paper with each change of tune, or give one large paper for students to paint all their responses on one page — in which case, the paper could be folded into the number of squares or rectangles

Ask students to let their paint brushes "dance" in time to the music. Switch music periodically.

When work is completed, display. Have students comment on each other's work, identifying paintings with the music they heard.

SUGGESTIONS FOR FURTHER DEVELOPMENT

Music, as we all know, has the power to set a "mood." Music can either stimulate or soothe — in both direct and indirect ways. "The Dancing Paintbrush" is a direct use for music, as is a lesson in which students will illustrate a song they have heard. Indirect influences include the playing of music while students are working — often a very effective tool for controlling behavior.

Music that relates to a given theme, such as Mexican Mariachi Bands (picture a celebration), Halloween music (Night on Bald Mountain — scary), and cowboy ballads (for western themes), can really bring a lesson to life!

ADAPTATIONS

INTELLECTUAL DISABILITY

Students respond to music. It's hard-wired in our brains. Reactions vary. Get students with profound intellectual disabilities moving (if they're not otherwise constricted) — help them move around in time to the music. After students are "loosened up," in the hand-over-hand manner described, transfer the body movement into the arm and let it come out through the brush on paper. Other students can "practice" with arm movements in the air before they register their marks on paper.

Use verbal cueing with all students when doing warm-up activities and lessons, such as "slow, slower, fast, faster, etc." This helps with their understanding of concepts.

EMOTIONAL DISTURBANCE

Word of caution: chose your musical selections for your students mindfully. Music can set students off, particularly very intense, fast numbers (as in Zydeco, with a student who is already hyperactive). Watch for reactions — if students don't respond in a suitable manner, change the tune. Jazz is often a fine choice, or classical.

You may want students to use pictorial imagery, drawn from the imagination while listening to music. Movie theme music works well for this activity, such as "Chariots of Fire," or instrumental pieces, such as "Rhapsody in Blue." (Avoid pieces with vocals for this approach.) Students can paint to music with whatever visual responses they are experiencing.

LEARNING DISABILITIES

What is the shape of a sound? Before you let paintbrushes loose, play some music (preferably instrumental) with a variety of musical sounds. Be "conductors" and let the arms describe the sounds, i.e., up, down, and around; overall zigzag; ladder steps from bottom to top (low to high), etc.

There are no "correct" answers; this activity helps students to translate what they hear into visual terms. It is an exercise of listening, then corresponding movement.

ORTHOPEDIC IMPAIRMENT

This is a great activity because it draws upon — and exercises — body movement. Students should be encouraged to respond to the music in any way that they are physically able. Use Adaptive Aids (page 122) to help with painting.

DEAF AND HARD OF HEARING

Students who are deaf are quite capable of enjoying music — and of dancing. Hearing losses may vary from student to student, but an all-around good bet is to select music that utilizes percussion instruments (drums, piano). Students can pick up the vibrations. If your room has a hardwood floor, it will help to carry the sound. Make sure that students understand the directions.

VISUAL IMPAIRMENT

Music has a strong place in the education of students on the visual impairment spectrum. Think about the late Ray Charles. Music is an important channel for artistic communication for individuals with visual impairments. Lessons can, generally speaking, be accompanied by music without considering it to be an overuse of method. In fact, music played during art class may be to the delight of students who may be grappling with visual concepts. If you are wondering if students who are blind enjoy painting, I assure you that they almost always do! The process provides an enjoyable sensory experience. *The Dancing Paintbrush* should be a hit, but consider also "dancing crayons" (on screenboard, see page 124) or any other medium that lends itself to making art with musical accompaniment.

GIFTED

Here's a group activity for gifted students: ask students for terms that describe music and list them on the board. Some terms are low, high, soft, loud, etc. If students know musical terminology (like forte, staccato, scherzo, etc.) use them, but make sure that students explain them to those who don't know the terms. Students get into a circle. Each student is assigned a musical term. Taking turns, students "sing" their word according to the word's meaning. For example, "loud" would be sung loudly in a strong voice, "soft" in a quiet voice, etc. After all students have participated, they go back to their seats and do a painting based on the musical word using patterns and colors that they feel best correspond.

When all work is complete, put paintings out for all to see. Ask the class to try to "sing" all the work before them as you point to one painting, then another, and so on. The class is a chorus and uses one common word, say, "paint." Now students hear what their art sounds like and see how well they interpret the music into paint. Go from this adaptation into *The Dancing Paintbrush* as presented earlier.

AUTISTIC SPECTRUM DISORDER AND ASPERGER'S SYNDROME

As always, the adaptation for this activity will be shaped by students' level on the Autistic Spectrum. Select music that would be described as mild...the term "background music" comes to mind. For many students who are autistic, loud music may upset them. In this lesson, knowledge of color identification will be reinforced. Materials will be distributed with the agreement that students wait until the teacher is finished the introduction before they begin to paint! Clearly demonstrate how to apply paint. As this is happening, ask..."What is the name of this color?" Students respond openly and respectfully each time. When actual painting begins (as determined by teacher), students may freely express themselves on large white paper, using the music as a relaxation element. Encourage students to softly call out names of the colors they are using. Scented markers (see p.145) could be used as an alternate approach. It might be a good challenge to see if students can print the names of the colors directly into appropriate area of their paintings. Note: teacher may want to create an informal color chart with the individual colors accompanied by the color's printed name. This is a reference board to keep handy! If all this isn't enough, the lesson can end with the teacher showing the sign language gesture for some colors (p.24-28).

Applause...sign language style (page 28)!

Designs in Wood and Cardboard

Materials

- Wood scraps of various sizes and textures
- Sturdy cardboard scraps
- White glue
- Sandpaper
- Braided picture wire (optional)
- Picture mounts (optional)
- Pictorial mementos

Teacher Preparation

Scraps can be collected from lumberyards and craft shops. You will need some larger squares, at least 4-inch or more, on which to mount the smaller pieces. If your scraps are very rough, have students sand them first. Wood is preferred. (If you are using the cardboard alternative, acquire and/or prepare a variety of sizes; this is not a large scale project.)

DIRECTIONS

1. Offer wood (or cardboard) to students. Ask them to observe the textures, colors, and wood tones, if appropriate.

2. Ask students to select the wood or cardboard they would like for their assemblages.

3. Experiment: move the parts around until a pleasing arrangement is reached.

4. Glue and let dry.

5. Paint surfaces. Add small "mementos" if desired

6. If students wish for their assemblage to be a wall piece, affix the picture mount.

Suggestions for further Development

Designs in Wood is a three-dimensional construction that can be built up, or can be created as a lower relief (bas relief) sculpture. If the piece is designed for wall mounting, the sculpture can expand laterally, rather than vertically.

Adaptations

Intellectual Disability

Guide student's hand in sanding wood. With student's free hand, "test" smoothness of surface. Repeat "wood is smooth," so that associations are made. Place wood shapes into a container within student's reach. Direct students to pick up wood from container and to glue wood to base. For those capable of stacking shapes, practice placing one shape on top of another before gluing.

For the cardboard alternative, substitute size for texture.

Sanding wood is a good activity for students on the Intellectual Disability Spectrum. It is a "job" that represents accomplishment. Have students sort the pieces to relative sizes (big, smaller, smallest). Create assemblage, glue, paint.

Emotional Disturbance

Show students a finished sample of the lesson. Ask what it reminds them of: a city, a parking lot, a space station on the moon?" Encourage students to think about an imaginary (or real) place when they design their assemblages. This allows students a chance to create their own spatial worlds in wood. The finished sculpture provides a sense of pride.

Learning Disabled

Designs in Wood is a "lesson without walls" — students can fully use imagination. Students with Attention Deficit Disorder are often among the most inventive. To add a challenge, you could include a concept in the activity.

Ask students to place some pieces vertically and some horizontally. Explain these terms clearly, giving examples of both. This approach makes good design sense because it will create a more harmonious balance of parts.

ORTHOPEDIC IMPAIRMENT

This is a good activity for students with orthopedic impairments because it is not exacting in nature. Students can also benefit from practicing the back and forth motion that sanding wood requires. Attach a sanding block to tabletop, or tape sandpaper to desk. Have container of wood pieces within reach. Students will sand wood until smooth. They will then build assemblages as they like.

Because students are able to complete most phases of the project independently, the results should be very gratifying.

DEAF AND HARD OF HEARING

Make sure that students understand the process before they begin their work. When all individual work has been accomplished, gather all pieces together. Treat assemblages like tiles and create a group wall. If parts are protruding, place arrangement out of way of traffic. Students will help decide how to arrange the tiles, which encourages positive interaction. In this way, students are less likely to experience any isolation.

VISUAL IMPAIRMENT

Provide a completed sample that students can touch and discuss. Concentrate on shape, size, and textural differences and similarities. Make sure that students use one hand to position the base, while working hand builds assemblage.

GIFTED

Gifted students can create an architectural fantasy of many levels and juxtapositions. Ask students to give the overall design a sense of continuity. This creates a design and building problem for students to solve. You might discuss the principle of a cantilever and ask students to include this concept in their design. (A *cantilever* is a rigid part of a structure that projects far beyond the vertical support on which it is built. It appears almost to defy gravity.) They may also want to include bridges, walkways, terraces, and so on.

AUTISTIC SPECTRUM DISORDER AND ASPERGER'S SYNDROME

The core activity will likely engage students in a positive way. Students may need design assistance. (It's not unimaginable for a student to try to build a teetering tower that will fail to stand — that could become a cause for frustration.) Also, application of the glue might be confusing. Be sure the proper side with the glue is placed down.

Face IT!

MaTerIaLS

- White paper
- Construction paper
- Scissors
- Paper fasteners
- Raffia (or yarn)
- Oil pastels, markers
- Paper hole puncher
- Paint-(choice optional)

Teacher PreParaTIon

Gather examples of African masks. Many African masks (particularly those from Zaire and Mali) use powerful patterns and details, often with symmetry. Providing material on masks of other cultures, such as China, Mexico, and Venetian Carnival would greatly enhance the activity.

You may want to precut a basic mask shape and slit the appropriate notches for 3-D paper features with mat knife or scissors for any group interested in trying that kind of paper craft mask.

DIRECTIONS

Introduce lesson with discussion on masks: What makes masks different from real faces? Masks usually distort or exaggerate features. Sometimes they simply look "unreal."

Present your reference material to class. Demonstrate cutting methods, which can vary. For example, fold a piece of construction paper length-wise. Cut half of an oval.

Open folded paper. Do we like this shape for our mask? If not, the shape can be altered — best to do this on the fold. Draw desired features and decorative patterns.

Student may refer to resource materials provided by teacher as masks develop.

Add raffia and paper fasteners. Use paper punch to make "accents" around shapes and features. Also use holes to pull strands of raffia through and knot.

Masks may be displayed or worn. If students wish to wear them, openings for eyes and nose should be aligned with students' faces. Attach string to sides and tie in the back.

SUGGESTIONS FOR FURTHER DEVELOPMENT

Do masks hide or reveal? The study of masks captivates the imagination. In many societies they are often regarded as having magical powers to heal the sick, ward off evil, and encourage good crops. In Western culture, masks date back to the beginning of history. There is an intrinsic element of classical Greek theater, where they were used to represent our strongest human emotions. In world art, they are rarely used without an accompanying garment. Teachers could certainly develop their mask lesson into one of the costuming arts — Mardi Gras for example. For our purposes, masks alone are engaging to students — delightfully decorative and visually inviting.

Masks can be made from just about any material you can name. Clay, papier-mâché, cloth, plaster, metal, wire mesh and wood are but some of the choices. You may later want to experiment with some other dimensional expressions.

ADAPTATIONS

InTeLLeCTuaL DISaBILITY

Precut mask shapes for students, who will apply paint directly to the masks with brushes, so the teacher may need to assist. Use verbal and physical prompting as you work, i.e., "We're painting the eyes now, we're painting the nose, etc." you can add simple expression to the mouth with an upward or downward movement of the paint. Again, explain that "The face is smiling" or "The face is sad." You can add sensory materials of raffia, feathers, or fabric by squeezing white glue onto the mask and pressing the materials on. Students will use their hands with those of the teacher in adding the textural materials. Fabric glue is your best bet.

emotional disturbance

Before you begin the lesson with younger students with emotional disturbances, say "Show me an angry face!" Do the same for other emotions (happy, sad, surprised). Ask students what happens to their faces as they change their expressions: happy, mouths turn up to smile; angry, eyebrows and mouths go down; surprised, eyes and mouths open wide; and so on. Ask students to choose one of the faces that they "made" for their masks. Let them cut and paste directly. Add in any materials that you think will enhance the mask's expression. Maskmaking has a high success rate with students of all ages with emotional disturbances.

Learning disabilities

Masks, because of their symmetry, are a perfect vehicle to help students with learning disabilities learn replication skills. Try this: Precut simple mask shapes for all students, then cut in half. Give students a single mask half to design with markers. Then, distribute blank half. Students affix the blank half to the mostly-completed side, using masking tape on the reverse side. Challenge: Reproduce the missing half, using the "worked on" side as a model. After the design has been symmetrically replicated, display! Discuss the experience with the students. Was it easy? Was it frustrating? How hard did you need to concentrate? Are you happy with the results?

orthopedic impairment

Students with highly restricted dexterity will have success using tactile materials. Fabric scraps can be used for features. Crushed tissue can be glued on to represent crowns, beards, etc. Crushing tissue is a good hand movement exercise.

A subject for masks that students can easily create is animal faces. Fake fur scraps can be precut, then glued by students. Wire or pipe cleaners make animal whiskers that are easy to manipulate. Add to masks.

Other students might also want to paint masks of animal skin patterns. The leopard's spots might be painted by making a simple movement with the brush. Stripes (zebra and tiger kind) are also easy to produce with adaptive tools.

deaf and hard of hearing

While the core lesson is suitable for the students who are deaf, demi-masks, which will leave the mouth exposed for lip reading, allow students to wear the masks and communicate with each other with greater ease. Flamboyant designs — elaborate butterflies, insects with antennas, or oriental fan shapes can make impressive demi-masks. Masks can be secured with string or elastic.

visual impairment

Students will give their masks a dazzling effect if they create parts of foil, fluorescent paints (or crayons), and glitter. All these materials will make the masks more visually stimulating! Masks are a fine activity for students who need reinforcement on location of facial features.

Students who are blind will appreciate precut mask shapes. Some assistance with location of facial features on the mask is in order. Students might enjoy paper curling — using one side of scissors to curl fringed paper. This makes good "hair" and clothing details. Students may need some teacher assistance learning this technique.

gifted

Gifted students might want to delve into history or mythology for inspiration. Minotaurs, dragons, gargoyles, and Greek gods/goddesses are some of the possibilities. Masks of other cultures — Japan, India, Africa — are also great subjects.

autistic spectrum disorder and asperger's syndrome

Some students with autism are affected with a condition referred to as "mind blindness." This means that it is often incomprehensible for the student to accurately "read" the expression of another individual. Note: this condition has been diagnosed in areas other than autism.

Refer to the adaptation under Emotional Disturbance to use the mask to better recognize basic facial expressions.

FACES AND TRACES

MATERIALS

- Brown butcher paper
- Markers
- Oil pastels (optional)
- Brushes — regular to 1/2-inch flat
- Costume jewelry, fabric scraps, doilies, etc.
- Scissors
- Poster paints
- White glue

TEACHER PREPARATION

Create a costume trunk. Some items you can gather are: kimonos, robes, uniforms, long dresses, men's suits, and Halloween leftovers, such as wigs and magic wands! Details such as hats, gloves, scarves, and fans are terrific.

For the production of this activity, you may want to precut student-sized lengths of brown paper.

Note: This lesson may require several art periods.

DIRECTIONS

Students select a costume and slip it over their street clothes. Decide on what the "character" of the clothes suggests and take an appropriate pose, such as a cowboy holding a lasso as shown.

Students will lie down on length of brown paper, while trying to retain a suitable pose for the costume of their choice. Note: this is a "partner project"...i.e. art "study buddy."

1. If costume is fragile, remove it before beginning the tracing, and pose in street clothes.

2. One student will trace the outline of his/her partner on the paper, using a marker.

3. Switch... so that there is an outline for each partner.

4. Using markers, and/or oil pastels, define this "self-portrait tracing."

5. Are you ready to paint? Decide on what areas need the most coverage. Think about facial expression, body language

6. Apply fabric scraps, jewelry, and costume details.

7. Display! Ask each student to stand near their painting and to introduce their personal character.

SUGGESTIONS FOR FURTHER DEVELOPMENT

Faces and Traces is a full-scale self-portrait in costume. Students definitely get involved. The activity has a theatrical quality and can enter many magic worlds of make-believe. But the tracing format can be used to teach the more "serious" subjects, such as anatomy, as well as increasing awareness of body proportions. *Faces and Traces* can even be turned into seasonal characters — Santas, scarecrows, and the Queen of Hearts for Valentine's Day!

ADAPTATIONS

INTELLECTUAL DISABILITY

Students who are somewhat mobile and have physical flexibility will be able to partake in the activity outlines as directed in the core activity. Teacher may or may not want to use costumes, depending on students' capacity for movement. If students can position themselves fairly straight on paper, either lying down or standing against the wall, trace them. Cut out whole figure. Assist students with facial features (in crayon or marker) using physical and verbal prompting. Print students' names in big bold letters across the front of their tracing. The whole figure might be too much to cover, so you might want the students to concentrate on painting hands, feet, and face. Help students to glue some fabric scraps around body. Display where students can see and touch their work. You can use the completed pieces to teach body parts and awareness of self.

Students with milder Intellectual Disabilities should be able to do the core lesson, but make sure that they understand what comes after the beginning (costume workshop). Clearly outlining the steps will help them to understand the logical sequence of the activity. It would be great if students could trace each other. They could practice before the lesson by outlining progressively larger shapes.

EMOTIONAL DISTURBANCE

The "acting out" part of this lesson is excellent for withdrawn students, as well as providing assertive students with an acceptable forum for their energy. Caution: If the group enters the lesson "charged up," it might be better to reschedule for next time. Otherwise, proceed accordingly.

LEARNING DISABILITIES

Faces and Traces is particularly useful for instruction of body parts and parts-to-whole relationships. Questions such as "What is your arm attached to? How far down do your fingers reach when you stand straight?" will help with this concept. Body tracing will increase awareness of closure — completing a whole outline, going all around the shape, and coming back to the beginning.

ORTHOPEDIC IMPAIRMENT

Costumes may be difficult to get in and out of so you might not want students to dress in "full regalia." Costume detail — hats, scarves, and so on — can carry the spirit of this activity very well also. If a student has a severe impairment, you may want to trace the outline according to the pupil's verbal direction. Taping the paper to the wall may be helpful in tracing the student in a wheelchair.

DEAF AND HARD OF HEARING

Students will enjoy carrying out the core activity, but there is another approach to the body tracing lesson that you might want to try: the Dance "Freeze." Tape two full-sized papers side by side onto an accessible wall. You will need a music player and a cd or stream of percussion music (see *Dancing Paintbrush*, page 42). Students will pair up as partners and dance in front of the paper. When you stop the music, students freeze against paper. You or another student outlines the couple. Partners paint their "pas de deux" together (black paint makes dynamic silhouettes). Repeat the activity until every student has danced and been traced. When all work has been completed, hang works collectively on your walls or halls — you'll have a display starring a lively dance troupe!

NOTE: If you do not want to use music, students can still pair up and move freely. Indicate to students when to freeze motion, then trace. Visual cues will be necessary. Be sure all directions and activities are clearly demonstrated.

VISUAL IMPAIRMENT

If the teacher is ambitious, you can trace the body outline by squeezing a line of white glue. Cotton yarn or string may be applied, which will define student body contour. Let dry, then paint (or glue fabric into the space) within yarn outline. For a more direct method, trace student's shape, then cut the whole shape out for the student. You might want to tape it to the wall to make it more manageable. Fabric application may be the preferred way to deal with the surface for tactile stimulation.

GIFTED

Students can research the design origins of costumes. They can then add more authentic details to their tracings based on the information gathered. Compatible environments may be created for figures. The costume should logically fit into the scene that the student develops around it.

AUTISTISTIC SPECTRUM DISORDER AND ASPERGER'S SYNDROME

This is an excellent lesson for students. It addresses the problem many students have in "understanding where he/she ends, and where the space around the child begins." Many students with Autism wear weighted vests to help them become more aware of their bodies in space. It stands to reason that teachers (and their aides) would want to help outline the contour of individual students, clearly defining the shape of the body with thick, black marker! Cut out shape and work with the student in much the same way as is described under Intellectual Disability.

For students with Asperger's Syndrome, the partnering aspect of the lesson is well-utilized to aid in the spirit of appropriate social interaction with peers.

Feat of clay

Materials

- Colored modeling clay (substitute plasticine or wet clay)

- Tongue depressors and/or other clay tools

- Manicure sticks (or dull pencils)

- "Wiggle Eyes" (readily available through arts & crafts catalogs, sewing notions, etc.)

Teacher Preparation

Cover work surfaces with paper or plastic cloth. What will be needed for cleanup is determined by the materials you use. Model Magic yields an easy clean-up.

Wet clay is another story...also depending on the viscosity of the clay. Plasticine can be greasy (see *Apples and Oranges*, page 30). Handle accordingly.

DIRECTIONS

Students decide on making clay animals or people, or both.

Students will roll out arms, legs, bodies, heads, in any order that suits them.

Assemble by joining parts. Small scale sculpture is easier to handle and suggested for this lesson. Also know that using a small wad of clay can work just as well for balance. Bottom-heavy, rounded animals and people (see activity photos) will surely stand solidly.

Add details. Oh, my...those wiggle eyes! They define the face so adorably! Hair, or any other "accessories" can be made more efficiently by using the clay tools suggested. Note: if you are using the wet clay alternative, treat your students to a garlic press! Placing a wad of clay into the garlic press and close — strands of what looks like hair will come out! Of course, this will then become a clay — not kitchen — tool!

SUGGESTIONS FOR FURTHER DEVELOPMENT

The "feat" of clay is to get clay to stand on its own two feet! Figures must be built so that they do not fall over. Rule number one is to build figures with a solid bottom and avoid top heaviness. You can incorporate "props" into clay sculpture, such as umbrellas, tree trunks, rocks, benches, and even furniture, to add support.

ADAPTATIONS

INTELLECTUAL DISABILITY

Brightly colored modeling clay is suggested to capture (and maintain) the attention of students with Intellectual Disabilities. The stimulation of color cannot be over-emphasized. Are your students somewhat limited in producing recognizable people or animals? Clay snakes are just fine to make. This provides a good movement exercise as well and offers practice in making coils for pot construction (see *Clay Pots*, page 38). You will need to help students get started. Whenever possible, fade away once students seem to understand the required motion, but keep them in your visual field. Clay snakes can be awfully cute! Apply smaller clay "dots" and "3-D squiggles" for sweet little patterns for "snakeskin." You can display snakes in their natural habitat with rocks and stones. If feasible, students can gather the rocks and stones in a nature walk. Other classmates can join in the nature hunt as well! Watch out for real snakes — don't upset *them*!

EMOTIONAL DISTURBANCE

Fantasy environments easily grow around clay figures. Let's consider people of power, such as kings, queens, super heroes, and so forth. When you introduce the lesson, tell students to think about a place where we might find these individuals — their own "Oz." They can start with the figures or with environment, whatever comes first. Figures such as elves, kings, queens, heroes, and magicians are more likely to fire up imaginations. Dragons and other mythical beasts will complete the scene. Make sure students have the chance to talk about the clay worlds they create.

Unlikely but lovable are "mixed-up creatures." Students will become "buddies" for this activity and work in pairs, with each student creating his or her own animal. When work is complete, divide each clay animal with a tongue depressor. Buddies will switch halves and join to make a brand-new creation, a sum of both their efforts. Results might resemble minotaurs, flying giraffes, or bears with kangaroo bottoms (pouches included). You might want to display them with name tags created by students to identify their creations. How about a lionoceros or a hippoplatypus?

Learning Disabilities

The flexibility of clay people can teach students more about the body's movement (see *You're a Doll*, page 120 for suggestions). Ask students to create figures that are active or in action: bending, leaning over, running, stretching.

Encourage students to assume some poses themselves. Posing and constructing figures will make students more aware of the body's movement in space and the balance to support it. Just as getting hit on the top of your head with a ripe apple falling from a tree can teach gravity (a la Sir Isaac Newton), toppling clay figures instruct students on weight distribution and the body's axis.

Orthopedic Impairment

Again, clay manipulation is an excellent isometric exercise (see *Apples and Oranges*, page 30). Students who are able to follow the core lesson should do so; other students may want to make very simple forms, such as turtles. Tools may help students with controlling the clay better. Adaptive tools can make the activity more accessible to the students — needs will vary. As we know, there is no one-size-fits-all.

If movement is severely restricted but present to some extent, you may want to abandon clay animals and people for simple theme that will at least allow for the art experience. One suggestion is "pancakes," which are extremely uncomplicated. Another, "spaghetti," can be made with the garlic press — and is that fun to make! Using the garlic press is also good for hand movement. Meatballs and dishes may be added. Remember: the suggested garlic press works best with wet clay and still requires grip.

Deaf and Hard of Hearing

After presenting hearing-impaired students with the steps of Feat of Clay, emphasize the theme of "two." "Two" stands for two people (or two animals) doing something that "takes two to do" as in the old saying — "it takes two to tango!" Some examples are dancing, playing, and shaking hands. Students will pair up for this lesson so that they can make figures interrelate properly. It might be advisable to look over examples of figure groups in sculpture in art history books

(or search Internet) to observe their relationships. When work is complete, the entire class will place all the pairs into a group display. Students show approval with "jazz hands."

Visual Impairment

Students can increase their awareness of body parts with the creation of clay people. A person can be divided into six units: the head — a ball; the arms and legs — coils; the body — a cylinder. Other parts (hands, feet, details) get added later.

Students who are blind will likely need assistance in assembling the parts. Verbal and physical prompting and a 3-D model (doll or sculptural reproduction) would be of value. The parts-to-whole relationship is a concept with which blind students can use some help. This activity does concern physical location and placement of parts.

Gifted

Students might want to design period costumes while they are creating their figures. Research would include observing styles and textures. Often traditional ethnic costumes (Russian folk costumes, Mexican festival dress) are challenging to replicate. Perhaps some students have dolls of other nations that they could bring to class as examples.

You might want students to study illustrations of classic Greek sculpture to see how folds and drapes can suggest the structure underneath the clothing. To help students with expressing the costumes and their effects in clay, clay tools of various sizes (particularly fine wooden sticks) will help.

Autistic Spectrum Disorder and Asperger's Syndrome

Once again, that "fat coil method" we learned in the *Clay Pot* activity (see page 38) will serve students well in the production of *Feat of Clay* people. The teacher is also referred to the adaptation suggested for students with Visual Impairment. What is of great importance for students on the Autistic Spectrum in this activity is body awareness. The idea that individuals know where they are in terms of the space that surrounds them does not necessarily apply to students with Autism. That is why lessons of this kind are quite helpful in learning how to recognize where one's body exists in the space around it.

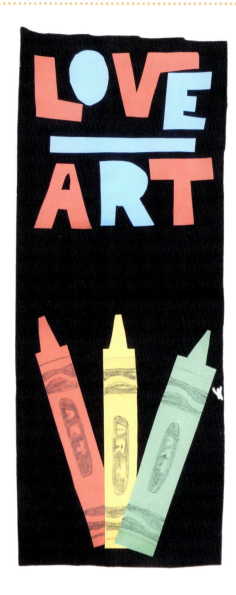

pieces precut to manageable sizes. For students with limited skills, you may even want to precut design elements (such as hearts, stars, circles, etc.).

If you want to use actual flag motifs, dictionaries and, of course, the Internet, offer full pictorial reference material.

DIRECTIONS

Flags are one way to present this lesson, but the banner theme offers a "broader" approach. Banners can be held, hung, or waved.

Students work their ideas out on paper before beginning fabric design.

Cut felt pieces according to plan. Glue pieces onto the banner section. Leave room at the top (and bottom if desired) for wooden dowels.

Sew, glue, staple the channels closed and insert the dowels through them.

What a banner lesson!

SUGGESTIONS FOR FURTHER DEVELOPMENT

If you decide on flags, plan to fly or mount them so they can hang indoors. Banners lend themselves to big, open space, but they can hang beautifully against a big wall.

Should you decide that you like working big and bold, a novel lesson you might want to try is *The Window Shade*. You can create a roll-up shade by purchasing the wooden bar and parts and designing the shade itself. The design should be painted (or sewn very flatly) so that the shade retains the roll-up action. This project is decorative and useful — form *and* function!

ADAPTATIONS

INTELLECTUAL DISABILITY

Precut 1- by 2-inch banner felt pieces for the student. In a hand-over-hand manner, you can help student cut a simple basic shape of contrasting color (see Adaptive Aids, page 122). This is a good opportunity to teach color. Repeat the name of the colors as you present the activity.

Glue the one basic shape on the banner. When dry, cut banner vertically to create wide streamers. Hang near students, particularly the less mobile ones. You will be providing an ongoing, student-made source of sensory stimulation as air currents move the fabric.

For other students, this lesson can be a tool for teaching colors. Try to find white felt. Cut into small, individual banners. Each student will be assigned a color from the color spectrum. The student will cut simple shape(s) out

FLYING COLORS

MATERIALS

- Felt
- Markers
- White glue
- String
- Crayon
- Scissors
- Yardstick
- Wooden dowels (substitute: the tubular cardboard cross bar that sometimes comes as part of clothing hangers)

TEACHER PREPARATION

You will need good lengths of felt to carry out this activity with flair. For easier handling, you might want to have felt of his or her color and glue the shape(s) on the felt. When banners are completed, they should be strung together on a clothesline (red-yellow-orange-green-blue-violet). This colorful display can be used as a reference when discussing color usage in the classroom.

Emotional Disturbance

When the students design the banner or paper, they should be expected to transfer their ideas from paper to fabric. This procedure will help them understand the consequential relationship between planning and final product. It will also encourage concentration and involvement with task. Consider doing the banner as a class project or in several small groups.

Learning Disabled

The flag motif will provide a very good visual exercise for students with learning disabilities. Students should select flag pictures or use real models as references. Duplicate the spatial design of the flag on paper first, using rulers if desired. Students will change the flag's color to make it their own color arrangement and can integrate their own "initials" as part of the design. The lesson done in this manner will aid visual perception, concentration, and eye-hand coordination. Students may enjoy considering the flag as their own flag by personalizing it with their monogram.

Orthopedic Impairment

Group the students according to a "balance" of skills. For example, students that have scissors skills can do cutting for those who demonstrate difficulty with fine motor grasp or use of hands.

To make gluing easier, pour glue into Styrofoam tray. Use a cardboard card to dip into the glue and spread it on the banner (before placing down the pieces). This simplifies the whole process.

Deaf and Hard of Hearing

Show students' pictures of banners or real models. Once students have selected a subject, suggest including the "sign" for the subject, if available. The "sign" will be cut out of felt in the shape of the hand's gesture. This slant to the activity adds a "communications" dimension.

Visual Impairment

For the students who are blind, why not create a multisensory banner that incorporates both textural materials and sound effects? Mount textural materials such as scraps of fake fur, sandpaper, velvet, steel wool, cotton balls. Add small pie plates, shells, old spoons and pot lids, and bells, if available. String up the noisy objects in such a way that they will clang together when banner is placed in a breeze. For students with some vision, you may want to follow the core lesson using yellow or orange felt, both of which are considered the most highly visible colors.

Fluorescent papers will also increase the visual interest with students who are visually impaired.

Gifted

Don't overlook other subject areas as motivation for "Flying Colors." For example, science provides weather, nature, plants, and the solar system. Even the common carrot can be a smashing banner. Some periods of history, such as the Middle Ages and Renaissance, are excellent for banners. Think about the Knights for banner shapes and sizes.

"Banners of the Future World" could be very exciting, drawing on a space age or technological theme.

Autistic Spectrum Disorder and Asperger's Syndrome

There is one reason why students with Autism might not enjoy making their own banner — felt is not the easiest fabric to cut, even with proper scissors. To avoid frustration (which can appear suddenly), paper is as a viable substitute. Otherwise, follow core lesson, assisting as necessary.

Guitars

Materials

- Oaktag — 18 x 20 inches if possible
- String
- Paper fasteners
- Scissors
- Crayons
- Markers

Teacher Preparation

The best introduction to this activity is a sing-along with a real guitar. If you don't play the guitar, chances are that you know someone at school or outside of school that does. However, to supplement or substitute the real article, provide a CD or electronic means of guitar music (country, folk, blues, etc.).

For the technical part, precut guitar shapes for students who need that level of assistance. You might also precut "guitar string" lengths out of the string (there are six strings on regular guitars).

Naturally, this is all a perfect reason to talk to the music department or instrumental music teacher— hoping that such resources exist in your school — about a cooperative lesson unit.

Note of Interest: The guitar and other stringed instruments show up in art history frequently enough for the teacher to take advantage of this idea. You certainly can't miss with Picasso — he uses guitar imagery on a regular basis. His Spanish heritage further supports the popularity of this instrument.

DIRECTIONS

1. Talk about the guitar and its distinctive appearance — the curvy shape, the wooden frame, the number of strings. Try to have a real guitar on hand that can be examined and plucked by students.

2. Students cut guitar shapes out of oaktag and design the surface.

3. Attach three paper fasteners to each side of the top of the neck. Draw a "bridge" across the bottom.

4. Wrap string around top of paper fasteners and punch through the bridge. Keep the acceptable tension of the strings in mind.

Suggestions for Further Development

The purpose of this activity is not to produce a real musical instrument that plays. It emphasizes artistic interpretation of the instrument's appearance and characteristic qualities.

Guitars, can, of course, lead into other instruments. This is an exciting way to familiarize students with the distinctive shapes — and personalities — of musical instruments.

Adaptations

Intellectual Disability

Play guitar music during activity. Try to get a real guitar that can be traced onto paper (or have a completed sample on hand). Show students how guitars are held, guiding their hands in a simple up and down strum. Using a paper of proper size and stiffness, help students to outline the shape of the real object with a crayon. Aid with cutting. Decorate by painting (or using crayons) while listening to the music.

To string, follow Step 3 of the directions, but make holes approximately ¼-inch round and use yarn. This is a good exercise for improving bilateral hand coordination and will help to improve focusing on a task.

Emotional Disturbance

Consider designing a "band." Some students will design guitars, others can make drums, horns, banjos, and so on. Be sure to have reference images on hand if the real articles are not available. Allow students to "name" their band!

Learning Disabilities

Having students trace a real guitar will increase awareness of the object's shape and the suggestion of dimensionality. After guitars are traced and cut, have students "pinstripe" along the perimeter of the guitar (thin line drawn along edge). This will reinforce awareness of closure.

Help students who have difficulty "stringing" the guitars; they might have trouble with the end-to-end parallel positions of strings.

ORTHOPEDIC IMPAIRMENT

Students will learn about the shape and function of the guitar by strumming it, holding it, and exploring it. To translate their sensory experience into 2-D, students will draw the guitar shape with teacher assistance. Students' manual ability will determine amount of teacher assistance needed in all phases of activity (particularly stringing).

You might want students to paint guitars in rhythm with the guitar music that you play for them.

DEAF AND HARD OF HEARING

Try to get a real guitar! When playing the guitar, let students touch the wooden part. Deaf students learn music through vibration. If you play the electronic substitute, let students place their hands on the side of the player; this can help with understanding the guitar music. Keep in mind that some students may have partial hearing, so compare the styles of two different guitarists — for example, the electric sounds of Jimi Hendrix and the traditional folk guitar of Bob Dylan.

Otherwise, proceed with the core lesson.

VISUAL IMPAIRMENT

It might be of interest to your students to learn that there are many accomplished and famous blind musicians. Guitarists such as late Doc Watson, Jeff Healey, and José Feliciano — students can research others. Share findings — listen and compare the styles played for the activity.

The auditory experience is very important for students with visual impairments, so try to make sure that a guitar is on hand for their examination.

You may want to help the student by tracing the guitar shape on paper in fluorescent crayon or marker for cutting purposes. Students who are blind may use screenboards (page 124) to help design the guitars. This will require a paper that is of a lighter weight than the oaktag. Many students require assistance in stringing their guitars.

GIFTED

Using pencils, let students draw the contour, using the real guitar as a model. Students will have the challenge of reproducing guitars symmetrically. When they have arrived at a "pleasing shape," cut out that desired shape. (It is wise to practice sketch first.)

It would be worthwhile to provide visual reference material on the decorative styles of guitars. Elaborate and ornate designs could be developed on guitars. Replicating various wood grains in a *trompe l'oeil* (translation from French means "trick the eye") manner might provide a nice challenge for the gifted student.

NOTE: *Trompe l'oeil* further means creating an illusion with paint (or pencil, etc.) that is so realistic that it could be mistaken for the real object.

AUTISTIC SPECTRUM DISORDER AND ASPERGER'S SYNDROME

Like any other students, music is pleasing for most students with Autistic Spectrum Disorder. However, be sure the music is not too loud or chaotic, since loud music can translate as disturbing noise to some students with Autism, causing an anxiety reaction.

As far as this lesson is concerned, bear in mind that tracing is always welcome — it reinforces fine and gross motor skills. Also, you may want to "pre-punch" holes, and assist with stringing the chords. Rock on!

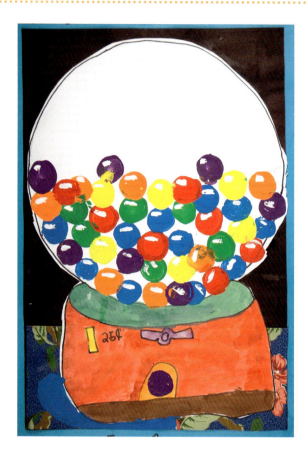

GUMBALL MACHINES

MATERIALS

- White paper
- Black paper
- Markers (scented, if available)
- Paper circles
- Glue/paste
- Colored paper squares
- Scrap wallpaper

TEACHER PREPARATION

Precut the gumball machine shapes. A circle can represent the glass bowl that holds the gumballs. The stand can be a truncated triangle (or any other shape you think is appropriate). You also have the option of precutting a one-piece machine by combining both parts (circle and base) and tracing them.

DIRECTIONS

Gumball machines are fun to operate and great to look at for their shapes and colors, which are the emphasis of this activity (clearly, we are not endorsing sugar)!

Cut out gumball machines. Select preferred materials for gumballs and other details.

Mount completed gumball machines against black paper. Add a "countertop" using scrap wallpaper.

SUGGESTIONS FOR FURTHER DEVELOPMENT

You can create a candy counter by displaying gumball machines side by side on the wall. This has an exciting, almost animating visual impact. Of course, other kinds of vending machines can be added, such as peanut vending machines, machines that dispense toy rings and whistles, etc. Gumball machines can be made to stand up if they are constructed from lightweight oaktag, and given a tabbed back.

Students often come up with a distinctive variety of "gumballs" — dabs, spots, circles, and so on. This gives their work individuality and shows that there are many ways to interpret subjects, even when they may appear to have a predictable outcome.

NOTE: Gumball machines are used in this activity strictly for their decorative quality — not their nutritional value. Again, you should make it clear to students that the aim is art, and that you do not want to promote tooth decay!

ADAPTATIONS

INTELLECTUAL DISABILITY

Precut gumball machine shape. Use tiddlywinks or paper circles for gumballs. Arrange by color in a sectioned tray. Students choose colors (with prompting), going from left to right, one color at a time. They arrange circles inside gumball machine shape and glue with your assistance.

Some students will be more capable of independence in this activity than others.

The tray arrangement is particularly helpful for its similarity to the techniques used in prevocational skills (i.e., sorting, sequencing, assembling).

EMOTIONAL DISTURBANCE

When students draw the gumball machines, ask that they put a "prize" into their bowls (like those you often see in vending machines). Suggest that the prize be an object that they would really like to have. When the class's work is completed, ask them to discuss their choices.

LEARNING DISABILITIES

Discuss the operation of gumball machines. Where does the money go in? Where does the gumball come out? Give your students the precut paper shape of the glass bowl; they can cut a base for it (or you can supply templates).

Students would benefit from outlining coins with fine-tip markers or pencils to create their gumballs. Apply color within coin shapes. This will require concentration on task as well as eye-hand skills. It is also fun and challenging.

ORTHOPEDIC IMPAIRMENT

You may want to present gumball machines as a printmaking activity. Fill shallow cups with different colored paints. Using corks in each color, student will print gumballs on paper machine. Bingo markers, which are readily available, would be just the ticket!

Another method is dabbing the paint with a round-tipped paintbrush. NOTE: This is an excellent activity for adaptive headgear (see Adaptive Aids, page 122).

DEAF AND HARD OF HEARING

The most authentic introduction to the lesson is taking your students to see the gumball machine at the corner store, if it's possible. You might even consider taking a snapshot of a gumball machine if no reference material is available. In addition, demonstrate the lesson.

Students who are deaf have no trouble drawing. Follow the core lesson — the results will be awesome.

VISUAL IMPAIRMENT

Since it is unlikely that you can bring a real gumball machine to class, have a discussion with students about what a gumball machine is (what it sounds like, looks like, what is does, etc.). As for students who are totally blind, offer tiddlywinks or paper circles to glue onto paper bowl shape.

Students can use scented markers to make circles (gumballs). Stationery stores may have fluorescent dot stickers that would be visually stimulating for students with sight impairment to use.

GIFTED

The challenge for the gifted can be in designing an extraordinary gumball machine. It can be elaborate or have moving parts in the "Rube Goldberg" tradition, that is, a contraption or device that could be done without complexity, but is made decisively complicated often having moving parts and mechanisms as part of the overall design. Think about what would happen if a pinball machine met a gumball machine. What would that look like?

AUTISTIC SPECTRUM DISORDER AND ASPERGER'S SYNDROME

The teacher is referred to the adaptation for Intellectual Disabilities and/or Orthopedic Impairment. Both are suited to students with Autistic Spectrum Disorder.

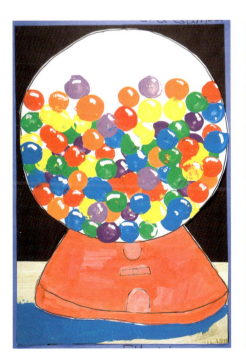
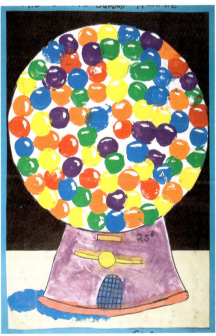
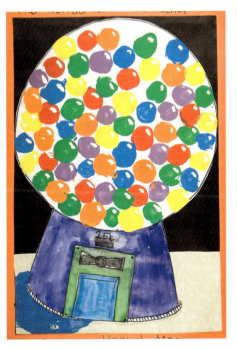

HanuKKaH's TOPS!

Materials

- White lightweight board (white on both sides)
- Colored tissue paper
- Paintbrushes — wide, flat
- Brightly colored ribbons or string
- Water containers
- White glue
- Paper towels
- Paper (or plastic cloth) to cover work surface
- Scissors
- Dreidels (see Teacher Preparation)

Teacher Preparation

Dreidels are small tops used to play a Hanukkah game. To introduce the lesson, it would be ideal to demonstrate with a real dreidel. If you don't have a dreidel on hand, provide pictures. Precut the dreidel shapes for students lacking scissors skills. Cover work surfaces before you distribute supplies. Dilute white glue with water in about equal parts.

DIRECTIONS

Discuss dreidels and significance of Hanukkah, based on reference materials. Pass around dreidels, letting students explore and spin them.

Give students white boards to cut dreidel shapes from, or offer precut dreidels.

Give colored tissues to students for cutting or tearing into irregular shapes. Lay torn pieces of tissue, one at a time, on dreidel shapes, and "paint" with white glue. (Do not be concerned by tissues that bunch up, tear, or overlap; this will create interesting color blends and textures.)

Students should decorate both sides. Glue dries fast, so you may want to allow a short time for drying between working on each side.

When dreidels dry, punch hole at top. Twist two or three ribbons together and string through the opening and hang.

Suggestions for further development

You can make a mobile out of several dreidels, hanging them together. You may want to add other elements of Hanukkah such as Stars of David and menorahs (Jewish candelabra), and cover them with colored tissues also. May be used as a hanging ornament.

ADAPTATIONS

INTELLECTUAL DISABILITY

Tape a precut dreidel shape to the table before beginning the lesson. Tearing, in itself, is a good activity for these students, so don't limit the amount of tissue they tear to what they really need to decorate dreidels. Use the hand-over-hand technique for gluing, and for tearing too, if necessary.

Students who are on the higher end of the spectrum should be able to complete the lesson as directed, with clear, explicit instructions from the teacher. You might want to spend some time with the last step of the activity — twisting and threading ribbons. This is a good opportunity to work on tying skills.

emotional disturbance

Students can work in pairs and collaborate on designs. Each student can decorate one side of his or her own shape and then switch with a partner. Decorating other side of partner's dreidel represents a cooperative effort between students. Hang dreidels together as one or several mobiles.

learning disabilities

By using a wide point felt-tipped marker in bright colors, students can add a decorative border to dreidels after they have dried. This will help closure skills and eye-hand coordination, while creating additional visual interest.

orthopedic impairment

Attach precut dreidel shapes to the table before beginning. If tearing is a problem, clip sheets of tissue to a clipboard. The student can then tear off pieces with greater ease. For help with other steps, you can try adaptive headgear, or paintbrush handles (see Adaptive Aids, page 122).

deaf and hard of hearing

It is important to present reference materials to your students, particularly those who are unfamiliar with Hanukkah and dreidels. If an actual dreidel or top is not available, you can indicate the spinning motion of a top in conjunction with pictures and reference materials. Be sure that directions are clearly presented and well understood before proceeding with activity.

visual impairment

Students would benefit from examining a real dreidel in order to better understand its shape and form. If a dreidel is not accessible, show students an ordinary top and explain that a dreidel is a special top used for a Hanukkah game.

Because tissues are brightly colored, they are particularly suitable for your students. Students who are blind will enjoy the textural surface interest of the finished product. Hang completed dreidels where your students with visual impairments can freely touch them — this provides repeated tactual enrichment experiences.

gifted

Gifted students who are presented with a real dreidel should notice that there are Hebrew symbols on each side. What is the meaning of these symbols? The answer to that question is a good opener for further research. Students could find out more about the Hanukkah tradition as well as the ancient language of Hebrew. You might want to carry the study of written symbols and calligraphic signs over to other areas such as researching Egyptian hieroglyphs, Chinese calligraphy, Sanskrit, and the cuneiform alphabet of the Sumerians. Gifted students should be fascinated by the possibilities for interpretations that these topics offer.

austistic spectrum disorder and asperger's syndrome

Once again, tactile aversion is not unlikely when it comes to gluey tissues! If student reactions warrant it, substitute markers and crayons for tissues to create a colorful dreidel. (Remember: encouragement is a good thing, forcing is not — and should be avoided.

It would be so helpful to have dreidel or toy top. The physical reality of the object, in this lesson, would be quite meaningful. It is also enjoyable for students to play with the top — chances are that it would be a big hit!

HOW DOES YOUR FLOWER POT GROW?

MATERIALS

- Lightweight boards or Manila tag
- Wooden sticks (tongue depressors, or popsicle sticks-or coffee stirring sticks)
- Green tissue paper
- Markers, crayons
- Paints (acrylic)
- Brushes
- White glue
- Green construction paper
- Scissors
- Sand or plasticine (florist's clay)
- Commercial clay flower pots (see Teacher Preparation)
- Optional — glitter

TEACHER PREPARATION

If each student brings a clay flower pot to class, you're in business! If not, you can either provide them for students or have students make a facsimile. Four to six-inch squares will serve students well for cutting flowers — other students will require precut shapes.

DIRECTIONS

Students draw basic floral shapes (tulip, daisy, etc.) on paper squares and cut out. Paint or sprinkle glitter into wet paint if desired. Let dry.

Paint sticks green; let dry. Staple or glue flower to "stem."

Paint simple patterns onto flower pot next, turning pot as it is decorated.

Place plasticene or sand into pot. "Plant" flowers.

Stuff green tissue into pot. Add construction paper leaves cut from simple shapes.

SUGGESTIONS FOR FURTHER DEVELOPMENT

You can create a "window box garden" by placing the flowers in a decorated shoebox. Or, place the flower pots on a table and draw a window scene. Flowers can also be made of felt (stuffed) and petals can be layered.

ADAPTATIONS

INTELLECTUAL DISABILITY

Use precut floral shapes. Students may use fluorescent crayons or fluorescent paints for decoration.

Some students may benefit by having materials laid out from left to right in order of sequence. For example, set up paper first, then scissors, paint, etc. Also, teacher might want to try glitter glue pens for more control and less mess.

Making the clay pot should be presented as a separate lesson.

EMOTIONAL DISTURBANCE

One way to use this lesson to improve students' social relationships is to have students design flower pots for someone special. Some choices are secretary, principal, friend, and teacher. It doesn't have to be an occasion — this is an expression of the students' caring.

Students can design a note that goes with the plant. A "John-a-gram" or "Mary-gram" can be created to get the personal message across.

LEARNING DISABILITIES

Cut paper in sizes to wrap around flower pot. This paper will decorate the pot by illustrating the stages of a flower's growth starting with a seed. Students will create a sequential "comic strip" of five blocks. The first block — planting the seed, second — watering the seed, third — the sprout, fourth — the young plant and bud, finally — the flower!

This is an approach that helps student understanding of sequence.

OrTHOPeDIC IMPAIRMENT

Students who have less manual dexterity can create a "newspaper plant." Tear sheet out of newspaper and paint it. Crush painted newspaper into a ball, and you have a newspaper flower! Attach to tongue depressor stems.

Another good source for "printed" flowers is an old telephone directory — simply tear out the pages. And, of course, brightly colored tissue paper will do nicely!

Deaf anD Hard OF Hearing

Show students a real plant in a pot. If you have illustrations of a plant growth sequence, also offer to students. Next, try to convince students to imitate the growth of a flower in pantomime body movement (you should demonstrate movement first). Present the precut flowers and other materials. Students then go ahead with lesson.

Visual IMPAIRMENT

Bring in fresh flowers for your students to examine. Enjoy the scent! Discuss the texture of petals as well as the anatomy of the flower. Cut petal shapes out of construction paper. Using the center of the flower as a focal point, paste petals in radiating pattern. Mount on stem, place in pot. Note: Students who are blind will likely require assistance from teacher or other support.

GIFTED

Combine flowers and fantasy — have students create their own "species" of flowers. Present illustrated examples of a variety of flowers and plants. Point out some interesting Latin botanical names to students, such as Collinia Elegans (palm family). Students will invent names for their flowers incorporating their subject ideas. For example, if a student wants a flower to represent a sport, it could be a "daisy basketball;" for a musical instrument, "cat o'harmonicus." You get the idea!

AUTISTIC SPECTRUM DISORDER anD ASPERGER'S SynDrOMe

Because students with Autism require support in communication and social interaction, the teacher is referred to the Emotional Disturbance adaptation in this activity. The students with Asperger's Syndrome may find the lesson quite rewarding. It's very applicable to students who are on the Autistic Spectrum.

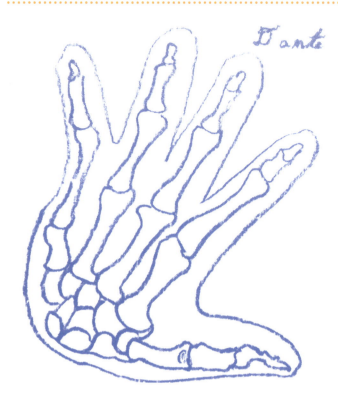

I SEE RIGHT THROUGH YOU!

MATERIALS

- Pencils

- White paper – 9 x 12 inches and 11 x 18 inches

- X-rays (see Teacher Preparation)

TEACHER PREPARATION

Get your hands on x-rays! Resources are your doctor, the local hospital or clinic, or anyone you know in the medical community. Old x-rays, your own x-rays, your family's x-rays — gather heads, backs, legs, arms, whatever you can to make a complete skeleton.

Try to have some print (or dimensional) reference material on the human skeleton available. Halloween skeletons may be used if they are generally anatomically correct.

DIRECTIONS

Hold x-rays up to the window. Have students guess what part of the body they are looking at, such as head, back, knee, etc. Ask students to defend their choice (i.e., how do you know that's an arm and not a leg?)

Hand out x-rays to use as reference (students should hold them up to the light). Students then draw the bones that the x-ray reveals. This represents a "study" of a body part.

Show students visual (or 3-D) reference material. If you have a 3-D model that moves, bend it and observe where joints are working. Have class get into various positions using bending, reaching, stretching actions.

One student volunteers to pose for the group. Announce that everyone is going to put on imaginary glasses: These glasses have the power to see right through to the model's bones!

Draw the model in action poses with "glasses on."

SUGGESTIONS FOR FURTHER DEVELOPMENT

Bones and anatomy are fascinating for children and adults to study. Although there is a definite connection between this art lesson and other subject areas (science, biology, health, etc.), the purpose here is to teach how the body is structured and proportioned and how we move. It is related to drawing and studio skills. Remember, drawing with anatomical perfection is not a requirement, and this is not a pre-med course.

Also, the bones of mammals and other creatures are quite interesting in their own right. Many artists have shown their appreciation for their unique qualities — artists such as Picasso, Georgia O'Keefe, Paul Klee, and Frida Kahlo. Art activities can explore this area with emphasis on shapes, texture, and structure of bones. Fish bones on a plate are wonderful as subjects for line drawings; the interlocking junctions of the bones will give the class ideas for bold designs. Experiment with your own ideas.

ADAPTATIONS

INTELLECTUAL DISABILITY

Students who are intellectually challenged are in need of body awareness. Do you know the lines of the children's song, "You put your right foot in, you put your right foot out..."? Maybe you know another appropriate tune ("the hip bone connected to the thigh bone...") That is a perfect movement activity for reinforcing location of body parts, and it leads into the art activity. You will need to guide students with physical and verbal prompting so that they move the correct arm, leg, etc. This introduction should be useful to all levels of students in the aforementioned exceptionality. You can move into the core activity from there.

The activity of body tracing is further suggested. (see *Faces and Traces*, page 46). After tracing student's body, cut it out. Assist students in painting the full-sized shape and name body parts as you work (i.e., leg, arm, body, etc.) You might even want to print the names of body parts in big bold letters on the appropriate area when the paint is dry. Display with student's name prominently printed on body tracing.

Emotional Disturbance

This lesson should go over very well with students because of its edgy flair and high interest content. When students are about to begin the bone "studies," follow the core lesson and try to have the class draw all the essential skeletal parts, (two ribs, hands/arms/shoulders, leg/foot, pelvis, head, and neck). When all parts are complete, assemble on a large length of butcher wrap or tape together. The class has created a full skeleton composed of everyone's efforts.

Learning Disabilities

Understanding how things work is often hard for some students with concentration issues. This exercise will make a point about body movement. First, have students stand. Then, tell students that a magic spell has been cast over them and they cannot move their joints. Now ask them to imagine that there is a basket filled with a million dollars on the floor. Could someone please pick it up?

This should make the reality of body movement less abstract. Proceed with core lesson.

Orthopedic Impairment

If you are fortunate enough to have some available windows, tape x-rays to them and ask your students to come to see them. In order to do a "study," materials should be accessible for close observation. Teacher will assist with mobility challenges to gain access to windows.

Students will discuss the details of the body parts. At the right moment, announce to students that they have just been granted a medical degree...so begin to call students Doctor! Their art projects will be their renditions of an x-ray of an injured body part. Black construction paper and white crayons or white oil pastels are ideal. Allow time for review.

Deaf and Hard of Hearing

Students can play a "connecting" game that will "move" them right into the activity, while encouraging positive social interplay. Students stand together. You touch student on a "movable" part, such as elbow, knee, wrist, or neck. Student moves that part and taps next student on a movable part. Repeat until all students have been "activated." The results are reminiscent of a gigantic robot or a big human machine.

If students can find an x-ray of their moving "part" (the place where they were tapped), do the study of it. Otherwise, follow the core. You will, of course, need to demonstrate the overall activity in physical and visual terms.

Visual Impairment

Students who are blind should firmly feel their arms and legs, ribs, back, etc. for the bone and cartilage; have the students describe what they are experiencing. It is helpful to get some kind of three-dimensional model (they are available in toy stores and some school science departments) or, at the very least, get a doll. Clear discussion about where bones are and what shape they are will help understanding also.

Students can make skeletons by gluing straws, toothpicks, or popsicle sticks to paper. Guide students in parts placement — in fact, consider precutting a human body shape to create the proper format (see Adaptive Aids page 122).

Gifted

Bones are an important component of anatomy, but what about muscles? After gifted students have followed the core lesson, let them research human musculature. Using an overlay of tracing paper on their skeleton drawings, students will draw muscle tissue. NOTE: Acetate is the ideal material for overlays, but it is more expensive than tracing paper and not as readily available.

Autistic Spectrum Disorder and Asperger's Syndrome

This lesson is about the human body — students with autism cannot have too many reminders on the topic of body awareness. Please refer to adaptation for students with visual impairment (minus the skeletal structure suggestion). Provide pre-cut people shapes (see Adaptive Aids page 122). Ask students to draw a face where it belongs, then draw the clothing (top and bottom) with crayons. Discuss, if appropriate, the students' completed figures. Note: this lesson is a good warm-up for *Faces and Traces* (page 48).

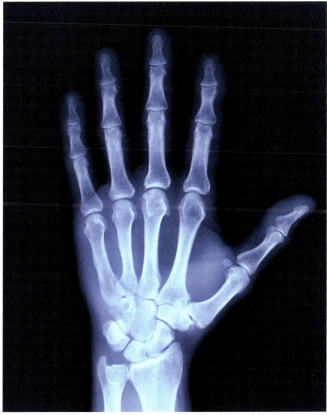

© itsmejust - Fotolia.com

I'M STUFFED!

MATERIALS

- Unbleached muslin cloth
- Straight pins, needles
- Acrylic paints, brushes
- Manila paper
- White glue
- Scissors
- Crayons, fabric crayons
- Stuffing (polyester fill or shredded foam)

- Fabric (assorted pieces)
- Thread
- Yarn
- Tape
- Cardboard
- Stapler
- Gloves

Recommended: Miscellaneous costume and cosmetic details — false eyelashes and false fingernails, scarves, hats, wigs, socks, sunglasses, plastic doll or wiggle eyes, clothing, fabric scraps — whatever you can collect.

TEACHER PREPARATION

Take up a collection of grand junk (see "Recommended" under Materials). You can ask students to bring in old gloves for the hands. White gloves are desirable because they can be painted to match the face. False fingernails lend realism (you can substitute with oaktag nails). You may want to cut the fabric either in proportioned pieces or as precut head/shoulders shapes. Fabric scraps and pieces, all sorts of yarn, buttons, and fake furs should be available.

DIRECTIONS

Discuss portraits. A portrait is simply a picture of someone's face, often including hands and upper body. But is it more? Can it tell us something about the personality of the person inside? Explain that these will be portraits in fabric and will have both fronts and backs.

Give students paper to sketch out the contour of their portraits. This will serve as the paper pattern for cutting fabric; keep it big, bold, and simple.

Measure the amount of muslin needed to accommodate the portrait. Pin down the cutout paper portrait to the folded fabric. Cut fabric to yield front and back.

If using crayons instead of paint to create the face, tape the cloth portrait shapes to a flat surface and draw.

Baste stitch the front and back cloth pieces together, wrong side out. Reinforce stitching on sewing machine or go over the stitching with smaller, tighter stitches.

Turn fabric right side out.

Cut out a section of cardboard to create a bottom on which portrait will stand. Stretch and pull fabric over cardboard. Staple closed. You now have a faceless, unclothed soft sculpture. Dress with costume items you've collected. Paint the portrait.

To make the hands, stuff the gloves. Use a dull pencil to push stuffing into fingers before you stuff the palm area. Add false fingernails and use white glue to attach them to gloves.

SUGGESTIONS FOR FURTHER DEVELOPMENT

"I'm Stuffed!" is the stuff that dreams are made of. Students can portray themselves in any way they fancy. If self-portraits do not appeal to you, here are some other suggestions:

Great artists	Egyptian pharaohs
Magicians	Movie and rock stars
Historical Figures	Monsters
Superheroes	Comic book characters

Portraits can be executed with crayons or can be elaborate productions. When they are completed by a group, display them all — they look like they belong together, no matter how diverse the characters.

ADAPTATIONS

INTELLECTUAL DISABILITY

Students can do beautifully with the lesson — the question is, how much of this activity should be attempted with your students with more severe intellectual disabilities? The answer depends on how much assistance you are prepared or able to offer and how much time you want to allot for the total project. Some teachers who have helpers can prepare the soft sculptures for their severely impaired students to paint and decorate. For other teachers who may want to know how to break down the whole activity, here are some suggestions:

The portrait on practice paper is a precut shape that students can use to identify the placement of the features.

Students can stitch the fabric halves together with you in a hand-over-hand method. You will need to reinforce stitches.

Stuffing the sculpture can be done in cooperation with the teacher. Help the student reach into a "stuffing bag," get a handful of stuffing (you may need to cup your hands with the student's), and push the stuffing securely into the fabric form. You will staple the bottom.

When 3-D muslin shape is stuffed and ready for painting, bring out the paper portrait for a frame of reference. Use the same technique for feature placements.

Help with the adding of fabric details. Hat and wigs make things easier. Glue (instead of sew) whenever you can.

When *I'm Stuffed!* is presented to the students with severe challenges, it can become a full-term project. But you are teaching concepts and skills: portrait reinforces body parts; sewing and stuffing eye-to-hand coordination; and sensory awareness through use of diverse materials. REMEMBER: *Each step* is an activity for students with profound intellectual disabilities and will need constant repetition.

Emotional Disturbance

This activity has great potential because it draws upon fantasy and imagination. It is like creating another "self."

Choices of subject are often heroic, powerful figures, and these superheroes are a great choice. However, if students get a little too "charged up," don't sacrifice classroom order for the sake of art (a rule to live by in general). This is the kind of lesson that can be picked up easily and worked on at varying intervals — so, "stop the works" if necessary.

When work has been successfully carried out, display projects in a prominent area in the school where they will receive much needed positive recognition.

Learning Disabilities

Learning disabled students need guidance on sequencing. To help students with directions, show them the project as it will appear at different stages — the paper pattern, the partially sewn shape, etc.

There are some basic concepts that might escape your students, such as where the hands go on the sculpture (body parts). Sewing will need some attention, mostly remembering to start at one end and go around, leaving room for stuffing.

Orthopedic Impairment

The way in which a student with an orthopedic impairment is challenged will dictate the type of assistance that will have to be provided. For instance, if movement is severely limited, sewing might be a problem. You might want to get another student to be an assistant to "fill in" what the other cannot physically do. Students with different strengths could help each other through various requirements of the activity. Of course, your assistance and support helps too — but so does a sense of independence. See the Adaptive Aids section for some suggestions (page 122).

Deaf or Hard of Hearing

I'm Stuffed! may easily be converted to animated activity. Soft sculptures can be turned into puppets by leaving enough room so that the student can insert his/her arm. The glove, loosely attached, is filled by the student's hand (therefore, you skip stuffing the gloves).

When students complete their work, they might want to get into groups of three or four to hold a play. A script can be developed or it can be improvisational. Simple situations like "Mary Lou is unhappy, and the Magician wants to help" can set up students for interesting interplay.

Visual Impairment

Precut the fabric and the practice paper to the contour of a portrait so that students have perimeters within which to place features. Students who are able to create, or simply want to try, noses, ears, and lips, should be encouraged to do so. This makes the dimensionality of portraits more concrete. Teacher assistance may be required for assembling of parts. This activity is a real enrichment for students with visual impairment, from sensory awareness to the placement of body parts.

Gifted

Use famous portraits to point out how artists observed their subjects' faces. The slant of an eye, a heavy eyelid, a droopy mouth — all helped give expression to the work. For the student with sewing skill, these details in fabric are achievable. Encourage students to try to create meaningful objects for the sculpture's hands: for example, a rabbit for a magician, an instrument for a musician, a book for a teacher.

Autistic Spectrum Disorder and Asperger's Syndrome

To do this activity with students on Life Skills curve of the Autistic Spectrum, follow the adaptation for Intellectual Disability. Students with Asperger's Syndrome, if otherwise capable, are referred to the Deaf and Hard of Hearing Adaptation. Why? Simply because it encourages playful interaction between peers and allows students with Aspberger's Syndrome to exercise their social skills in an upbeat, artistically meaningful way.

1 of 4   Emily Saitone

IT'S A PRINT!

MATERIALS

- Linoleum blocks
- Brayers
- Paper – newsprint, colored construction paper
- Wooden spoon
- Printmaking tools (V gouge and U gouge)
- Felt-tipped markers
- Newspapers

- Print foam or Styrofoam
- Manila paper
- Sheets of Plexiglas (or cardboard)
- Paper towels
- Printing ink (water-based) in desired colors
- White or black crayon
- Rice paper (optional)

TEACHER PREPARATION

All materials should be on hand for a demonstration before you begin the activity. Tools are sharp, so it is absolutely imperative that you show students their proper use! Consider the sizes of the blocks in relationship to the time needed for the activity. HINT: Linoleum blocks can be made easier to cut by placing in a warm spot prior to use.

DIRECTIONS: FOR LINOLEUM PRINTING

Introduce lesson by asking students if they can think of anything that is printed. Show them a dollar bill to get them started. Some other examples are books and newspapers.

Students should plan their designs on paper using thick markers (this discourages fine details, which are not suited for the activity).

Draw the image on the block with a crayon that contrasts with the linoleum. This helps students to visualize the reversed look of the print. It is important to explain that the printed image will appear as a mirror image of the design.

Show cutting method. Place non-working hand behind the working hand. All cutting movement must be done away from the body. Supervise students closely during the activity to make sure that this method is being strictly followed. (A bench hook, or holding jig, may be used to secure the linoleum block in place. See Adaptive Aids, page 122)

To ink the block, first squeeze a line of ink across the top of the Plexiglas or cardboard. Use the brayer to "pull" ink over the board until it becomes tacky, then roll ink over the block.

Place your paper carefully on top of the block, leaving a reasonable border. Use the back of the wooden spoon to rub the back of the paper. Make sure the paper doesn't shift.

When you think you have it evenly rubbed, gently pull the paper away from the block. You have just printed your first "proof." Repeat the process for as many prints as desired. NOTE: It may take some practice to get the ink "right" on your prints. You will notice you have too much ink on the block when it pools in the incised areas; too little when the print is light. String up prints to dry in class.

ADAPTATIONS

INTELLECTUAL DISABILITY

Using sharp printer's tools is NOT recommended for students who lack the understanding, grip, and deductive process to carry out the lesson. Yet printmaking is an excellent activity for older students with mild Intellectual Disabilities. Students who would benefit from printmaking, but not sharp tools, should draw their images directly into a Styrofoam tray. Lines should be deeply incised, but be careful not to poke the pen through the tray. You might need to water the ink down a little to pick up the print. Students will use the brayer and perform other parts of the process, with you assisting in a hand-over-hand manner if needed.

EMOTIONAL DISTURBANCE

This approach ought to suit your students to a tee: T-shirt prints. Ask students to design self-portraits, portraits, or a symbol of a favorite place. Symbols or abbreviated scenes are much easier to cut than entire landscapes. Some suggestions are the Eiffel Tower, palm tree, or a Ferris wheel.

Students will need white or pastel cotton T-shirts. Painting will be done with fabric paint, available at art supply stores and hobby shops. (Acrylic paint and printer's inks do not hold up in the wash.) It is sometimes easier to brush the paint onto the linoleum blocks instead of rolling it on. Place a clean board inside the shirt to keep the print from bleeding through to the back. Turn the block over and carefully press onto the shirt in the desired location. Students can use the block for other prints with paper and printer's ink.

CAUTION: Printing tools are sharp and can be a real hazard! If students are showing aggressiveness or are not following directions, DO NOT proceed with lesson! An alternative is Styrofoam block prints (see Intellectual Impairment). Monitor behavior closely and make sure that all tools are returned. Behavior must be compliant and respectful. Only allow sharp tools if you are certain your students can manage behavior and they demonstrate their best conduct!

Learning Disabilities

What's funny about money? When it has students' faces printed on it and their own original borders. Use real dollars as samples and discuss the process of printing currency.

Review the activity, going over the steps clearly, particularly the cutting instructions. Linoleum or wood blocks should be rectangular shapes that resemble the size of paper currency.

Students will decide on a motif for the border and put their portraits in the center. If they want to show monetary value, numbers will need to be inscribed backwards (remember, block prints are reversed). This lesson is not only fun, but it also exercises closure and helps with replication skills.

Orthopedic Impairment

Students with limited hand and arm movement may have difficulty with the lesson. Manipulating tools requires grasp and motor control. For students who cannot use gouges, use a pen and Styrofoam (see Intellectual Disability). Also see Adaptive Aids (page 122) for improving grip.

Another idea is the Texture Collage Print. Gather fabric scraps, lace doilies, sandpaper, corrugated paper, etc., and glue them to a piece of cardboard. Let dry and print as you would a linoleum or wood block. Using the brayer and rubbing the paper are both good arm and hand exercises.

You can adapt sanded wooden block scraps of various shapes and sizes for press on prints. Simply screw in furniture drawer handles. Set up shallow trays of paint for students to dip into and press assorted designs on paper.

Deaf and Hard of Hearing

Presenting the lesson as it is outlined in the core should give your hearing impaired students a good idea of what printing from blocks entails. But, be sure they understand all the details, particularly how to handle the tools.

Another direction for this lesson would be to create cards. Students must use paper that is twice the size of their blocks and think about where their prints will come out on the paper with respect to the folded card. The idea is to use the art to encourage communication via the written card.

Visual Impairment

Visually impaired students can use printing tools. Students who are more severely sight-limited may require hand-over-hand assistance and should stick with very simple designs.

Something exciting for students to try is to take the cut block (when printing is done) and wash it off. Roll out a clay tile cut to the block's size. Press the block into the clay. The raised image will provide a tatile "picture" of the print. Poke a hole through the top of the clay tile, and let dry.

Other printmaking "plates" can be made with yarn and white glue. Yarn can be glued to the board in a pattern, and when dry, it can be printed. White glue can be used to create a linear design, and when it has thoroughly dried, can be printed? Try it. NOTE: Again, watch hands and tools closely to avoid mishaps!

Gifted

Gifted students may become very involved with printmaking as an expressive means because it has so many technical facets and is so challenging. It would be interesting to bring in reproductions of a variety of different printed images in art (engraving, lithograph, silkscreen, etc.) and see if students could guess the technique by looking at the finished product. Students might even want to set up a lab where they can bring in and experiment with techniques and materials.

Gifted students should use their technical ability to the fullest, cutting the block with a variety of textures and using all available tools. Prints should be pulled at various stages of the print's development so that students can decide on what "goes" and what "stays."

The printed image works beautifully with poetry and prose. Students may want to create a book as a class (a great group project), illustrating their favorite poem or making up poems of their own. Or students could do books individually.

Autistic Spectrum Disorder and Asperger's Syndrome

The choice of printmaking techniques to offer will depend on where students are on the Autistic Spectrum. Students with Asperger's Syndrome can follow the core activity. Check adaptations for Deaf and Hard of Hearing and Orthopedic Impairment for further activity suggestions. Adaptive Aids can also be quite useful (page 122).

Macaroni Townhouses

Materials

- Milk cartons (single serve)
- Lace doilies
- Construction paper
- Glue
- Crayons, markers
- Watercolors
- Scissors
- Uncooked macaroni of choice
- Absorbent cotton or stuffing
- Steel wool (optional)

Teacher Preparation

Collect milk cartons, the small size that children get at lunch. Rinse them out. Not all stores carry macaroni wheels, so substitute whatever pasta will make good roof shingles or siding. You will also want to acquire some lace doilies for "curtains." Provide precut paper to cover the milk carton's sides to eliminate the students' having to measure them (unless you wish for them to do so).

DIRECTIONS

With the milk cartons in front of them, ask students to imagine they are looking at houses in a cute little neighborhood.

Cut out the necessary house parts — windows, doors, walls — from paper.

Cut the milk cartons to the desired size. Measure walls, decorate.

Glue the macaroni to the flat roof, leaving room for a smoke stack. First, cut slits in a 3- by 4-inch piece of paper. Then roll the paper into a cylinder, fold up the bottom slits, and glue the smoke stack together and onto the roof.

Add "smoke" out of a mixture of steel wool and cotton. (optional, but a crowning touch).

Houses are now ready for immediate occupancy!

Suggestions for Further Development

While *Macaroni Townhouses* appears to be an activity for younger students, there is potential for more advanced projects. Elaborate structures can be built by placing several milk cartons on each other, creating architectural interpretations of Greek temples, skyscrapers, apartment complexes, neighborhoods, etc. The macaroni wheels when painted white have a visually impressive effect.

Adaptations

Intellectual Disability

Students who will benefit more from process than product might concentrate on the cube as a shape, rather than making it represent something else. The dimensional cube will have greater meaning as a solid shape and as a tactile experience — if fabric is applied to it. Corduroy, velvet, burlap, sandpaper etc., can be precut to fit the milk carton sides. Students will paste these on with your assistance. Result: a sensory cube. This can be used repeatedly after it is made to reach simple discrimination between textural differences.

Other students on the spectrum would be receptive the meaning of making a house from a milk carton. Direct discussion of "Where do you live?" and "Tell us what a house looks like?" will generally bring the house concept into focus. Proceed with the core lesson, giving assistance when indicated.

Emotional Disturbance

Open with a discussion about students' own neighborhoods. What kind of stores are near you? Are houses close together? Far apart? Ask students to think about houses or stores in their community when they create their houses. It is good if one student can create a shoe store, another a grocery store, etc. When all projects are completed, the group will display houses together as a community. Note to teacher: Please be aware that student circumstances for housing may be a sensitive matter. Poverty may force alternatives that bear little resemblance to "home sweet home." Sleeping in a car at night, living in abandoned houses, shelters, and homelessness are unfortunate realities for many students.

learning Disabilities

The basic shape of a house and its square dimensionality may not be understood clearly by students. It may help to demonstrate how the box shape is formed by dissecting a sample like the carton. Students can help reassemble it. The concept becomes more concrete through this "discovery" method.

Let students decorate milk carton walls, but be sure to discuss the placement of windows and doors. Why are they located where they are? Follow the core lesson for decoration.

orthopedic impairment

Materials should be laid out in an organized manner. (See Adaptive Aids, page 122). Small and loose items, such as cotton balls and macaroni, can be placed in shallow cups. This will make the lesson more accessible for students. The empty milk cartons are so lightweight that students may have trouble applying decorations to surfaces, so stabilize them by temporarily placing a heavy object inside, such as a paperweight, rock, etc., or used rolled masking tape on the bottoms.

Some students lacking fine motor control may require teacher assistance when applying the smaller parts, such as macaroni and cotton.

Deaf and Hard of Hearing

Show pictures of houses or, better yet, take students on a neighborhood walk. Observe and touch various wall surfaces, such as brick, stone, and stucco. Bring some paper to make simple sketches of different surfaces. Students will apply this information to their macaroni townhouse walls.

Be sure that students understand the steps of the lesson before you begin. Presenting a sample finished product would be helpful.

Visual impairment

Students who are blind can use the screen board for making textures on the paper that will go on the carton as walls. Other materials, such as sandpaper and aluminum foil, can be added to enhance tactile experience. These materials are close to real building materials (sandpaper feels like stucco and foil resembles aluminum siding).

Students with some sight will be able to draw brick and stone patterns. This is generally a very tangible project for the students who are on the visual impairment spectrum.

Gifted

Ask each student to save several milk cartons. They will be asked to create a neighborhood using as much architectural variety as possible. Encourage students to make observations concerning their neighborhoods — the stores, buildings, schools, etc. In a city, students should "look up"... because often architectural detail is above the storefronts.

Posterboard or panels of cardboard boxes are recommended for the base of these milk carton neighborhoods.

Autistic Spectrum Disorder and Asperger's Syndrome

Please refer to orthopedic impairment. Student exposure and enjoyment of sensory materials (found in Adaptive Aids, page 122) provide tactile learning. If the teacher wants a house form for the outcome, use a communication board or pictorial images to convey outcome desired. An actual finished product as an example cannot hurt!

MIRROR, MIRROR ON THE WALL

MATERIALS

- Mirror squares, 8 x 10 inch, by 9 x 12 inch or smaller

- Paper, 12 x 15 inches

- Cardboard that can be cut with scissors

- Sharp scissors

- Masking tape

- White glue

- Acrylic or poster paints

- Yarn

- Gesso (or substitute white paint)

- Braided picture wire for hanging (or other appropriate hardware)

- Papier-mâché ingredients (see Teacher Prep)

TEACHER PREPARATION

When presenting this activity to young children or students with limited technical skills, production of frame parts is going to be your assignment. If older and more skilled students are available, enlist their assistance in precutting the frames. Exercise extreme caution with the glass mirrors — they often have sharp edges and are, of course, fragile. Mirrors are available in variety stores, home improvement centers, discount stores, department stores, etc. If possible, use metal mirrors. You can substitute tinfoil or foil paper for real mirrors, but it's not the same thing.

INGREDIENTS FOR PAPIER-MÂCHÉ

- 1 cup flour

- 1 cup water

- Black and white newspaper

- White glue (optional)

Mix flour and water a little at a time in a bowl. Some people prefer adding flour to water, believing that it makes a smoother paste. Add white glue if desired. Avoid "clouds" of flour in the air by sifting the flour directly into water. Tear newspaper into strips. Cover work surface with newspapers. When lumps in mixture have disappeared, dip strips in. Slip excess paste off of strips by pulling them through your first two fingers.

Apply strips to cardboard shape. Add dry paper strips between very wet ones to absorb extra wetness. Wrap strips in overlapping manner with respect to original form. Squeeze and manipulate to control shape if needed. Let dry.

DIRECTIONS

Day One: Show your students the sample that you prepared for demonstration purposes. If you have not decorated the frame beforehand, do it along with the students.

Cut the oval pattern to be traced on the cardboard. First, fold the 12 by 15-inch paper in half lengthwise. Then fold again into quarters. Cut a curve along the outer edge and the inner edge. Be sure not to cut the fold! Now open the cut paper to reveal your oval pattern. If you are using lightweight board, you should do parts as doubles — two frame backs, two frame fronts.

Punch two holes in back for picture wire. Knot one end and thread through, then knot the other.

Glue to second back cardboard. Turn over, glue mirror down. Glue frames to each other; mount with glue on top of each other.

Papier-mâché is next. Prepare according to the recipe (see above). You might want to protect the mirror's surface with a piece of paper taped over it temporarily.

Begin laying newspaper strips onto frame. Build up; this provides the strength for the frame to support the mirror on the wall. Let dry for at least 24 hours.

Day Two: Paint gesso on the frame. Allow 20 minutes to dry.

While gesso is drying, students can sketch out design ideas on practice paper. Suggestions: simple patterns, hearts, rainbows, birds. Mirror can serve as the center of a flower; artists such as van Gogh or Monet could be honored. Or try an "Under the Sea" theme? The mirror suggests a porthole!

Paint the designs on the frame. Squeeze out white glue in curvy patterns to add the yarn. Keep paints rich; avoid watery, weak color. Tip for teacher: Model Magic can be incorporated into frame design. For example, fish, seahorses, diver's helmet would embellish the "Under the Sea" mirror. Attach with white glue. Let dry thoroughly.

ADAPTATIONS

INTELLECTUAL DISABILITY

Prepare papier-mâché mixture. Break down the steps of papier-mâché. It may take an entire lesson to properly tear the newspaper into strips. Students will apply newspaper to frame. Note that papier-mâché is another one of those materials that may trigger tactile defensive behavior. Assist students with mirror installation.

Another approach to decorating the frame is the application of fabric scraps. White glue, thinned with water, is poured into shallow cups for students to dip fabric scraps into before applying to frame. By building a variety of textures, students will be provided with sensory enrichment and a touchable, visually lively frame.

EMOTIONAL DISABILITIES

Make sure students know how special this activity is and how they will treat materials respectfully. Point out that mirrors are fragile and that you are sure they will be careful. If your students are acting-out or aggressive on the day that the lesson is planned, reschedule and let them do the sketches for the frame design instead. (Papier-mâché can become a behavioral mess if students are not cooperative!)

LEARNING DISABILITIES

Students should enjoy the activity — just make sure they understand the sequence of events. Showing the sample and all the parts that led up to the finished product should help with perceiving the logical progression. The oval shape is a good format for the concept of closure. Measure yarn (with students) that will fit the frame, with extra for design. Apply glue in a pattern all around the frame and affix yarn.

ORTHOPEDIC IMPAIRMENT

Students with use of their hands can take this activity all the way through... others will want to start with the papier mâché. Papier-mâché is a playful activity for students with orthopedic impairments, yet is also excellent for manipulative experiences. Exacting design ability is not a prerequisite for frame decoration — even simple patterns look fine. You might place mirrors securely against flat surfaces for easier decoration.

DEAF AND HARD OF HEARING

Demonstrate to make sure that students know what is expected of them. The demonstration should include a sample of each major stage of the frame's completion. Papier-mâché is a separate technique that must be clearly shown within its sequences. Once understood, follow core.

VISUAL IMPAIRMENT

Some students will be able to cut and prepare frames. Squares are sometimes easier to cut than other shapes. Some students may be tactually defensive toward the papier-mâché, so ease them into it. For decoration, add yarn. Yarn may be dipped in a container of glue and then applied. Papier mâché is actually quite popular with students with varying levels of visual impairment, including those who are blind. It can be readily applied to flexible armatures as a sculptural process...a fine experience for all ages.

GIFTED

Gifted students should be able to accomplish this lesson smoothly because of their ability to handle procedures with multitasking steps. When they design their frames, they should think in terms of sculptural relief. For example, they can make a landscape and build up selected parts, such as trees and mountains, with papier-mâché. Art history images can provide inspiration for subject ideas; the classical Greek and Roman periods have good examples of relief works.

AUTISTIC SPECTRUM DISORDER AND ASPERGER'S SYNDROME

The point where teacher support ends and greater student involvement begins is so entirely dependent on the level of student's capability to follow instructions, with this activity in paricular. It is not unheard of for teachers and support staff to prepare mirrors with frames for students to decorate. On the other side of the autistic spectrum, students with Asperger's Syndrome could more than likely follow the core lesson. Generally speaking, the hands-on part of papier-mâché is tactually joyful — so the more the student is involved with the project, the better!

MITTENS, MUFFLERS, HATS, AND GLOVES

MATERIALS

- Paper — Manila or white
- Paper — lightweight tag board
- Crayons
- Yarn
- String
- Scissors
- Clothespins

TEACHER PREPARATION

You and your students can bring actual winter gloves, mittens, etc. to class to examine patterns. You can precut the hat and scarf.

DIRECTIONS

What is a pattern? It is a repeated design, as on wallpaper. Ask students, "Who is wearing a pattern? Are there patterns in your house? Where?"

Present pattern samples. Talk about varieties of patterns.

Make enough paper available to carry out the parts of the lesson you want to tackle. You may want to sequence the lesson into parts such as gloves, hats, mufflers, etc. A "set" looks great.

For gloves, trace hands on paper and cut. Scarves can be measured on a straight fold. Scarves can be fringed with scissors. Hats can be drawn freehand (or also on a symmetrical fold).

Decorate. Hang "sets" or parts on a clothesline for display.

ADAPTATIONS

INTELLECTUAL DISABILITY

Help students who want to make gloves by tracing their hands onto paper. Cut out. Offer fabric scraps for gluing onto gloves, which provides a sensory experience for students. To make sets, use same method and precut shapes. Talk about change of seasons. These students should try "their hands" at doing their own outlining. Offer assistance in cutting sets.

Be sure to practice zigzag patterns, etc. before students begin their projects.

Students generally should be encouraged to hang their work on a clothesline — they should squeeze the clothespins. This helps develop the pincer grasp!

EMOTIONAL DISTURBANCE

For a little extra fun, while prompting positive class interaction, try this: each student designs a winter pattern on a 3 by 5-inch card. All finished cards are collected and the deck is shuffled. Each student picks a card (without looking). This becomes the pattern design for their set.

When all sets are displayed, hold a class discussion on how the students feel their original designs were interpreted.

LEARNING DISABILITIES

Once the student has established a design motif, it will be used on all the clothing accessories (hat, gloves, scarf, etc.). Repeating the same pattern faithfully will require visual concentration. Establish linear pattern outlines and block in colors; this exercises fine motor skill.

ORTHOPEDIC IMPAIRMENT

Do parts of the set that make sense for the student. A student with severely contracted hands might prefer to make mittens instead of gloves (since fingers cannot be easily outlined).However, teacher is well-advised to not make assumptions about students' creative ideas, based on their physical appearance. When decorating, students with good motor control can create "stitchy" geometric patterns. Other students may want to paint instead.

Again, the manipulation of the clothespin is a good manual exercise (see Adaptive Aids, page 122).

DEAF AND HARD OF HEARING

To introduce this lesson, be a mime. Pretend to put on your gloves, your hat, and your scarf. Throw in a ("brrr") shiver for good measure. Present a complete, finished product ("set") before handing out materials. Perhaps students might want to try their mime skills too!

VISUAL IMPAIRMENT

Let your students do their own tracing when possible. Fluorescent crayons or paint create a visually stimulating quality. Offer precut scarf or hat when necessary.

Assist students who are blind in tracing their hands on screenboard for gloves (see Adaptive Aids, page 122). Cut gloves out. Other items may need to be precut.

One way to present geometric pattern possibilities to students is to have students draw zigzags and other linear patterns in a "moving" way. For students with blindness, the teacher can create pattern samples with crayon outlines on the screenboard that students can feel. Yarn may also be used to demonstrate linear patterns.

GIFTED

The world of woven fabrics and fibers can be examined through illustrations and example. Have students use crayons or markers in their work to reflect the look of "stitches." This gives the project a colorful, intricate appearance. Students can sew actual stitches into their flat work using light oaktag paper, light embroidery thread and sewing needles. Sewing will require good control in order to avoid tearing the paper. The student should have no real problem with the skill and still regard it as a challenge. Perhaps some research on popular winter patterns (Sweden is a treasure trove of such designs) would be appreciated. Feel free to embellish this lesson with bold color combinations and original patterns.

AUTISTIC SPECTRUM DISORDER AND ASPERGER'S SYNDROME

You can trace the student's hand for the glove shape — which is a body part(s) learning experience in itself. Use your "teacher judgment" as to which scissors will best serve activity (see Adaptive Aids: Scissors, page 122). As for the other choices in the lesson (hats, scarves)... students are encouraged to select at least one other item to reinforce the concept of "what goes together and why." It also helps to bring real scarves, mittens, and hats into the mix. Student names on hats and scarves will top it off!

MOSAIC MAGIC

MATERIALS

- Construction paper (several colors)
- Manila paper, 9 x 12, 11 x 18 inches
- Glue sticks or white glue
- Scissors
- Thick marker
- Ruler
- Crayons
- Ceramic tiles (optional)
- Clay (optional)
- Cardboard or posterboard (optional)

TEACHER PREPARATION

Precut construction paper into strips. (Be sure to have uncut papers of contrasting color on hand for background.) The mosaic technique — the joining of smaller parts to form larger shapes and patterns can be demonstrated in several ways: with small colored tiles (available from craft catalogues and tile stores), or with cut paper squares...even with loose coins from your pockets! Simply move pieces together to create designs.

DIRECTIONS

What is a mosaic? Ask students if they have ever seen murals, coffee tables, or floors made out of small colored tiles. Demonstrate mosaics (see Teacher Preparation).

Have students pick a simple subject to use for mosaic design. Some suggestions are: boat, fish, fruit, face, animals, house, tree. NOTE: Mosaics do not lend themselves to very fine details, so keep that in mind when choosing subjects.

Practice ideas on manila paper with thick markers; plot out color areas.

Cut paper strips into squares as needed. Paste squares on to background paper until surface is complete. NOTE: There is no "right" order to pasting down paper squares. Some students may start with tile outline, while others will start from any point.

SUGGESTIONS FOR FURTHER DEVELOPMENT

Once a paper mosaic project is completed, ceramic mosaics are a cliché. Ceramic tiles may be fixed to wood or heavy board with white glue. Craft possibilities include trays, plaques, decorative boxes (e.g. covering a cigar box), mirror frames (see *Mirror Mirror on the Wall*, page 70), etc.

Alternative to buying tiles is making tiles: roll out clay with rolling pin, use ruler, and cut out tiles with appropriate knife. Let clay harden and paint with acrylic paints.

Other materials that can be used for a "natural" mosaic are seeds, beans, stones, and shells.

ADAPTATIONS

INTELLECTUAL DISABILITY

You can draw a simple shape with marker on paper for students who may require more assistance. Students then tear paper squares with hand-over-hand assistance. Using prompting and verbal cues about the shape (i.e., "We are putting our paper into a circle."). Some students may be able to use scissors (see Adaptive Aids, page 122). Students glue their own paper "mosaics" into the "target" shape. Remember, some glue may cause tactile defensiveness, so use the gradual approach.

Other students can create their own mosaic using this plan: teacher precuts (or assists students in cutting out) a simple object, i.e., a ball, a house, a tulip, etc. Cut paper squares of basic colors and place in trays for organization. Paste appropriate colored squares into the precut shape, then paste the precut shape down on the larger paper. Now paste other colored squares on the larger paper (which is blank) and you have a complete mosaic!

EMOTIONAL DISTURBANCE

It is important that your students carry through ideas from start to completion. *Mosaic Magic* lends itself to this process well. Ideas must be thoroughly thought out in order to succeed.

Students should try out several ideas before selecting one. Set up a color plan on practice paper, indicating each color group that is needed. Prepare colored squares and proceed.

Once students are involved with mosaics, it's like popcorn — you can't stop until you finish it all!

LEARNING DISABILITIES

Students with learning disabilities could easily become confused by this lesson if it is not presented in the proper sequential order. To prevent confusion, try using graph paper (which is conveniently broken down into squares) for plotting out the mosaic design. It is a good idea to start with a strong outline of the shape, then block in the colored areas with crayons. Use the (filled in) practice grid as a reference and pick out corresponding colors, then proceed with the core lesson.

Mosaics exercise eye-hand coordination as well as organizational skills and help with closure of contour. Students with attention deficit issues will likely find this activity absorbing.

ORTHOPEDIC IMPAIRMENT

For students with reduced dexterity, mosaics provide an excellent motor exercise. However, cardboard or posterboard mosaics would probably be easier to grasp than paper. This will mean precutting boards into small — not tiny — tiles for students. (Many paper cutters are constructed to handle the cutting of boards and save you time — otherwise mat knives or extra sharp scissors are in order — for teachers only.)

You may want some of your students to practice their scissor skills and cut their own paper squares (see Adaptive Aids, page 122 for adaptive scissors). Once squares are cut, use cups or divided trays to hold colored squares, so that students can reach them and handle them with greater ease. Dividing by color is highly recommended.

DEAF AND HARD OF HEARING

Once the basics are understood, expand the project into a small group activity. Two or three students should plan a "wall" mosaic, using a length of butcher paper (two feet to three feet). Outline the agreed upon design (after sketching it first) and block in the tiles. The subject choice is open, but one suggestion is a class portrait, stressing the characteristic features of each student.

It is important to go through all the steps of this lesson. Even if it is not to scale, include a sample finished product.

VISUAL IMPAIRMENT

Fluorescent or intensely bright paper would be exciting for visually impaired students to use as mosaics. Mix them in with construction paper squares, and offer fluorescent crayons to color white paper (before cutting into paper tiles.) For students who are blind, tiles can be cut from sandpaper, corrugated paper, oaktag, etc., to create a texture mosaic. These tiles can be cut from strips (you may need to assist with cutting). A shape may be precut on which students can apply tiles, or a yarn outline of a specific shape can be glued down to create boundaries for contour.

Students will need to place their nonworking hands on the last area where they worked for points of reference. This indicates to the students where further work needs to be done. Some guidance may be needed for logical placement of elements within students' design scheme.

GIFTED

Mosaics have a rich history dating back to ancient times. Art history texts or Internet research should illustrate examples of mosaic art. Gifted students may enjoy the challenge of reproducing early designs (e.g., Pompeii still lifes, Byzantine wall mosaics, Islamic patterns). Students' work should reflect various characteristics of tile work within specific periods, such as differences in shapes, sizes, and styles.

AUTISTIC SPECTRUM DISORDER AND ASPERGER'S SYNDROME

To ensure against frustration, assist with spatial divisions of image placement. (Please refer to Learning Disabilities for helpful suggestions for successful completion.)

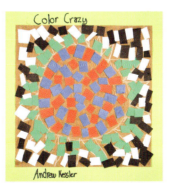
Color Crazy
Andrew Kessler

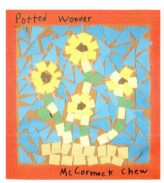
Potted Wonder
McCormack Chew

NATURE WEAVE

MATERIALS

- Yarn
- Pencils
- Tape
- Cardboard (approx. 9 x 12 inches)
- Ruler
- Scissors
- Twigs or dowels
- Feathers and other decorative pieces (optional)

Teacher Preparation

Cardboard looms should be notched vertically about one inch apart on both ends. You might want to precut yarn in desired lengths. Twigs or dowels will be needed for the cross bar on which weaving will hang. NOTE: If students need an introduction to weaving, see *Weave a Turtle*, page 112.

DIRECTIONS

Wrap yarn around one end of the cardboard. Start at first notch at top of cardboard (tape yarn to back side of loom); bring yarn down to notch at bottom. Continue wrapping yarn to next notch from bottom to top. Repeat until you finish winding the yarn on all notches. Tape end to back. This is called "warping" the loom.

For a closed weave, simply follow the left to right, under over following with right to left, over under technique starting at the bottom and working to the top. Yarn can be continuous from one row to the next. When you want to change colors, clip off the yarn you are using through the back of the piece. Start the new color where you stopped the last one.

For an open weave, set up the loom as you would for the closed piece. Weave yarn lengths randomly through the front of the loom in various directions, including diagonally. You can work section by section or in any free form manner. Just make sure that some of the yarn goes all the way across the piece so that it holds it together. To ensure stability, a few straight rows can be woven across the top and the bottom.

To remove piece from the loom, first trim and tie off loose threads. (NOTE: You may want to let yarn endings intentionally hang for decorative purposes. They can be tied into tassels and cord, adding beads, shells, feathers, etc.) Next, insert twigs into loops, one by one. Gently lift weaving away from board (board may need some bending).

SUGGESTIONS FOR FURTHER DEVELOPMENT

A wide variety of objects can be converted into looms. Shoeboxes, cartons, wooden crates, twigs, cylinder drum container lids, wheels (without spokes), frames, cut cardboard shapes, upside down chairs, even plastic soda straws (they can be used for belts). Professional weavers use large, standing looms. But beautiful weavings can be created on just about anything n which you can string yarn.

As for the fabric of your weaving, the possibilities for creativity are just as varied: gift wrapping ties, hair ribbons, silk cord, fabric scraps, socks, assorted trimmings (braiding, gimp, fringe) and lots of natural items (dry grasses, dried flowers, weeds, bark trips, bamboo shoots, etc.)

ADAPTATIONS

INTELLECTUAL DISABILITY

In advance preparation for the lesson, you might gather fabric sample books. Look for books that have woven and textural samples with paper backings. Some sources for out-of-date sample books are home decorating centers, furniture departments in stores, and fabric stores.

Precut strips of paper backed fabric for students who require it. These strips should be easier for students to grasp. Remove a full page sample for your "loom" or use oaktag. Cut three or four slits into it. Using a few fabric strips, assist students in the hand-over-hand weaving method. If you prefer to skip the weaving, students can paste strips directly onto cardboard. Assist with pasting and with applying strips, going from the bottom to the top. Use physical and verbal prompting — describe what you are doing while you are doing it. The motion that weaving provides is a good movement experience, but either approach provides sensory enrichment. Feathers are a welcome addition in either case. Display where students can touch them.

Many students should be able to follow the core lesson but will need the steps clearly outlined and demonstrated. If a nature walk is possible, it is an opportunity to gather not only twigs, but possibly pods, bark strips, and other weavable natural things. In the classroom, textural materials should be sorted into containers marked SMOOTH and ROUGH, or HARD and SOFT. Students can organize materials themselves, which adds to the learning experience.

EMOTIONAL DISTURBANCE

As mentioned in *Weave a Turtle* (page 112), weaving is a structured activity for students who need to focus their energy. In addition, to make the project more personalized, try using a favorite color scheme. Ask students what their favorite colors are and what it is about the colors that they like. Other possibilities are school colors or team colors.

LEARNING DISABILITIES

Constructing a loom is a recommended way for learning disabled students to begin this activity. Rather than notches, try the clothespin loom. Use a sturdy piece of cardboard or a wood board and wooden spring-type clothespins. Students will first measure and draw vertical lines about 1¹⁄₂ inches apart with ruler and pencil, going from left to right. The lines should be fairly even. Clothespins will be clipped on corresponding ends of the loom. Set up yarn by looping it over and around pins (tape ends to the back). Clothespins should fit board snugly so that they do not slip as student weaves the yarn. When work is completed, slip twig into the piece as directed and remove clothespins. NOTE: You can secure clothespins with tape, wrapping tape around the top and bottom. Loom will then need bending to remove piece.

You may also want students to try weaving a shaped cardboard loom. Create an oaktag template of simple shape — a fish, a flower, a heart, a kite, etc. Copy template onto cardboard and cut to make the loom. Weaving a specific contour should improve closure skills, while weaving is, in itself, an excellent eye-hand coordination exercise.

ORTHOPEDIC IMPAIRMENT

The kind of loom that your students will use will depend on their range of motion. Wooden crate looms can be placed in an upright position and may allow for a little more freedom of the "under-over" movement. You might want to experiment with different looms (see Suggestions for Further Development) but to adapt the cardboard loom to students' needs, consider clamps, vice, and reading stands. Also, try using a shuttle (available in hobby stores and art catalogs). They can also be made by notching a tongue depressor at both ends. Yarn is then wrapped securely around the stick.

Weaving is a good activity for students with orthopedic impairment. Using a flat cardboard loom can help with finger dexterity. Larger, open looms also add exercise to the arms and shoulders. Teacher discretion is required.

DEAF AND HARD OF HEARING

Here are two ways to implement *Nature Weave* as a group activity with your hearing impaired students, once the steps of the lesson have been demonstrated.

Variation 1: Students will stitch their finished weavings onto a large felt banner. Shaped looms (see Learning Disabilities) will yield a more varied visual effect. Skip the individual branches or dowels; instead, you will use a large wooden strip to hang the banner (See *Flying Colors*, page 52).

Variation 2: make an ongoing group weave. Set up a frame or box loom in the classroom. At a designated time, each student will add their yarn lines to the piece. Each student should have a turn. When the work is done, it will truly have everyone's efforts woven into it!

VISUAL IMPAIRMENT

Fluorescent (Day-Glo) and intensely colored yarns are available in craft stores. These, along with metallic yarns and trim, make visually stimulating weavings. Students with impaired vision can mix these bright and shiny materials with yarn in contrasting colors for dazzling effect. Blind students will need hand-over-hand guidance. To help students tactually differentiate between the "over-under" lines, use one distinct texture for "over" (smooth), another contrasting texture for "under" (rough). You might want to use fabric strips in combination with yarn.

GIFTED

Show gifted students examples of tapestries and other textiles. Weaving magazines are an excellent source for this. Ask students to design a representational subject that would work well in the woven medium. Some suggestions are sunsets, landscapes, seascapes, and sand dunes. Students will want to plan their ideas and color schemes on paper before they begin to "weave a picture." Encourage students to experiment with open spaces and creative knotting techniques in their piece. They could also try threading the yarn through previously woven sections to build textures.

AUTISTIC SPECTRUM DISORDER AND ASPERGER'S SYNDROME

Please refer to *Weave-a-Turtle* (page 112) to learn the "x" and "o" method in adaptive weaving. Also, please keep in mind that the definition of weaving may be broadened, such as making a spider web from thick yarn by gluing down directly on to paper. A "spider story" — of which there are many — would be an ideal way to introduce this lesson, followed by a teacher demonstration before students begin. And a great time for this activity would be October...a magical month!

OVER THE RAINBOW

MATERIALS

- Lightweight board or heavy paper

- Ribbon or string

- Markers, paint, crayons

- Scissors

- Dowels (approximately 12 inches) or wood alternative (recycled paint brush handle). Note: coat hangers can also be used.

- Hole puncher (optional)

TEACHER PREPARATION

You might want to precut the rainbow arch shape. You might also want to have paper squares and rectangles on hand for the clouds, stars, and so on. Hint: 3 x 5 or 5 x 8-inch unlined index cards can work, too.

DIRECTIONS

A discussion on rainbows should precede lesson. Just what are rainbows: When do they appear and why are they considered so special, so magical? What other elements can we use with them (e.g., stars, clouds, lightning)?

Distribute materials.

Decorate both sides of all elements.

Punch holes at the tops of all parts. Attach string to elements and to dowel. You will need to experiment with placement to achieve the right balance.

Ready for hanging? Windows that allow room for some rotation are perfect.

SUGGESTIONS FOR FURTHER DEVELOPMENT

Rainbow elements can be also be constructed from pre-colored and scented clay (see Adaptive Aids, page 122) if dimensionality is desired. They are easy to make and perfect for mobiles. They can be hung with fish hooks (be careful!), opened paper clips, or holiday ornament hangers.

ADAPTATIONS

INTELLECTUAL DISABILITY

Precut the rainbow arches for your students with profound intellectual disabilities. This lesson may then involve finger-painting on one side of the rainbow and crayoning on the other. Students will follow rainbow's arch with crayon: you can prompt student to use several colors.

Another approach: teachers will put out five cups of finger-paint, each filled with a different "rainbow color." With assistance, student will dip each finger into a different color using all five fingers. Guide student's hand in painting the curve of the arch. Let dry and hang either on hanger or hanging freely, within student's view for visual stimulation.

Many students can do the core lesson with or without precut rainbows. This is a good opportunity to teach and reinforce color. Provide an example of a rainbow that illustrates the basic colors and their order. Make sure, too, that students have concrete concept of what a rainbow is.

Emotional Disturbance

Your students can create "mobiles with messages," so they should make the elements a bit oversized. Paint bright bands of color on shapes and let dry. Write a personal response to each color on the mobile, following the band of color: e.g., "yellow is warm; it makes me feel good," etc. Messages can be different on both sides of the mobile. When mobiles are hung, students should have a chance to read and react to each other's remarks.

Learning Disabilities

Make a demonstration rainbow, with colors in a given order. Ask your students to replicate the successive order of the colors on at least one side of their mobile. The problem of the mobile's balance might be shown by giving students a heavy object (like books) to hold in one hand, then asking what the "other hand" feels like it needs. Follow core lesson for the rest of the activity.

Orthopedic Impairment

See "Suggestions for Further Development." A dimensional experience would allow for greater physical involvement. Scented clay is enjoyable, but not necessary.

Deaf and Hard of Hearing

Show illustration of rainbow or sample of finished lesson: verbally point out colors. The Sign Language Guide (page 24) has colors listed: why not try signing them as well? Take students through the steps of the mobile's assemblage before attempting it.

Visual Impairment

You might use the rainbow to further teach color concepts. Scented markers or flavored clays (see Adaptive Aids page 122) will help reinforce color to students who are blind. If you choose to use the screenboard, give students the precut rainbows and have them follow the rainbow's curve in their designs...do keep in mind that lightweight paper and crayons are required for effective screenboard activities.

Gifted

Rainbows can be multileveled mobiles. Students would benefit by studying the physical principles of more complex mobiles in order to construct them correctly. They may research mobile artists such as Alexander Calder who is credited with developing the idea of the mobile. Experiment with balance before launching into final projects.

As an added attraction, students can visually try to "catch" a rainbow by using a plant mister near the window light. Rainbows do appear in the mist in a certain angle. This is a close as you are likely to get to a real model — unless a rainbow happens outside your window on cue with the activity!

Autistic Spectrum Disorder and Asperger's Syndrome

Teachers are advised to precut rainbow shape(s) and cloud forms. Allow students to follow the contours as they apply colors of choice. The materials that teachers offer for the lesson is wholly dependent on students' functional level(s) and tactile sensitivities...wet or dry media work well, even when combined. Mobiles will be displayed together for maximum visual effect.

PIECES OF THE SKY

MATERIALS

- White paper
- Brown butcher paper
- Acrylic or tempera paints
- Brushes, all sizes
- Scissors
- Paper towers
- Cups or containers
- Glue

TEACHER PREPARATION

This is a mural lesson that can be done with several students at once, or just one to a paper. This decision will determine what size you cut the brown paper. For larger surfaces, keep flat paintbrushes on hand. Plastic cups or containers should be available for mixing colors.

DIRECTIONS

How does the sky look at different times of day and in different weather conditions? See how many sky "changes" students can name.

Students select colors appropriate to their choices. Encourage the mixing of pastel tones for sunsets, clouds, fog, etc.

Paint large area with big brushes. For "sky details" such as stars, birds, snowflakes, and so forth. students can paint them into their work directly or create parts separately on another paper, cut, and apply to mural.

NOTE: This is an excellent subject for studio painting (on canvas with acrylic). It is colorful and "loosens up" the hand.

SUGGESTIONS FOR FURTHER DEVELOPMENT

The sky is blue? Who said so? The sky is also pink, orange, purple, gray, and black — and is often in multicolored combinations. Skies can be painted loosely and freely in the style of "action" painting. They can be treated like Monet's Waterlilies," which is a delightful sum of color parts dots, dabs, etc.). They can be graphically designed for clean-cut, dramatic contrast. The sky's the limit!

ADAPTATIONS

INTELLECTUAL DISABILITY

Painting in a big, loose manner is both a kinesthetic and sensory experience. Your students will enjoy painting "Pieces of Sky," big brushes. Brushes that are easier to handle (see Adaptive Aids page 122) and require less fine-motor skill are simply ideal! Offer hand-over-hand assistance when necessary. When painting is complete, glue on "cotton clouds" for further tactual enrichment.

Students whose intellectual disabilities are moderate are capable of the concept of painting the subject of the sky. Use the view from your window. If possible, take students outdoors to make experience more concrete; e.g., what does the sky look like today?

If you plan to use pastel (or mixed) colors, you will need to instruct students clearly on how to mix them. This is the kind of lesson that lends itself to teaching color blending. Proceed with core.

EMOTIONAL DISTURBANCE

This lesson is a natural for a multiple group activity. The entire group should decide on one theme, e.g., times of day, seasons, weather conditions. Once that is determined, smaller groups of three or four will carry out the aspects of the bigger theme. For example, if the theme is "weather," one small group does "rain," another does "snowstorm," and so on. Within each group, students decide who wants to do details. This approach teaches cooperation within the larger groups as well as within the closer, interpersonal one.

LEARNING DISABILITIES

Students should enjoy a lesson that is as open and unstructured as this one — and one that is free from organizational demands. Students still need to think about covering the paper in a logical manner, i.e., composing the space effectively, using the materials to express their ideas successfully. The only possible caveat is the "overly enthusiastic" student. Since this is such an engaging lesson, playing soft, relaxing music while students are painting should help assure a calming atmosphere.

Orthopedic Impairment

The big broad movement that painting "Pieces of the Sky" affords is a healthy exercise for those with the range of motion to do it. For those with greater restriction of motion, try using a shelf paper roll in a tear off dispenser. (If it does not come with one, see if you can find a wax paper or foil paper dispenser that will work.) Use double-faced tape to secure dispenser to the left or right side of work surface, leaving enough paper out for student to start work. As student paints (or draws with oil pastels), he or she can pull fresh paper to continue in the mural size panel until complete. NOTE: You may need to assist in pulling paper from roll and in finding the most convenient placement of paper on the desk for the student.

Deaf and Hard of Hearing

An intriguing way to do this lesson with your hearing impaired students is to create a giant puzzle! Students will develop, as a group, a big sky mural. Another piece of butcher wrap is cut to the same size as the first. The finished painted sky is cut into large puzzle pieces when dry, then scrambled up. The class must put it back together on top of the other cut butcher paper (rolled masking tape on the back of the puzzle pieces will make puzzle stick to uncut paper). This all needs to be demonstrated, even in a smaller sample size, before the project begins. It is a project that benefits students by combining play with creativity while encouraging positive student interaction.

Visual Impairment

Students will enjoy using fluorescent paints. These can be used in combination with the poster paints to create a dazzling visual effect. Sunsets would be particularly dramatic.

Some students who are blind may have some difficulty with the concept of a sky. It is not a tangible object. You can talk about weather, the smell of the air when it rains, and most importantly, the spatial expanse of the sky, which students can relate to when they stand in a large open space without nearby walls (with the teacher present)!

Students with visual impairments will enjoy the pure sensory enjoyment of painting "big." To add to this experience, you may want to add texture to the paint (e.g. sand) for variety.

Gifted

Your gifted students might be interested in discussing how cloud formations and sky conditions are used to predict the weather. It would be fun to learn about skies — researching what cloud patterns can mean and using that information in painting *Pieces of the Sky*. When work is complete, the class can become "weather reporters" and "read" each other's work for probable forecasts!

Another direction for this lesson is "celestial bodies." Paintings that include the stars, the planets, and the constellations would definitely be out of this world!

Autistic Spectrum Disorder and Asperger's Syndrome

This is an opportunity for a small group project. As we know, if there is one major feature across the autistic spectrum, it is the need for learning how to socially communicate with others. Even for students with mild conditions, here's a place where art will reinforce social skills.

Teachers are referred to the Emotional Disturbance Adaptation found in this activity. The goal is similar... group cooperation. Frankly, even if students aren't highly interactive, at least they are working together — and that's a step in the right direction.

PIZZA TO GO

MATERIALS

- Paper large enough for at least a 9-inch circle

- Markers

- Crayons

- Scissors

TEACHER PREPARATION

Here's how to make the pizza:

Cut a square to the size you want.

Fold in quarters, then fold again for "slices."

Cut as shown in images. Open the paper to reveal the "pizza."

DIRECTIONS

Be a waitress or waiter (server) and take orders. After students state their favorites, ask them to name as many pizza toppings as they can: pepperoni, mushrooms, sausages, cheese, and so forth.

Cut out pizzas.

With a dark marker, delineate crust and slices.

Add "the works." Serve!

SUGGESTIONS FOR FURTHER DEVELOPMENT

The overwhelming appeal of pizza speaks for itself! You might consider turning a corner of your classroom into a temporary "pizza parlor" to display the pizzas. (You could put brown paper up as the "window," and give the pizza parlor its name.) Tomato pies are really loved, but if you want to turn the lesson into apple pie (or blueberry pie) — help yourself!

ADAPTATIONS

INTELLECTUAL DISABILITY

Precut mushroom slices out of brown construction paper. Red paper circles can represent pepperoni; yellow corrugated paper can be your cheese. If needed, provide help for your students in pasting these parts onto their pizzas, with verbal cueing as you progress.

Students with moderate disabilities can search magazines for photos of appropriate food for pizza toppings. They can cut out illustrations (see Adaptive Aids, scissors, page 122), and use glue stick to place on slices.

Other media (crayons, watercolors) may be employed.

EMOTIONAL DISTURBANCE

Because the activity is exciting, don't overdue your presentation! Students will be asked to create a giant pizza, which will contain a combination of everybody's favorite toppings. You can do several oversized pizzas or one enormous pizza, depending on class size and available classroom space.

When pizza is completed, encourage students to create their signatures out of topping, e.g., TIMMY (in pepperoni)! Display finished product in a prominent place in the school.

LEARNING DISABILITIES

Have students trace the circle that is the pizza shape. Clearly instruct students in method of folding pizza into slices (see Teacher Preparation), and assist when necessary. Draw lines on folds to indicate slices. Students then cut along line to "cut slices" out. They have just made a "pizza puzzle." If desired, students can paste pizza slices back onto white paper. You might want to help students with their understanding of the parts (slices) to whole (pie) relationship by using the "fraction" approach, i.e., a slice is 1/8 of the pizza. Focus skills will be summoned ...and reinforced.

orthopedic impairment

Some students have cutting skills but need practice (Adaptive Aids, scissors, page 122). The pizza is a great exercise for staying on the lines of the slices and cutting the slices out — if reasonable for student. Once slices are cut, students can paste them onto a larger circle that they will cut. That will be the pizza plate. Decorate pizzas as outlined in the core lesson.

For those students with less dexterity, precut pizzas and decorate with finger paint using "pizza colors" such as orange, red, and yellow. For decoration, dip string into white glue and drape around pizza (it resembles cheese.) Add paper circles for pepperoni if desired.

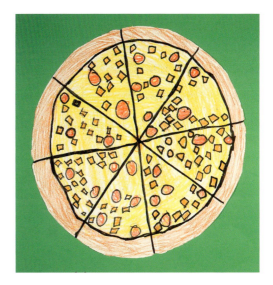

deaf and hard of hearing

Save a frozen pizza carton or take-out box to show students that they will be making a pizza. Present the pizza circle, and indicate that the students will decorate it. Provide colored construction paper that students will cut for toppings. You may want to look up sign language color names (see the Sign Language Chart) and "sign" colors with students.

visual impairment

Do you know that pizza cutters and tracing wheels are almost the same tool? (Tracing wheels are sometimes used as adaptive aids.) Students who are blind enjoy using tracing wheels on surfaces that allow raised marks, somewhat like the screen board — there is tactile contour, and they are perfect for the imaginary slicing of pizza. Students enjoy the movement of the wheel on the paper — a wad of newspaper below helps the marks become more tactile. Tracing wheels can be used in combination with crayon on the screenboard to decorate the overall surface. NOTE: A curved line (such as the crust) is hard to do with tracing wheels. The students with great visual acuity may want to cut out toppings and paste them on the pies. They can share their mushrooms, pepperonis, etc., with all the students.

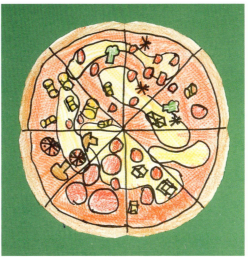

gifted

Not only can gifted students create fabulous pizzas but they can also make pizza boxes. Bring in a take-out box as a sample. Supply class with paper of suitable weight and size. Students can look at the sample box, then figure out how to construct their own. Students can design logos for their pizza boxes, which brings in possibilities for a unit on advertising art and food product design.

autistic spectrum disorder and asperger's syndrome

Once again, this lesson is an opportunity for working with others on a widely shared experience. The directions given in the adaptation for emotional disturbance fits into the autistic spectrum disorder. Attention to individual names, as well as group activity, are of interest here.

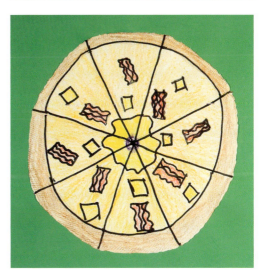

POCKET PLANTERS

MATERIALS

- Wet red clay
- Tape
- Tongue depressors
- Burlap

- Rolling pin
- Containers for water
- Wire or string
- Newspaper

Optional:

- Clay tools
- Toothbrushes

- Old shirts (smocks)
- Dried or artificial flowers

TEACHER PREPARATION

(See *Clay Pots: Pinch and Coil*, page 38 for advance preparations.) NOTE: You may want to precut burlap into 8 x 12-inch pieces and tape to work surface in advance.

DIRECTIONS

Give students a chunk of clay about the size of a grapefruit, and a piece of burlap. Tape burlap to work surface.

Students will roll out clay with a rolling pin on top of the burlap. They will need two slabs to form the "pocket." Use tongue depressor (or clay tool) and ruler to cut appropriate matching shapes. Squares are recommended, but other shapes can be used.

Wet and score inside edges of the two clay tiles. Fold a wad of newspaper, and make a "sandwich" — two "slices" of clay, newspaper in the middle. Pinch along the three sides of the clay tiles to join the two sides.

Pierce a hole in the tile for later hanging.

When thoroughly dry, carefully remove newspaper. Thread wire or string through the hole. Place dry materials inside and hang on the wall.

SUGGESTIONS FOR FURTHER DEVELOPMENT

In creating pocket planters, you have learned the slab method. Slab, along with the pinch and coil, is among the most versatile techniques in handbuilt ceramics. Stabs readily become tiles and plaques. Slabs can also be wrapped around and over existing bowls, vases, and cardboard molds to create new replications of the object. It is also the slab technique that is best suited for making clay boxes.

Slabs deserve lots of experimentation. They make tall, sturdy vessels and can be combined easily with other handbuilding methods, such as pinch and coil.

ADAPTATIONS

INTELLECTUAL DISABILITY

Students with severe disabilities will likely need your assistance in rolling out the clay. Show students how to use the rolling pin in a hand-over-hand manner (see Adaptive Aids, page 122). Students may want to use a one-piece slab to create their pocket planters. Slab should be of a shape long enough to accommodate the double-sided fold. Place the newspaper in the middle and fold clay slab over. Student will pinch the sides of the clay together or press one finger against edge to close the pot. Let dry as directed.

Students should enjoy the novelty of pushing the rolling pin. It is also a good exercise for the hands and arms. Some students might enjoy using a cookie cutter. Encourage "people" shapes; gingerbread men are perfect. Assist students in stamping out a man; use a dull pencil to create features on the face. Physical and verbal prompting should take place as the cookie man is coming to life (i.e., "Here are the eyes, here's the mouth, etc."). Decorate pot with cookie cutter shaped people. Teacher may need to help students with attaching the forms using score and slip.

EMOTIONAL DISTURBANCE

Consider taking your students on a fresh-air adventure that will expand upon their daily experience with the outside world. Your students could become young "archeologists" (once the terminology is understood, and the nature walk will become a mock "dig." Collect items such as stones, leaves, twigs, and pods. See also what artifacts of man-made civilization you can find: bottle caps, empty matchbooks, keys, pens, etc. (NOTE: Supervise the "found" objects so that they appear reasonably safe and clean. You may even want to "plant" some items along the trail in advance for students to uncover later such as broken clock parts, furniture coasters, jar lids, etc.)

Back in the classroom with the collection of items — what happens next? You create instant fossils. Roll clay out directly on work surface (skip the burlap). Press objects into the clay and encourage sharing. Follow the core as directed.

Why use this particular adaptation? Students with emotional disturbances are typically responsive to clay (please forgive this generalization, yet it happens to be the case). With the receptivity of clay in the lesson's favor, including the "outdoor" elements could prove expansive.

Learning Disabilities

The pocket planter as presented in the core requires matching and measuring. Students often need reinforcement in these areas. It might be a good idea to use a cut oaktag or cardboard template for slab shape. Place on top of clay and cut clay out with tool. Pull clay away from work surface. Proceed with core activity.

You might want students to do other projects using slabs and patterns. Students can design a simple shape out of oaktag — apple, fish, house, etc. Roll out clay slab, place template on clay, and cut. Push away excess clay and pull the paper off the clay. Decorate surface. Let dry. (These can easily be converted into wall plaques... just remember to punch a hole for hanging while clay is still wet.)

Orthopedic Impairment

If students have the range of motion that is required to operate a rolling pin, it is an excellent exercise. Pressing the object into the clay to create textures is not a physically difficult movement, and it is something that students enjoy doing. Offer clay tools to students who are very limited physically. It is sometimes easier to use a tool to accomplish a task, such as closing the seam between the two sides of the planter. Students who cannot pinch the clay will want to press the seam closed with a tongue depressor (a one-piece foldover slab is suggested, instead of two pieces).

Even students with limited dexterity can make "a dozen long-stemmed colored tissues." Students can crush colored tissues into flower "balls" (another good hand exercise). Stems are made of pipe cleaners poked through tissue to hold in place (you might need some tape inside flower.) Plant flowers into pocket planters; it makes a dazzling array!

Deaf and Hard of Hearing

This provides students with a unique way to develop literary skills. Bring in some poetry books that include nature themes. Haiku (short Japanese verse) is perfect. After demonstrating technique (skip burlap), provide students with books from which to choose poems. Demonstrate by picking one line from a poem and inscribing it in the clay. Draw a compatible motif (flowers, stars, clouds, etc.).

Of course, students have to know how to read to do the activity in this manner. If they don't, follow core as directed. Make sure students understand the lesson in either case.

Visual Impairment

Clay slabs receive textural impressions beautifully. Students can particularly enjoy and learn from this characteristic of clay. Kitchen tools that make a great "impressions" include forks, spoons, egg beater, whisk, meat tenderizing hammer (less common, but terrific, is the Swedish rolling pin).

Students will enjoy using these objects in the clay to create textures and patterns. They will also delight in using the rolling pins. Students who are blind may require some guidance as to the location of the water cups, the tools, and the edges of the clay. Direct student's hand when needed.

One more object that is suggested for clay impressions: the alphabet block. Pressing letters into the clay makes a playful and appealing design, but also helps the younger student with visual impairment in identifying the alphabet.

Gifted

The planters themselves can grow and grow in the hands of students who are gifted. Students should be shown the basic lesson, then asked how they could make planters with additional pockets. Pockets can go on top of pockets or students can create a clay "shoe bag." The challenge is to create a greater design complexity out of a basic idea. When dry flowers are planted in the pockets, the effect is quite charming.

In addition, students should give thought to decorating clay surfaces. They may want to treat slabs like tiles and use a different texture for each pocket's surface. Some suggestions are shells, rubber bands, clips, lids, string — the choices are endless. Rubber stamps are quite "impressive!"

Autistic Spectrum Disorder and Asperger's Syndrome

Please refer to the adaptation listed in the *Clay Pots* activity (page 38).

PRETZELS

MATERIALS

- Manila paper
- Large sheets of brown butcher wrap paper, about 2 by 3 feet
- Markers
- Crayons
- Scissors
- Newspaper
- Stapler

TEACHER PREPARATION

The most solid introduction to this lesson would be a clay activity. Students roll out clay "snakes" and create a pretzel (see *Clay Pots*, page 38). This may help to understand how pretzels are formed from one piece (See images in this activity). To precut the paper pretzel for students, you need only to cut along the outside contour. Negative or open space can be cut later.

DIRECTIONS

Students can use one large folded sheet of brown paper or two sheets of the same size.

Practice drawing a smaller pretzel before attempting the full-sized outline.

Draw pretzel shape to edges of paper. Decorate. Cut negative (open) spaces with scissors. (Note: the term of negative space commonly refers to space that is not part of the concrete object. It can occur between, within, or around the object. It is also known as open space.)

Avoid making the pretzel shape too narrow — it's easier to stuff a "fatter" pretzel than a "skinny" one!

Newspaper that has been torn and crushed into small balls will provide pretzel's dimensionality. Students will be stapling along the sides of the shape.

Stuff portions of newspaper into the pretzel until it is finished. Students may need some assistance with the stapling and stuffing.

SUGGESTIONS FOR FURTHER DEVELOPMENT

In Philadelphia, Pennsylvania, putting mustard on pretzels is a tradition. Perhaps there are other regional or personal garnishes for pretzels? Allow students to decorate the pretzels with their ideas!

ADAPTATIONS

INTELLECTUAL DISABILITY

Students with profound intellectual disabilities may explore the basic pretzel shape by examining precut pretzel forms. Help students draw shape following the pretzel configuration template made by teacher. If reasonable, place newspapers in a place where students can locate them independently. Help students to tear and crush newspapers. Offer aid when necessary, especially in stapling and stuffing the form. Display pretzels within students' view.

Students may benefit from a clay introduction to pretzel shapes. By using clay "snakes/coils" to create clay pretzels, students will become familiar with the unique pretzel shape. In addition, students can physically imitate pretzel curves with their arms and legs! Continue with the regular directions for paper pretzel.

EMOTIONAL DISTURBANCE

What's your favorite kind of pretzel: crispy or soft? Get students involved, then ask them to "cook up" their own unlikely specialties. Decorations for pretzels could include cherries, stars, whipped cream, etc. Hence, pretzels become students' own creations, i.e., "Billy John's star-studded pretzels," "Maria's rainbow pretzel," and so on.

LEARNING DISABILITIES

Draw pretzel shape as a guide for students. After they draw and cut shape, students can decorate to simulate a traditional pretzel. Flowing linear patterns that follow the pretzel's shape will improve students' tracking and closure skills. Stuff and staple to complete.

orthopedic impairment

Try to do the clay introduction (see Teacher Preparation). Have students with arm mobility draw their own pretzels on a stable surface; others may opt for precut pretzels. Tearing the newspaper and crushing are good movement exercises for the many students.

deaf and hard of hearing

Students can "pair up" for this activity. Explain clearly in written words and draw a pretzel on the board. Students will share the designing, cutting, and stuffing of the pretzels. This makes a nice opportunity for communication as well as cooperation between students.

visual impairment

If you don't do the clay introduction (as appears in Teacher Preparation) then bring some real pretzels to class. Students can feel their shapes (and later devour them)! For teacher to precut pretzel shapes with the "negative" parts cut out will be helpful in better understanding the project. For a 3-D touch, the "salt" could be paper fasteners, Styrofoam packing chips, or even sugar cubes (Paper fasteners should be inserted before stuffing begins.)

For body awareness, students could also imitate pretzel shapes with their arms and legs.

gifted

Why not make a mock pretzel vending business! You could construct a vending cart out of cardboard cartons to display the pretzels.

Another approach that engages abstract thinking is to ask students to identify other "pretzel" configurations that are not food; for example, highway ramps, figure skating on ice ("figure eights"), etc.

autistic spectrum disorder and asperger's syndrome

Depending on where students are on the Autistic Spectrum, a template — generally speaking — is recommended. If student are on the severe end, please refer to Intellectual Disabilities. Otherwise, follow core lesson.

REFLECTIONS

MATERIALS

- White crayons or white pencils

- Black paper

- Mirrors (portable sizes)

TEACHER PREPARATION

If it is not possible to provide each student with a mirror, students can share mirrors. Remind students to handle mirrors with care! If available, use metal mirrors.

DIRECTIONS

Students may study their images in the mirrors. Observe individual characteristics such as hair style and texture, size and shape of features, etc.

Draw self-portrait with white crayon or white pencil on black paper.

Selectively develop areas that further describe details. Block in details with white crayon as you would with a black pencil on white paper.

SUGGESTIONS FOR FURTHER DEVELOPMENT

This approach to self-portraits allows students to study their own faces. However self-portraits that are created solely from the mental image that students have of themselves can be just as revealing. Mirrors provide a reference and are fun to use, but should not necessarily dictate an approach for perfect duplication of reflected images. Show portraiture examples from art history to back up this point, using a few diverse images (see Art Heroes Section, page 139 — Frida Kahlo, Chuck Close, and van Gogh). Discuss differences.

To develop compositions around self-portraits, ask students to add a personal background — either real or imaginary.

ADAPTATIONS

INTELLECTUAL DISABILITY

For students who will need teacher assistance for reflected self-portraits, teacher holds mirror so that student can see his or her face. With free hand, engage student's hand and place his hand on facial feature with verbal prompting, i.e., "Joey's eyes, Joey's nose, Joey's mouth," etc. Put down mirror and introduce black paper. In a hand-over-hand method, guide student in outlining shape of "portrait" on the paper. Further guide student in drawing simple representations of facial features. Continue verbal cueing. To create a sensory quality and touch of realism, you can add yarn or fake fur to represent hair.

Some students will need reinforcement regarding the placement of facial features when looking in the mirror. Remind students that eyes are in the middle of the face, nose between eyes, and mouth, mouth near the bottom, at the top is the forehead, at the bottom is the chin. Ask students to physically locate these features on themselves. Follow core as directed.

EMOTIONAL DISTURBANCE

What is a portrait? Is it merely a visual account of a person's face? Is it a report on the particular order in which hair and facial features are arranged? Portraits can do more than report facts; they can express character and personality.

Your students should be encouraged to observe their faces in the mirror and try to show many different expressions. To create them, students should think of specific incidents or feelings that make them feel happy, relaxed, or angry. Ask them to describe what happens to their faces when mood change (i.e., cheerfulness — eyes open wide, corners of mouth turn up, posture straightens). Students select the mood they want to capture by "posing" for themselves in the mirror. Class can brainstorm words that describe feelings.

Another way to explore moods is to do multiple self-portraits. Using a larger paper, do several "selves" — reflecting many expressions. Have a class discussion when all work is complete.

Learning Disabilities

Ask students to examine the anatomy of their faces with their fingers. Press fingers gently around the eyes to feel that eyes are set within the face, not on top of it. Feel these from its bridge to the tip to make students aware of the nose's protrusion from the rest of the face. Place tips of fingers firmly against lips to understand that it is the teeth and the jaw that define our mouths.

This exercise should help with understanding volume and dimensionality. Follow core.

Orthopedic Impairment

The degree of students' movements should determine where mirrors are placed. It may make sense to hang a mirror on the wall if it is possible to do so — and to assist the student so that he can see himself comfortably. Be sure that drawing surfaces are compatible to mirror level. See Adaptive Aids, page 122 for drawing aids that may help with manual grasp.

Deaf and Hard of Hearing

Try this movement activity that is often used in drama workshops. Two students sit opposite each other, face to face. One student begins a motion, such as a circular movement of the hand. The other student "mirrors" (follows) the movement with his or her hand. There is no leader; students take their own "turns" spontaneously within the exercise. The challenge is to anticipate the other person's move – keen concentration and observation are needed. This game requires a form of kinesthetic communication. It will also serve to loosen students up before drawing and active observational skills. Studying the mirror image ties directly into the lesson of *Reflections*.

Of course, you will need to demonstrate clearly the fact that students will follow the game with a self-portrait from mirror's image.

Visual Impairment

To increase sensory awareness through tactual means for students with visual impairments, use the introduction suggested under Learning Disabilities. The student will enjoy using the mirror as a reference and may need to get very close to see himself. The white on black drawing will increase the visibility of the line work through contrast (in advertising art, this is known as "reversed" and is recognized to have greater visual impact.) Students who are blind may be curious about the object known as a mirror, so let them explore it carefully. The teacher will then become the "talking mirror" and describe to the student what the mirror is reflecting of each student's face. Portraits may be done on screenboard (see Adaptive Aids, page 122) with physical and verbal prompting regarding placement of features. Students may want to add sensory materials and real effects such as a tie, a scarf, earrings, yarn hair, etc., to further enhance their experience.

Gifted

The gifted student should also have an opportunity to do the self-portrait as presented in the core activity. However, after that has been accomplished, you could follow up with the "magic mirror." Tell students to imagine that they are holding magic mirrors that can add or subtract years (making you older or younger) or can change your identity (i.e., your face is still your face, but you are a spy, a king, a rock star, etc.). Mirrors can also go back or forward in the history of time, turning you into a caveman or a spaceman!

Autistic Spectrum Disorder and Asperger's Syndrome

In the realm of autism specifically (although not exclusively), the recognition of the human face and its expression is often poorly understood at best. A condition broadly known as "mind blindness" may effect a student's inability to identify any particular facial expression correctly. What can an art teacher do? Actually, art activities such as this one can begin by locating features on the face (See Adaptive Aids for face-shaped paper). Note: Since the mind-blindness condition is prevalent in the autistic spectrum, don't concern yourself with the white crayon on black aspect of the lesson.

If students appear ready to proceed (after placement of facial features is reasonably understood), acquire magazines and cut out a wide variety of eyes, noses and mouths. Students using face-shaped paper or other paper will select from (presorted) facial features.

Using a glue stick, students will arrange "collage-style" features on the paper face. To top off this lesson, provide simple drawings of basic visual symbols (or representatively drawn examples) that convey the basic emotional scale: happy, frightened, angry, surprised, sad. Now see if students can match the expressions they created in the "collage" portraits — both their own and their classmates — with the emotions stated. This is a step in the right direction in mitigating a widespread communication problem!

Students with Asperger's Syndrome can either follow the core lesson or the Adaptation for Deaf and Hard of Hearing.

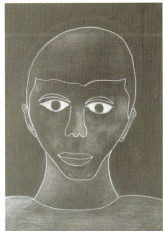

SHE SELLS SEASHELLS AND OTHER SURPRISES!

MATERIALS

- Paper (lightweight, i.e., newsprint, tracing paper)

- Crayons, broken or stubs (also see Adaptive Aids: Crayons, page 123)

- Shells (flat shells work well)

NOTE: If shells are not available, see Teacher Preparation.

TEACHER PREPARATION

Did you ever wonder what to do with those shells you saved? Bring them into class — encourage students to bring them in, too. Besides the beach, seafood restaurants are a good source for shells. Pet stores selling aquarium supplies should stock seashells. If shells are not available to everyone, shell shapes can be created from corrugated paper. Show students a real shell (or picture of one). Draw shell contour (or trace the real one) on the wrong (flat) side of the corrugated paper. Cut out and use for rubbings as you would use shells. You may want to precut shells from corrugated paper or other objects that are good for rubbings for some students (See Adaptive Aids for plastic rubbing plates, page 124).

DIRECTIONS

Give each student at least one shell. Other objects to use in rubbing may also be introduced.

Place object(s) under paper; use broad side of crayon (wrapper removed) until texture emerges. You may need to manipulate paper over shell and other objects to rub whole shape.

Move shells and objects around under paper to create a multicolored and varied overall pattern, using many colors from the crayon box. Students should exchange shells and objects to make their designs more interesting.

SUGGESTIONS FOR FURTHER DEVELOPMENT

Seashells are one group of natural objects that make good rubbings. Leaves, in the fall, are another. Rubbings can easily have seasonal themes, but there are many kinds of approaches and materials. Simply emptying your pockets can provide many items for rubbing — combs, keys, ticket stubs, paper clips, and especially coins. Remember, pencils can be used as well as crayons, to create your rubbed images on paper.

ADAPTATIONS

INTELLECTUAL DISABILITY

A shell should first be explored tactually with you guiding the student's hand. Hand over hand assistance should be given to the student in learning the drawing motion (with the crayon) that produces the rubbing.

Students should be clear on the steps that will lead to a finished rubbing: placing shells under papers, moving them around; feeling for shells and rubbing crayon over the paper; using side of the crayon. Demonstrate the activity. You might want to talk about the size differences and how you will mix sizes in the rubbings to make designs more interesting.

EMOTIONAL DISTURBANCE

Memories associated with shells and the seashore should prompt students to "open up" and share pleasant experiences. Vacations, summer camps, etc., evoke good feelings. This is an excellent opportunity for students to have a positive exchange around their art activity.

LEARNING DISABILITIES

Try to have students rub the whole shell for its entire shape. Students will become more aware of its contour by rubbing the outside edge of the shell. Shape and texture awareness will help with the concept. Ask questions: Where do you find shells? Have you ever pressed them into wet sand? What mark did it leave? Does the shell feel the same on the outside as it does on the inside? Which side is rough, which one is smooth? And so on. A discussion of this kind leads to a broader understanding of the subject.

ORTHOPEDIC IMPAIRMENT

Students may need teacher assistance with the rubbing motion, which is a good hand and arm movement activity. Another way to do it is to wrap shells with paper tissue (arts and crafts or wrapping type). Rub the wrapped shell, then open. Repeat for other parts of your design. This is fun to do, it has an additional surprise element when results are "unwrapped." Also, wrapping the shells provides another manual dexterity exercise.

DEAF AND HARD OF HEARING

Your students should be able to follow the core after it has been presented in a step-by-step demonstration. After your students have accomplished their rubbings, here's an adventure you could send them on: the Texture Safari. Students will pair up. Armed with pencils and lightweight papers, students will go on a hunt for interesting surfaces around the school that they can rub. Brick walls, fences, gratings, doors, etc., are fair game. When students return to the art room or classroom, see if students can identify the objects (students may want to write out their guesses). This project not only expands on the seashell lesson, but it also gives students an opportunity for some independence and decision-making outside the classroom. The "Buddy" system will help with social relationships.

VISUAL IMPAIRMENT

This activity is excellent for students because of its very nature — rubbing and the sense of touch go together. Experiment with fluorescent crayons for rubbing with your students. Students who are blind will enjoy the experience of the rubbing of the shell texture, but you might want to add to it by sprinkling sand on the paper (use white glue first) when rubbing is completed. Students with low vision might find the combination of sand and glitter visually stimulating — and there's always glitter glue! For your absolute finishing touch bring in some suntan oil. Lightly scatter some drops on the paper to round off the complete sensory picture!

GIFTED

Students can use their shell rubbings as part of an undersea composition that they will develop. At the beginning of the activity, students select a particular ocean environment to draw or paint, using a specific example of tropical, or arctic, waters. Based on their choices, students will create appropriate flora and fauna. Students will need to research the project so that their underwaterscapes are correct; i.e., tropical fish belong in a coral reef, not in the North Sea. The one exception will be the rubbed shells, which will not necessarily match in the environmental picture, but will add the textural interest.

AUTISTIC SPECTRUM DISORDER AND ASPERGER'S SYNDROME

Here's a perfect opportunity to learn the techniques of rubbing with the side of the crayons. Note: students often need encouragement to try new methods when using an alternative to the expected and known way. This sort of approach provides assurance that change isn't always threatening (see Adaptive Aids, page 122).

SILHOUETTES OF PLACES NEAR AND FAR

MATERIALS

- White paper or brown butcher wrap
- Black construction paper
- Scissors
- White glue
- Pencils
- Watercolor or tempera
- White oil pastels or white pencils
- Glue sticks

TEACHER PREPARATION

You may want to use *Pieces of Sky* (page 85) as the backdrop to this lesson. If mural paper is being used, cut to size. Try to provide visual reference material that illustrates appropriate subjects for silhouettes such as skylines or tropical plant life (see student examples here). For dramatic use of silhouettes in art, look for examples of cut paper folk crafts, using sharp contrast silhouettes (e.g. Haitian oil drum art, Pennsylvania Dutch, Polish papercuts, etc.)

DIRECTIONS

Paint colorful "backdrops" to silhouettes that will represent the sky.

Select a subject for a silhouette. Deserts, tropical islands, cities, and bridges are some possibilities.

Students draw outside contour of silhouette and cut it out.

Decide if white outline on drawing adds or detracts from silhouette. Glue silhouette on paper.

SUGGESTIONS FOR FURTHER DEVELOPMENT

There are many ways to create exciting backgrounds for your silhouettes. You can use watercolor (see *Working Wet with Watercolor*, page 118), color broad bands with crayons, or apply foil stars on bright blue paper.

You might want to "reverse" the elements of this lesson by creating a colorful foreground (e.g., brightly patterned buildings) against a black sky!

ADAPTATIONS

INTELLECTUAL DISABILITY

The core lesson may be too abstract for many students. However, the high contrast of a dark area against a bright area is visually stimulating. So, the skyline silhouette can be traded for a torn paper collage. Black paper will be folded, pieces torn out of center. Repeat — fold, tear — until paper looks like Swiss cheese! Reminder: tearing is also a skill, but if the teacher prefers cutting, there are adaptive scissors that can be used (See Adaptive Aids, page 122). Paste perforated black paper against a fluorescent or brightly colored paper. You will still have an eye-popping display

Students may or may not be able to comprehend the concept of a skyline. If you think your students would be perplexed, have them work on simple images of a house and/or a tree. Cut out the objects and mount them on bright backgrounds of choice. When all of the class's work is complete, they can be shown side by side as silhouettes. At that point, the teacher can discuss silhouettes and skylines. The concept should then become more concrete.

EMOTIONAL DISTURBANCE

Where is your favorite place? The seashore? The city? An amusement park? An imaginary place you like to think about? If you don't have a favorite spot, invent one.

Once the special place is established, your students can draw the details on black paper, cut, and mount it against the colorful backdrop they created. They should be encouraged to title their work (e.g. Fantasy Park, Paradise Mountain, etc.) Class discussion on why their places are unique should follow.

LEARNING DISABILITIES

It is worthwhile to remind students that silhouettes are flat representations of three-dimensional volumes. Spatial reality may also be confusing to student with learning disabilities — or not. Students may want to sketch out their ideas before proceeding with one activity.

A corresponding lesson you could try is "Shadows." Have students fold a piece of paper into four blocks that will represent morning, high noon, afternoon, and night. Students pick a single object, such as a cactus in the desert or a cat on a windowsill. In each block, students will show the object, the sky, and its shadow reflecting the time of day. Students may need to observe an object at home or at school at different times to carry out this lesson with confidence. The "night" block will be a silhouette, but what is valuable is that students will better understand the time sequence that led up to the darkened object. Sequencing is also an area that generally needs building with all students.

ORTHOPEDICALLY IMPAIRED

Creating a cut silhouette requires scissors skills. (See "Adaptive Aids" for scissors.) If student's hand movement is too severely limited for working with scissors, consider "City Lights." Offer students several sizes of rectangular and square construction paper. Cut a dry sponge into strips (about the size of a pen). Students will dip end of sponge into bright paint (orange, yellow, white) and print "windows" on the paper. You can assist students in mounting the "buildings" against a backdrop to create a lively city. (See "Adaptive Aids, page 122" for other tools to use for printing.)

DEAF OR HARD OF HEARING

Skylines can be considered the "autograph" of a city. Much like well-known personalities, many skylines are famous and recognizable — New York, Paris, San Francisco, Athens, Istanbul, and Moscow are good examples. Travel brochures and pamphlets are free and available from national tourist bureaus, travel agents, and chambers of commerce. You can also collect "famous city" reference materials from travel magazines or from the travel sections of the newspaper.

Provide posterboards on which students will paint their skyline. When everyone is finished, tape the boards together to create a panoramic fanfold of international skylines!

By presenting "Silhouettes" in this way, you are widening your students' world and giving them an important role in an exciting group project where their efforts can be displayed with pride. NOTE: Students should do all work either horizontally or vertically so that boards will "match" each other for fanfold. Of course, make sure that students understand all phases of the activity beforehand.

VISUAL IMPAIRMENT

The high contrast qualities of this lesson contribute to positive visual stimulation. The black silhouette against the bright background, the white drawing on the black paper serve this purpose. You may want to add a little "extra" by including fluorescent (or brightly colored) paper squares as windows and other details on the black silhouette.

Students who are blind will need to understand exactly what you mean by the term "silhouette." Students with "light perception" may see the world in a somewhat similar way (forms, not details, appear against a contrasting backdrop).

You may want to precut basic skylines and let students explore the outline. Explain to them what they are feeling (i.e., roof, top of skyscraper, etc.). If you have 3-D models,

bring them into the lesson. Students can use screenboards (see Adaptive Aids, page 124) to draw windows onto the buildings. Mount against background paper.

GIFTED

Observe the student work for a moment or two. Does it begin to remind you of something familiar? If not, here's a hint: "Wish you were here" often appears on the back. That's right, when scaled down, this activity closely resembles a postcard. Your gifted students may be intrigued by creating a travel poster of an exotic place (let's say a tropical island with the palm tree). Design the travel poster to include another view of this island (maybe an aerial view or map). This will require other materials such as brushes, markers, etc. Places your students choose can be real or imaginary — from the land of Oz to a resort in France. Do drop us a line!

AUTISTIC SPECTRUM DISORDER AND ASPERGER'S SYDROME

A perfect chance to use Adaptive Aids (page 122), particularly bingo markers and other bright spongy applicators. Provide black paper on which students will "make their marks." You have probably guessed that these round and square patterns — random or otherwise — will soon become "bright lights, big city." Teacher can assist in the forming of building shapes — either before students begin or after work dries.

Students with Asperger's Syndrome can follow the core lesson — yet might want to take advantage of an adaptation that invites social interaction (see Emotional Disturbance).

Floating into the Sunset — Lauren Klunk

When the Amusment Park Opens — Daniel Pyle   Luke Kelly

THE SKETCHBOOK: OBSERVATIONS AND INTERPRETATIONS

MATERIALS

- Pencils

- Fine-tip markers

- Sketchbooks or white drawing paper

- Newsprint or other inexpensive paper (optional)

- Charcoal drawing sticks (optional)

- Kneaded erasers

- Chamois (blending cloth) — simple facial tissues can be substituted

TEACHER PREPARATION

If your budget does not provide for sketchbook purchases, students may want to buy their own sketchbooks, if financially feasible. Other alternatives are: clipping papers together (with paper fasteners, staples, or paper clips) and working on a hard board (drawing board), keeping papers in large oaktag-weight folders. The idea is to keep the artwork together for reference and to note the continuity and progress of visual expression.

DIRECTIONS

To Do: Outdoors

Take your students for a neighborhood walk, or simply explore school grounds. (Reminder: please check your school's policy on classes held outside of the usual, designated classroom.)

Bring sketchbooks, drawing boards if needed, and other stated materials.

Ask students to find an object or area (such as a tree, a bench, a fence) that interests them.

Students will then do a study of the chosen subject, with attention to texture, shading, and line.

Allow an appropriate amount of time.

Share!

To Do: Indoors

1. Students will model for each other. It is best to "warm up" with short poses before drawing students in longer poses. ("Props" such as an umbrella, fan or hat might relax the "studio" atmosphere.)

2. Students will begin with sketches of student modeling in an "action" pose, which should last no more than five minutes. Poses include bending, pretending to catch a ball, dancing, etc., all in a "frozen" motion (model tries not to move while posing).

3. Use charcoal and newsprint. Draw in a big, loose manner. The goal is to capture the direction of the pose, not the details. (note: charcoal is friendly but can be messy...students need to be forewarned.)

4. After students have "loosened up" with their drawings, use sketchbooks for the longer poses (at least 20 minutes a pose). Student models may pose in seated, standing, or reclining postures.

Suggestions for Further Development

Keeping a sketchbook is a stimulating and exciting experience for children as well as for older students. You may want students to have two sketchbooks, one for home and one for school. Students may surprise you with their enthusiasm for their out-of-school sketchbooks: they are often eager to share their world with you in this visual form.

You may want to create a studio-like atmosphere at school around the modeling setting. You and your students can collect props: hats, empty bottles, used musical instruments, old lamps, scarves, fabric lengths, etc. These are welcome additions to the modeling sessions and are worthy of attention for their own qualities and for their value in still life arrangements. The transition from sketchbook to easel is a natural one. Painting from palettes on canvas boards (with acrylic paint) epitomizes the studio experience, which is strongly backed up by the drawing skills that the keeping of sketchbooks helps to develop.

ADAPTATIONS

Intellectual Disability

Some students may not be able to respond to an object or subject with a drawing that explains its qualities. However, students can learn about the movement of line and mass by keeping sketchbooks. Using a fat crayon (see Adaptive Aids for ideas, page 122), students will be shown various lines in a hand-over-hand manner by you. You might want to start with a straight line, moving into a curvy, wavy line, then circles. Try varying width of line by rubbing the side of the crayon (crayon wrapper removed) and experimenting with different hand pressures. After students have practiced line work with you and can do it with a minimal amount of prompting, draw combinations of these simple lines with color and texture. NOTE: the element of play and exploration of materials is meaningful in this sketchbook activity.

Other students who are able to work independently should be given charcoal (or chalk) and large paper before working in sketchbooks. Save the charcoal sketches in large folders or portfolios. Boldly print students' names in marker on the portfolios. Sketchbooks may also be slipped inside. On a regular basis, review all the work with students individually and in a group. This will reinforce their learning experiences and give you an opportunity to observe their progress.

Emotional Disturbance

Sketching nature and the environment raises awareness and develops appreciation for the world we all share. There is something relaxing and humanizing about spending time with a tree or sitting on a grassy hill in a park. Students should be given a specific time frame for selecting objects, observing and drawing them, and should be encouraged to complete their work within it.

Studio modeling is a wholesome vehicle for students to "act out" in a pose or costume. It is closely akin to role playing. Students should have input in taking poses. Teacher might want to resist "directing" the activity completely, allowing students to find what feels right for them.

Sketchbooks are in themselves a healthy vehicle for self-expression, personal thoughts, and feelings. They are in many ways like visual diaries.

Learning Disabilities

Students with learning disabilities, while often quite bright in certain academic areas, may have spatial issues that can be identified in their artwork. These perceptual distortions often exist in the student's misunderstandings of spatial depth and the placement of objects in space. Remind students of logical perspective by asking "What tree is closest to us? Which is farther away?" etc. This is also useful with studio work, e.g., "What part of that object does the model's head hide? What part of the chair is nearest to you?" Sometimes, what may appear obvious needs to be verbally distinguished.

Another approach that helps students to organize their thinking is to provide a reference point immediately. The first thing that goes down on the paper can do it. For example, suppose the student draws a tall tree. Establish its location on the page compared to the rest of the landscape. Is the park bench on the right or left of the tree? What about the little bush in relationship to the tree? And so on.

Drawing from objects and people is indeed an exercise that develops observational skills and helps with ability to respond to the visual world in a cohesive manner. Also it is a way of improving eye-hand coordination.

Orthopedically Impaired

Drawing is not merely an act performed by two well-coordinated hands. We don't really draw with our hands — they are subservient to our mind's interpretation of what we see. Sensitivity, determination, and spirit also have a lot to do with it. Think about the mouth and foot painters (Art Heroes, page 153-154) who create exquisite images by holding a pencil or brush between teeth or toes. There is more to drawing and painting than learning mechanically correct technique.

Students with orthopedic impairments will need to experiment with adaptive aids and methods until they find the ones that best express their own individual style (see Adaptive Aids, page 122 for ideas). Sketchbooks may also need to be adjusted so that the surface of the page is accessible. Reading stands and, of course, drawing tables that are adjusted properly can be of great help.

Deaf and Hard of Hearing

Nature walks and neighborhood trips with sketchbooks will continue to expand the world of your students. Please keep in mind that students with hearing impairments may not hear oncoming traffic as well as other warning sounds! Keeping "outside" sketchbooks — where students draw about the events and people in their lives outside of school — is highly recommended. The sketchbook provides students with a way of making visual notes and impressions in the universally understandable language of art.

The modeling experience can offer students a social exercise through group poses. Use two to four students as models together. Try this: Demonstrate to students that they will be having an imaginary tug-of-war. This will create interaction, as well as animate the poses. Indicate to the class that they will all have a chance to pose; and that they should leave room on their paper for add-on figures. Through this method, visual interest and movement are introduced, and everyone gets into the act! Make sure your students are clear on what the activities require.

Visual Impairment

Some students who are visually impaired might benefit from using a magnifying glass when doing studies outdoors — particularly when drawing small details. Magnifying glasses can also be fascinating and may aid visual understanding for some sight losses.

For studio work, a spotlight, which is fairly inexpensive and easy to mount, can be used. Direct artificial light on a model or still life can often help. Note: Albinism (and some other eye conditions) can include extreme sensitivity to bright lights. Even though this is far less common than most students' need for illumination, be aware of it. If a student complains that the light is hurting his/her eyes, giving him a headache, or making him feel sick, remove the student from the bright area immediately. This extreme light sensitivity had a medical term with a somewhat misleading name: photophobia (students with albinism do not necessarily have a "phobia" of intense light. Due to the lack of melanin in their eyes, light is not properly filtered. Even sunlight can be overwhelming.)

Students who are blind can keep sketchbooks, but the paper should be lightweight enough for screenboard penetration (newsprint sketchpads are good). Screenboards (see Adaptive Aids, page 124) can be slipped under each sketchpad page as students draw. Students will actually need to "feel" outdoor objects tactually in order to draw them. Three-dimensional anatomical models that can be held and explored are suggested for studio work. Also, students might enjoy using yarn or string as their "line." Drawing with yarn provides tactual information for students who are blind when they touch their work.

Gifted

Students who are gifted are able to comprehend the effects of light on a figure or object, and can interpret texture, scale, and spatial relationships. Ask students to bring into class some illustrations of master drawings, from the Renaissance to the twentieth century. Examine how the artists handled these elements. Students' work should reflect dimensionality through shading, plastic line (line that varies in expression), and textural richness. Drawings should also suggest students' selectivity; i.e., students should choose parts or details of the object or setting, and avoid "reporting "everything in front of them.

Here's a related activity that gives students a chance to analyze action poses and understand the basics of animation at the same time. Students can use small unlined notepads or precut 30 small pages (about 3 x 5 inches). A model will select one action pose, such as lifting an imaginary balloon from the floor to above his or her head. Each pose (which lasts about two minutes) will be drawn on a separate page showing each movement that comprises the whole action; the first page shows the model with hands above the head. When all phases of movement have been sequentially drawn, staple all pages together at the top. Flip pages with thumb for a moving experience!

AUTISTIC SPECTRUM DISORDER AND ASPERGER'S SYNDROME

Using an oversized "writing" pad or newsprint sketch pad, you can divide pages with marker and yardstick into six to eight blocks. Because we know that students with autism respond well to visual cues and supports, the "sketchbook" can be an ongoing picture diary. Referencing the visual supports shown on page 123 in Adaptive Aids, each block, starting with block number one, can represent an image of his/her face — even if drawing skills are developmentally delayed — along with student's name. This is important... the student next draws a symbol of a task that he accomplished on that same day. What is different about this activity is that the amount of time allocated to each block

— 45 minutes is suggested. The theme might be...What (student name) did today! The time sequence should be somewhat accurate.

It is suggested for art teachers to expand the time, as in What (student name) does in school on (art day)! This activity represents a communication board. Picture cards can also help students in depicting ordinary images. Markers and crayons are suggested. Note: parents can reinforce this activity with the student at home.

ASPERGER'S SYNDROME

Often students with Asperger's Syndrome fixate on a single subject, of which they become extremely knowledgeable. This has earned them the dubious nickname of "little professors." While subjects may vary from student to student, trains are exceptionally popular. While there are varying theories about this, there is reason to believe that the predictability of trains may help qualify the attraction. Students on the autistic spectrum do crave predictability and, in many instances, display rigidity in their behavior.

Older students with Asperger's Syndrome can follow the core lesson, whether or not they are experts on trains!

A SNAKE IN THE GRASS

MATERIALS

- Paper (construction or plain)
- Scissors
- Crayons, oil pastels, or markers
- Black felt-tip pens (optional)

TEACHER PREPARATION

Be a snake charmer and present your class with a basket full of precut snakes. Have some good reference material around or create sample snakeskin patterns for them.

DIRECTIONS

Introduce snakeskin patterns.

Either give students paper to cut out snakes or give them the snakes you pre-cut for them.

Students will create designs based on either real snakeskin or whimsical ones. Add forked tongue – don't forget the "snake eyes"!

SUGGESTIONS FOR FURTHER DEVELOPMENT

Snakes have notorious reputations. They inspire fear and awe, so naturally they are fascinating to children. There are lots of ways to develop this activity. Students can use snakes to "weave" through the tall paper grass in larger theme formats, such as "rainforests." Compositions can expand to include lizards and other reptiles that might make some say "yuck" — but they secretly adore them. It cannot be denied that crawly creatures have a design impact that is perfect for art room study. They are part of our natural habitat, so let's treat them with respect!

You may also want to turn *A Snake in the Grass* into a rubbing activity (see page 90 for more on this technique).

ADAPTATIONS

INTELLECTUAL DISABILITY

Give your students practice paper, and help them to draw curvy lines over and over. Next, present them with the precut snakes. You may need to tape snakes to the work surfaces to keep them from slipping. Offer students hand-over-hand assistance in transferring "big movement" used in practice to the smaller movement required for drawing the precut snake. Try fluorescent crayons; they are more visually stimulating.

Completed snakes can be tied on to a coat hanger to create a coat hanger mobile. Display mobiles where children can see them.

Suggestion: students can practice snake-like motion in the air with their arms. Explain to them that this is how a snake moves — showing pictures of snakes will help them understand more as well. Assist children in cutting their own snakes (see Adaptive Aids page 122 for scissors). Decorate in whatever manner is desired.

EMOTIONAL DISTURBANCE

You can precut a "jumbo" snake large enough to provide each student with a (precut) snake "section." Students design their own part. When everyone is finished, reunite the snake. You have an instant group project and a dazzling display of everyone's patterns!

LEARNING DISABILITIES

A Snake in the Grass can be a perfect connect-the-dots lesson. Use a precut snake as a pattern and trace in the dotted line. Students then connect dots, which is great for eye-hand coordination and closure. Decorate snakes as desired — prompt students to cut them out.

You may want to display finished snakes in a group mural, encouraging students to develop an appropriate theme (e.g., rainforest, desert, garden).

Orthopedically Impaired

For students in wheelchairs, place a length of brown wrap paper across the floor. Draw a big wavy line that becomes "a snake's path." Wheelchairs can be navigated by students over the wavy course. To further imitate a snake's journey, chairs could become "trees" that the student will need to go around — this adds a little drama.

If your students have some motor ability (yet still restrictive), gently ease into the "snaky" line drawing by practicing S-curves, then draw on the precut snakes.

Deaf and Hard of Hearing

See if the science department has a spare snake to lend you. It's the perfect model for drawing snakes. Show students a finished sample snake (and a picture if available), pointing to markings. Proceed if all is understood.

Visual Impairment

Students who are blind may draw designs on the precut snakes on their screenboards (note photo next page) — or let them use yarn to decorate the snakes, following the serpentine. If you have a toy rubber snake, let your students explore it, but tell them that it's not real and that it might feel funny! If you want to add dimensionality to this lesson, students can fold snakes in an accordion manner, but that does alter the wavy contour of the snake shape.

Gifted

Gifted students can do some fancy snakeskin designs — use felt-tip markers. Students can create coiled snakes, cobras, interlocking snakes, etc. In addition to the common garden variety, students who are gifted can capture some exotic designs. Their scissors become the drawing tool for executing the contours. You might want to talk about the amazing nature of snakes... specifically, the fact that some snakes are able to swallow animals whole. A snake contour that reveals another shape within it could be amusing and unique!

Autistic Spectrum Disorder and Asperger's Syndrome

The challenge of the teacher is to make sure that the idea of the paper snakes (precut) is a representation of a real snake. In this case, a nature dvd that clearly shows snakes in motion — in their habitat — would be very helpful. Check the Internet, too. Choice of materials to best show snakeskin patterns are crayons and markers. (Check out Adaptive Aids page 122 for other appropriate art tool possibilities.)

Students with Asperger's Syndrome proceed with core activity.

SOMETHING'S FISHY!

MATERIALS

- Paper
- Newspapers
- Watercolors (silver and gold watercolors are great)
- Paintbrushes
- Cellophane (optional)
- Glass fishbowls

- Pencils, markers
- Stapler
- Coffee stirring sticks or popsicle sticks
- Scissors
- Paper reinforcements
- Aquarium gravel

TEACHER PREPARATION

If you or your students can get real goldfish bowls, the results will be terrific. You might want to precut squares and rectangles that will be folded for cutting of fish shapes.

DIRECTIONS

1. Talk about fish and their undersea environments. Ask students to imagine that they are scuba divers who plunge deep into the ocean. Ask have them to describe what they see and hear.

2. Hand out papers. Let students select the sizes they want for their fish.

3. Students design contour of fish shape with pencil or marker. Decorate with paint and/or markers (add glitter if desired-perhaps as a finishing touch). Let dry a bit.

4. Cut fish out of folded paper.

5. Staple around edges of fish leaving room for stuffing.

6. Tear newspaper into strips and crush into fish-size balls.

7. Stuff fish with newspaper. Staple closed.

8. Insert coffee stirrer or popsicle stick into the "belly" of the fish. Put aside, then fill bottom of bowls with gravel.

9. Add details like "air bubbles," which can made out of reinforcements that can be glued inside the glass.

10. Plant other end of the "fish on a stick" in the gravel. Fish should appear suspended inside the bowl. If desired, add colored cellophane.

SUGGESTIONS FOR FURTHER DEVELOPMENT

Shoeboxes can substitute as aquariums. Add blue tissue paper or cellophane — and other details (starfish, coral, seaweed, etc.). Students could paint waves on the sides.

ADAPTATIONS

INTELLECTUAL DISABILITY

Divide students into small groups. Precut fish large enough for several students to stuff — staple edge, leaving a gap in one area for students to later insert newspaper stuffing. Students take turns in applying color to fish (see Adaptive Aids, page 122). Help students tear newspapers and guide them in stuffing the fish as it is passed from one student to another. Staple the fish closed and hang them in a prominent place.

If possible, introduce this activity with a real fish in a fishbowl. Point out the special features of a fish: fins, tail, scales, placement of eyes — and the way fish appears suspended in water. If students are able to draw the fish, encourage them — if not, use teacher-made fish patterns or precut fish. Tear newspaper and stuff fish, staple it and insert it in a bowl or reasonable equivalent.

EMOTIONAL DISTURBANCE

Why not use the undersea world as an reason for a group project? Use cardboard box or a real glass aquarium. All fish to be placed within the container provided. A few students could be the designers of the box/aquarium — others work on oceanic elements besides fish, such as seaweed, coral, and — buried treasures! A treasure chest provides a "lesson within a lesson." Each student will be asked to draw and cut out what they would like to discover in a treasure chest!

LEARNING DISABILITIES

Students should be made aware of the fish's dimensionality. Point out both sides of the fish to add an element of realism; to exercise eye-hand coordination, have students create and attach fins using small pieces of colored paper and a simple fan fold technique. Wiggle eyes would really top off this lesson!

ORTHOPEDIC IMPAIRMENT

Crushing newspaper is an excellent activity for manipulation skills. Assist when needed in stuffing the fish. Some students will cut the fish themselves while others will require precut ones (See, Adaptive Aids: Scissors, page 122). All should be able to find a medium for decorating fish that suits their skills. Some students may draw scale patterns, some might paint freely, etc. Ahoy there, mates!

DEAF OR HARD OF HEARING

Bring in real fish or pictures for observation. Point out scale patterns. You might want to draw some sample patterns for student to consider. Then explain basic elements of the lesson so that students can see the progressive steps.

VISUAL IMPAIRMENT

Use watercolor...yes, students who are blind do enjoy watercolor! It is a sensory experience. Be sure that the watercolor cups are secure on the desk (cut a piece of masking tape, roll it, and place under cup so it sticks to desk). Use precut fish for students who lack cutting skills that may occur in severe vision losses. Point out to students that there is a connection between the watery quality of the painting method and the fish's world — this adds meaning to both the lesson and the painting experience. Other materials to consider using are fluorescent crayons and/or paints. Fluorescent materials are reminiscent of fish's iridescence. NOTE: See *Working Wet with Watercolor*, page 118, for suggestions on painting for students who are blind.

GIFTED

There are so many gorgeous tropical fish that the gifted students can study before creating their own fish. Researching scale patterns, intensive fish colorations, and the variety within the names of the different species should provide the initial stimulation for this lesson. Students may be asked to draw more than one species...and to be able to report on the details associated with their choices. You could easily extend this lesson into marine biology.

AUTISTIC SPECTRUM DISORDER AND ASPERGER'S SYNDROME

If the student is confident in drawing a simple fish, do allow it — ditto for cutting out the form. Other students can trace a fish template (with teacher guidance) of the fish shape provided. Decorative colors and designs should follow. Note: if you provide sturdy paper, stuffing may not be unnecessary.

If you are able to collect the clear plastic containers in which lettuce is sometimes sold, students would have an ideal aquarium. Place florist's clay, plasticene, or modeling clay across the bottom and help students "plant" their fish. Be sure to point out that fish are not really planted in the sea — they swim. Students with autism are prone to take things literally, so make sure they understand the difference between this art activity and the natural world.

SPECTACULAR SANDWICHES AND 12-LAYER CAKES

Materials

- Brown butcher wrap paper
- Poster paint, brushes
- Oil pastels
- Scissors

Teacher Preparation

Because the subjects of cakes and sandwiches are so similar in this activity, it is being presented here as a "double choice" lesson. In order to make sandwiches or cakes "spectacular," you will need 3- to 6-foot lengths of brown paper. Since it is a good idea to provide images — do employ visual resources for both wedding cakes and layered sandwiches.

DIRECTIONS

Discuss wedding cakes — how are they different from everyday cakes? Answer — more than one layer. How about the decoration? Pastry guns create rosettes and frilly designs.

Now, for the sandwiches. Again, layers are the key here. If you keep adding layers to your sandwich, you can have a giant sandwich as tall as a wedding cake — but who could eat it? Since we are having "fun with food" in art, who could actually eat it is not of concern (though still an interesting question...).

Unroll brown butcher wrap to desired size. Cut.

Create the sandwich or cake of your dreams.

Suggestions for Further Development

There are other food fantasies besides cake and sandwiches that can be oversized wonders. Visit *What's the Scoop?* on page 114. You may want to take a look at it before starting this activity...it lends itself to a thematic unit.

ADAPTATIONS

Intellectual Disability

Pprecut comic strips, fabric widths (lace trim is great), colored paper strips, etc. Assist students in pasting various strips, starting at the bottom and working your way up. As students progress in layering, they will be exercising their abilities to reach physically from one point to another. Teachers are reinforcing a very important concept—bottom to top! To illustrate this point (along with an image of a layered cake) try stacking colored building blocks.

NOTE: If student can't manage this even with assistance, see the Orthopedic Impairment adaptation.

Emotional Disturbance

After introducing the lesson, have students decide to make either sandwich or cake. Pair students with each other on the basis of their choices, as well as their potential for working together. They should decide on materials, designs, etc., together. When work is completed, have a group discussion. Allow partners to explain how they reached their mutual decisions on their work. Give much positive recognition for partners who worked well together.

Learning Disabilities

Whether they choose sandwiches or cakes, students will need to examine the idea of layering. Both the sandwich and cake start at the base and are built up from there. You can illustrate this principle by using your hands and the students' hands — stacking them all up together (you know that playful old trick, right)? Once students start building the layers, they should catch on to this concept.

Orthopedic Impairment

You may want to assign some student to create sandwich "food components" on smaller paper, such as pickles, olives, tomatoes, onions — and, of course, the meat(s) of choice. This gives students with limited physical reach an opportunity to work independently. When completed, gather all sandwich fixings — with the incorporation of green tissue paper for lettuce or other materials if desired. Students will collaboratively mount their super-sized sandwich vertically on butcher paper.

A suggestion for students who want full control of the project is to drape butcher paper over the table. Paper can be moved or rolled forward as students complete each layer.

Deaf or Hard of Hearing

Try this fun approach: Each student has a brown paper panel for either sandwich or cake. Allot a given time per layer, say, ten minutes. When time is reached, student passes his or her paper to the next student. This process is repeated until determined number of layers is reached. Divide time according to number of layers and time allotment. The results will be an amusing mixture of everyone's efforts, and lots of exchange will have taken place.

Visual Impairment

Your visually handicapped students might use textural materials to represent various parts of the sandwich or cake. For example, green tissue can become lettuce, and red circles can be pepperoni. For cake, fabric trim and lace doilies can be added for decorations.

To make the idea of layering more understandable to blind students, try accordion-folding the brown paper. Open and lay flat. Lines provided by folds will cue students, on the layers' boundaries. Take students' hands; lead them from bottom "up the ladder" to the top.

Gifted

Use the cake activity (since it most closely resembles architectural facades) for a "cake-tower" theme. The theme could be a city, country, or period of history. For example, if the theme were "New Orleans," the cake could have a layer of mardi-gras mask faces, a layer of jazz instruments, a layer of iron grill work, etc.

Students might need to research themes. When projects are completed, students should not reveal the theme's identity — other students must guess!

Autistic Spectrum Disorder and Asperger's Syndrome

The extent to which students will take this lesson will likely depend on where their individual abilities fall on the autistic spectrum. Students with Asperger's Syndrome can readily follow the core activity. Students on the other side of the spectrum will accomplish the cakes or sandwiches on a smaller scale — for example, a double layer cake — or a three layer sandwich (i.e., Big Mac, club sandwich). Students will require visual ques. Teachers also may want to precut forms, although that isn't really necessary. For choice of materials, teacher may want to visit Adaptive Aids (page 122). Oil pastels may not be appropriate. The main idea here is that students "get it" — they are creating their own special cake or sandwich. Student names can boldly accompany finished products, as in Jason's Great Big Yummy Cake!

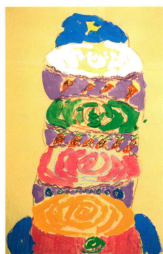

STAMP IT, PRINT IT!

MATERIALS

- Modeling clay (plasticine may be substituted)
- Tongue depressors
- Manicure sticks
- Clay tools
- Poster paint
- Brushes
- Paper
- Paper towels

TEACHER PREPARATION

Modeling clay is soft enough to manipulate. You may want to collect — and then offer — objects that can be pressed into the clay to make prints more interesting, such as bottle caps, combs, forks, etc.

DIRECTIONS

Give students a portion of modeling clay in the appropriate size to be divided into stubs.

Grip the tongue depressor at both ends and divide the clay into two or more pieces. Roll into stubby cylinders.

With tongue depressors, clay tools or orange sticks, students carve out a simple design that they will soon print.

Using brush, apply paint to the "business end" of the clay stumps.

Press clay firmly on to the paper, (but not too hard or you will dull the stamp).

Give thought to the overall design. Clay stamps can be lightly wiped in order to apply other paint colors. New patterns can be cut by removing a thin slice from end of clay.

SUGGESTIONS FOR FURTHER DEVELOPMENT

You might want to show the class some rubber stamps and explain the difference between the stamp print and the block print. Some other materials for stamps are vegetable prints (potato, carrot, onion, etc.), corks, and rubber erasers.

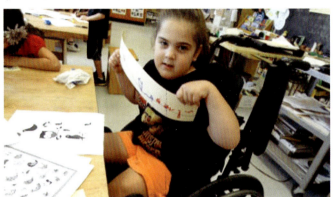

ADAPTATIONS

INTELLECTUAL DISABILITY

This is an excellent activity for all levels of students. They will enjoy rolling the modeling clay into a cylinder. Teacher assistance will be needed for students to create simple stamps. Cut away enough to give stamps some definition — one stamp per student is fine.

In a hand-over-hand method, instruct students in the printing technique. (Teacher "fades away" as student gets the idea.) Stamps are "dipped" into shallow cups of poster paint. You may want to stay with a small range of bright colors that contrast with paper. Black paper will really make the print images pop! Most students should be able to accomplish this activity once it is clearly understood.

EMOTIONAL DISTURBANCE

Prints and greeting cards go well together. Make lots of construction paper available in assorted colors. Students create their stamps and design their own hand-crafted cards from them. Each student will produce a stack of cards, varying their stamp cuts and colors. Prompt students to experiment with each other's stamps. Note: Be sure that students know how to fold cards before beginning activity.

When cards are completed, students may want to keep them to send to others or package them with a string or tied ribbon around a pack of cards to give as a gift or sell at school fairs. Make sure students put their own "logo" on the back of the card. This emphasizes personal pride in one's own creative product, while supporting a positive interchange of ideas between students.

Learning Disabilities

Ask students to create a border print. Select two or three colors. Have students vary their prints in some way, either by overlapping or by alternating colors. Students decide whether they want a "free-form" or a geometric border. Leave center blank. After the border dries, either write a poem or draw a picture inside the "frame."

This approach will help with learning to follow directions, better learn visual closure, and reinforce fine-motor control. Besides the learning merits, the activity is joyful!

Orthopedic Impairment

Students will benefit from the rolling of the clay. Even if arm movement is limited, try to help them to do it (but don't force it). The carving of the clay does require some fine-motor ability, so students who lack those skills will need assistance. The "press and print" part of this activity is achievable and should be made available for all students.

Deaf and Hard of Hearing

Create "wallpaper" for the classroom. This is a group activity that will encourage communication and interplay between students. Demonstrate the rolling out of the clay and the carving, etc. Students may use brown mural paper upon which they will print. Allow students to decide whether or not they want freeform printing or a specific pattern. Cover a substantial area in the classroom for display.

Visual Impairment

Assist your students in rolling the modeling clay and carving the stamps. You might want to use acrylic paint to print stamps, which is thicker than poster paint, or add sand to poster paint for texture. By doing this, students who are blind can feel their designs when they are dry.

When a blind student prints, it may be of random nature. If printed impressions overlap excessively, you might suggest that the student start printing on a new page — do

help move hands over surfaces. Finished (and dry) prints should have a slightly "embossed" quality that students can appreciate tactually. You might want to offer the original modeling clay stamp to students with their finished prints, so that they can explore both paper and modeling clay surfaces to understand their relationship better.

Gifted

Students can recreate symbols and signs of historical significance, such as *fleur-de-lis*, Egyptian hieroglyphs, Roman numerals, etc. Another stimulation can be reproductions of the work of artists whose strong yet simple designs would translate well into stamps, e.g., Matisse, Miró, Calder. Remember, students may be capable of producing fine details as well as incisive line work.

Autistic Spectrum Disorder and Asperger's Syndrome

There is nothing wrong with vegetable printing — it is always in season! Direct printing with vegetables that teachers have precut, such as sliced peppers, make wonderful patterns! Brightly colored poster paint applied on appropriate side of vegetable is recommend, as is black paper. Teacher assistance is suggested!

STITCHSCAPES

Materials

- Felt scraps (assorted colors and sizes)
- Yarn and/or embroidery thread
- Sewing needles
- Scissors
- Printed cotton fabric
- Canvas stretchers, embroidery hoops, pins (optional)

Teacher Preparation

Gather print fabrics that suggest "sky" backgrounds, such as stripes and dots. Felt will be difficult for many students to cut, so you might want to precut simple shapes that easily could be made into trees, houses, clouds, sky, and so forth.

DIRECTIONS

Ask students to describe what is outside their window, either at home or at school. Ask students to think about outdoor environments.

Students select print fabrics for their backgrounds and felt for houses, trees.

Cut and arrange elements on the background fabric. Students may want to tape the felt parts on the fabric, pulling tape away as they stitch. (Pins may be used if appropriate.)

Stitching directly on the fabric should be fine as long as students don't pull on the thread (embroidery hoops or stretchers may be used). Stitches may be practiced on scrap fabric. Encourage variety and experimentation.

SUGGESTIONS FOR FURTHER DEVELOPMENT

Themes such as "The Four Seasons" or "The Time of Day" (day, night, stars, sunsets, etc.) will extend this lesson into an activity of more than one appliqué. You can create "sets" that have sequence.

NOTE: For sewing presentation tips for the classroom, please (re)visit *Bags Beautiful*, page 32)

ADAPTATIONS

INTELLECTUAL DISABILITY

Assist student's hands in moving sewing needles (See Autistic Spectrum Disorder for suggestions). To prepare students to understand the motion of " in and out "of holes, punch holes in oaktag or heavy paper, then prompt students to sew through the punched holes for practice.

EMOTIONAL DISTURBANCE

When your students achieve a task, it is very gratifying — but frustration should be avoided. Be certain that the technical aspects of sewing are understood before launching the project. Each student will have a patch of fabric into which they will sew an important event in their lives, using simple, symbolic shapes. They may want to work out ideas (and simplify them) on paper first. Choose appropriate fabric scraps. Teacher may be pleasantly surprised with students' level of focus.

At the finish, assist students in assembling a "story quilt" — by stitching pictures together. A quilt is tangible evidence of a cooperative effort — as well as an opportunity for each student to tell an autobiographical life story. Display!

LEARNING DISABILITIES

This is an excellent activity to reinforce eye-hand coordination as well as endorse understanding of directionality. To help students who are having difficulty, draw marker lines of felt to illustrate where stitches should go. Make sure that students know where to begin and that they leave enough thread at the end to knot easily.

As mentioned in the previous Adaptation, sewing has the magic touch when it comes to total engagement. If the teacher has students with Attention Deficient Disorder, sewing activities may help with concentration on task.

ORTHOPEDIC IMPAIRMENT

It may be worthwhile to secure fabric in embroidery hoops or canvas stretchers so that some students can better manage. Offer assistance on threading needles, cutting felt, etc., as the need arises. If sewing is really not practical, use fabric glue. Suggestion: "glitter glue" is sure to enliven this activity!

DEAF AND HARD OF HEARING

Show students reproductions of landscapes (or outdoor scenes), cityscapes, or any related appropriate subjects. Then present a sample stitchery picture of any of these subjects so that students understand that they will be translating "scapes" into fabric stitch pictures. Make sure to demonstrate the variety of stitches, such as running stitch, saddle stitch, etc. Otherwise, follow core lesson.

VISUAL IMPAIRMENT

Students who are blind can sew with help. Fabric should be taped to indicate where stitches will go, along with hand-over-hand instructions ("in-out," verbal cues). Students with visual impairments need needles with large eyes for threading (sometimes called Crewel Embroidery needles). Precut fabric (and lightweight felt, if available) may also be used. A patient teacher will be rewarded with fine results!

GIFTED

Students who are gifted are typically up for a challenge. The Bayeux Tapestry is the most famous tapestry in the western world. This medieval embroidery is 230 feet long and 20 inches high. What stories it depicts are a matter of research and dispute. The Battle of Hastings in the year 1066 is associated with it. The stitchery and storytelling of this still preserved artwork are amazing.

Students will create their own Bayeux tapestry. Students will work cooperatively in their research, studying not only history but the patterns and prints set against each other within the fabric pictures, creating rich designs. Teacher will decide the scale of this tapestry interpretation and present materials accordingly. Students should be able to experiment with many varieties of stitches and should have excellent technical control of the materials. Sound the trumpet when the project is complete!

AUTISTIC SPECTRUM DISORDER AND ASPERGER'S SYNDROME

For this activity, plastic needles are recommended, as is burlap cloth and bright yarn. If the teacher plans to incorporate appliqué in lesson, fabric shapes for students to cut will need to be prepared. Some students may be able to cut their own shapes (See Adaptive Aids, page 122)...others may do better with simple, precut felt forms. To start, mark cloth edges with marker circles so that students can follow in a dot-to-dot manner. Assist in threading the yarn through the needle. As for the choice of subject, the act of learning how to sew may be a goal achieved by itself. Students who are more advanced along the spectrum may indeed want a recognizable image. House, tree, and person are reasonable expectations. Perhaps the family dog or cat can be included. Happy stitches to all!

Thanksgiving Feasts and Picnic Days

Materials

- Paper plates (not waxed)
- Colored paper (12 x 18 inches)
- Tissue paper (various colors)
- Crayons
- Paste
- Plastic utensils
- Wallpaper samples
- Scissors
- Markers
- White glue

Teacher Preparation

You will need enough plastic spoons, forks, and knives to go around your class. Provide paper plates unless you want to cut large paper circles as a substitute. Wallpaper samples can be acquired by approaching wallpaper and paint stores for outdated books. You can precut food shapes if you wish, such as corncobs, drumsticks, asparagus, etc. as examples for students who will be drawing and cutting their own food. Precut squares and rectangles work well, generally speaking.

Directions

Talk about the meaning of Thanksgiving — how it started and why we have big dinners to celebrate it. If it does not confuse your students, compare it to a family picnic. Ask students to select one or the other for this "dual" activity — both can take place at the same time.

Offer students the paper, crayons, scissors, and paper plates. They can create turkey drumsticks, potatoes, sandwiches or whatever their tummies tell them to do. Students might also crumple up tissue paper and glue to the appropriate place. For example, green tissue makes great lettuce — either for salads or sandwiches.

Cut and paste food to the paper plate.

For placemats and napkins, use wallpaper and construction paper. Glue all parts of the setting on the placemat.

Suggestions for Further Development

One lesson has very strong motivation before Thanksgiving. Teacher may want to separate the lessons. Teacher may also want to save the picnic lesson for in the spring or summer seasons. It is presented here as a dual lesson...the decision of when to offer the lesson(s) is at the teachers discretion.

Adaptations

Intellectual Disability

Would some of your students put inedible objects in their mouths? Because the place setting is suggestive of meal times, you might want to avoid confusion. Concentrate on decorating the plate. Students will tear colored paper by holding the paper stationary with one hand and pulling with the other hand. Help students to glue down colored tissue on plate. With physical and verbal prompting, guide students in the gluing and placement of plate and utensils.

Let your students draw their own interpretations of Thanksgiving dinner food (even scribbling can be cut out for "spaghetti"). Place food on plate. Major emphasis will be on placing setting in proper location on placemat. To help students toward independence in this task, outline in marker the plate and utensils on the placemat. Students will then match the objects to their outlines.

Emotional Disturbance

Thanksgiving is a good occasion to discuss the art of "getting along," as in the case of the pilgrim settlers and the Native American Indians.

Create your own "togetherness" banquet in the classroom; have students mount their individual settings on a length of brown paper representing a table top. Have everyone sign a

"place card" and glue it in place with student work. The table top (of brown paper) can be a replication of wood, created by two or more students.

If you go with the picnic theme, it's likely that most students can answer the question "describe a picnic" prior to the distribution of materials. It's important to allow students to express themselves, yet the teacher might want to tell the students in advance how many minutes they have to talk. Keep a timer in your classroom (it's a helpful device anyway) — or simply be very aware of the clock. Follow core lesson, stressing cooperation. Make sure it's a well-stocked picnic... students should decide what they can bring.

Bon Appetit (fun fact...the French claim they invented *Le Pique-nique*)!

Learning Disabilities

Provide students with magazines that they can use for food pictures. Have students tear out as many pages as they think have the appropriate food items, then decide those items which best reflect Thanksgiving or a picnic. Cut out items and paste on plate. When setting the places, make sure students understand which utensils go on the left and on the right. Why is this a good approach for students with learning disabilities? It helps with organizational skills.

Orthopedic Impairment

Rather than cutting out the food, you might want your physically handicapped students to paint food directly on the paper plate. Painting will allow more freedom of expression when muscular control is limited. Try to get students to choose colors that relate to the food (green for vegetables. Brown for meat, etc.) The placemat as well as the napkin can be painted also. If you want students to practice cutting, use the wallpaper (not the coated kind.) Paste down the scraps on the painted placemats when paint is dry.

Deaf and Hard of Hearing

The spirit of Thanksgiving is sharing and communicating. Students will do both with this approach: assign partners to a specific part of the banquet preparation — "cooking" (drawing) vegetables, meat, etc., "designing" — plates, napkins, table settings. When all work is complete, everyone joins in to contribute and exchange their specialties. Have pictures that illustrate Thanksgiving or picnic on hand and samples of finished products before beginning lesson.

Visual Impairment

It's somewhat tricky for students who are blind to cut the precise shapes representing the food. Give students freedom to do it their way without imposing standards (e.g., vegetables might be represented by shredded paper). It helps to keep "fake food" models in the art room. You could aslo have students apply color to the plates: the borders often have a ribbed texture that's tactually interesting. For the placemat, try to find paper samples with texture.

Gifted

Students can develop a place and silver designs by looking at traditional and contemporary patterns. Department store catalogs may provide ideas. When students design plate patterns, they can use paper plates but they will want to design flatware out of oaktag. Napkin rings can also be created out of cardboard rolls. In short, they are designers.

Autistic Spectrum Disorder and Asperger's Syndrome

Students on the autistic spectrum would benefit from visual cues before the lesson begins. Further, it is advised to pick only one of the two themes offered — either Thanksgiving or picnic. On a 12 x 18-inch sheet of paper, draw a place-setting. If possible, make photocopies for students. Once they understand the concept, materials may be offered. Verbal prompting about the "food" would be suggested. Again, lesson elements may be presorted prior to help the lesson along...tissues in one box, "food colored," precut construction paper in another box, and so forth.

When ready, students can cut and glue the available food choices....it's a bit more of a collage or assemblage lesson. This is a more orderly way of creating a delicious plate and cheerful placement! Less confusion is a good thing.

UP, UP AND AWAY!

MATERIALS

- White display or butcher paper (on roll)
- Markers
- Crayons
- Poster or acrylic paint
- Scissors
- Glue
- Wide brushes
- String
- Construction paper
- Magazines (optional)

TEACHER PREPARATION

The emphasis in this lesson is big and bold. For huge balloons, you need to precut shapes (balloon, basket). The net part can be cut as part of basket or of balloon. Otherwise, cut out in one piece — fold first for symmetry. Remember to use visual images of hot air balloon — they are not hard to find online or in cinema clips; for example, a hot air balloon appears at the end of *The Wizard of Oz.* Note: Students can use open coffee filters for balloon shape. Also, students could be asked to bring photocopies of themselves, pets, even world leaders!

DIRECTIONS

What are hot air balloons? Where and when can you see them? How are they different from party balloons? Talk about their monumental size. Use visuals.

Roll out the paper. With a crayon or pencil, sketch out the balloon shape freely — or design half on fold. Cut out. Teacher will determine sizes required.

Student will outline bands of color and design for balloon body. Paint with bright colors.

Now for the basket — discuss basket shapes and weave patterns — and the purpose of the basket.

Cut all needed parts — sand bags, people, etc. Assemble with glue, tape and staple if feasible.

Time to lift off...up into the big, bright imaginary sky!

ADAPTATIONS

INTELLECTUAL DISABILITY

Make the largest work surface in your room accessible. Guide your student's arm, using a thick crayon in broad circular motions over craft brown paper. Decorate surface with bright, strong colors. When cutting out balloon, include gondola (carrier basket) in overall contour. Put aside. Create "passengers" by drawing or by cutting out magazine images (or student's photocopied image of self). Combine, or fly solo. Note: some interest may be given to the texture of the carrier basket before or after people are added.

EMOTIONAL DISTURBANCE

Once the main part of this lesson is accomplished (the balloon), you might want to stress the "people" part. Students can create figure groups for balloon to carry in the basket. They can be based on self-portraits and friends, or just from students' imaginations. Teacher may want to extend the "togetherness" part of this lesson with questions such as, "Who are these people-do they know each other?" and/or "Do you think their trip has a purpose...if so, what is it?" The goal here is fairly obvious: the reinforcement of positive social interaction between students.

Learning Disabilities

The sheer size of the balloons lends to exploring the concepts of big and little. Talk about the differences between the scale of real hot air balloons and the ones that you are making out of paper. Awareness of the size of the surface students are required to cover will bring the "wholeness" of the project into focus — remind students to paint surfaces fully. It's also important to follow the contour of the shape. This will lend a great reality through optical illusion.

Orthopedically Impaired

Please refer to the adaptation for Intellectual Disabilities. To carry the "people" part of the lesson forward, you might want to check out the *You're a Doll* Activity (page 120) to stimulate further concentration in creating the people, using student's own self for inclusion in the basket.

Deaf and Hard of Hearing

Do some movement exercises that say "UP!" Stretch, reach, jump. Then make a circular shape with arms. Show pictures of all kinds of balloons in motion, point out the hot air balloons, then launch lesson! As always, be certain that you- as a teacher — have properly communicated the expectations. It's always a fine idea to show the finished product first...even if you simply share the images in this book with your students.

Visual Impairment

Try to bring some party balloons to class (the kind that have been blown up through tanks at party stores, gift shops, etc.). Ask students to feel their elastic surfaces. If possible, take the students outside and suggest that students imagine that the balloons are easily one hundred times bigger! Be sure all students hold the string in order to understand the concept. Talk about aerodynamics, even everyday physics, that allow objects like air balloons and air planes to stay up in the sky! There is science in this lesson- why not use it? In class, give students large precut paper balloons that include carriers. Allow use of bright yarn. For people shapes, you might want check out the the precut commercial packet on page 125. A screenboard (see page 124) can help with students who are blind to draw details. Attach yarn with white glue to the outside contour of balloons. Apply color with mixed dry media, or roller applicators (see page 122 in Adaptive Aids).

Gifted

Students should be able to cut balloon parts on their own. Perhaps they can paper weave the basket part. If they make people you might suggest a "period" theme, e.g., "The turn of the previous century," to create corresponding styles and costumes. History and research are needed to support this approach. Students might also enjoy designing their own "air ships" — blimps, zeppelins, etc. — from streamlined to ornate. The sky's the limit!

Autistic Spectrum Disorder and Asperger's Syndrome

One of the most prominent features of students across the autistic spectrum is their difficulty with communication. In fact, autism is a communication disorder. For this reason, the teacher is referred to the adaptation suggested for students with emotional disturbance adaptation — the focus is social interaction and communication.

WEAVE A TURTLE

MATERIALS

- Construction paper (assorted colors)
- Scissors
- Crayons

TEACHER PREPARATION

Students will need to understand the concept of weaving to do this activity. Precut the turtle shape for students lacking in scissors skills. The paper cutter will help with preparing the paper strips you will need for weaving.

DIRECTIONS

Demonstrate the basic weaving movement to students who do not know how to weave. The easiest explanation is to start one line with under, over, under, etc... begin the next with over, under, over, etc. (or vice-versa) with paper strips through paper.

Students cut turtle shell shapes on a fold as indicated. Cut either wavy or straight lines to weave paper through slits. Note: Leave enough remaining paper to provide paper's strength.

Weave in paper strips. Trim ends. Draw turtle's face.

SUGGESTIONS FOR FURTHER DEVELOPMENT

This is a good introductory activity to weaving. It's simple to move from paper weaving to fiber weaving (see *Nature Weaving*, page 76). Other creatures work for paper weaving... consider snails, fish, and butterflies!

ADAPTATIONS

INTELLECTUAL DISABILITY

Students draw with crayons on precut turtles. Cut four to six straight slits. Use oversized paper strips. In a hand-over-hand method, weave paper strips into turtle shape. Use verbal cues of "under-over-under-over" to reinforce weaving movement.

Some students may be able to cut the outline of the turtle — particularly from a template they can trace. Otherwise, provide precut turtles. Students on the higher end of the spectrum should be able to learn to weave. On the lower end of the spectrum, students will probably benefit the most from the physical motion of weaving, but may not fully absorb the "how to" knowledge.

EMOTIONAL DISTURBANCE

Weaving is an absorbing activity that requires concentration. To promote student interest in weaving, treat paper weaving as a first step to many other projects. You might want to present examples of the many forms of weaving, from paper to fabric (See *Nature Weaving*, page 76).

For a group activity, think about a "paper weaving bee." Students can weave individual components of a larger subject such as paper cityscape. Students will weave their own skyscrapers, storefronts, building facades, etc. (How about yellow or white strips into dark buildings to represent windows?) Cooperation, as always, is key.

LEARNING DISABILITIES

Turtle shape may be outlined from a template created by teacher or drawn freehand. Assist student if necessary before cutting.

Weaving is an excellent activity for learning disabled students. The weaving process exercises directionality: left-to-right, over-and-under. Students may have trouble understanding the sequence and alternation of weaving. Try this: Use two colors only for the paper strips, say, orange for over and green for under. The turtle should be a contrasting color. Make sure strips are woven into the turtle in the proper order. That should do it. Success is a beautiful thing!

ORTHOPEDIC IMPAIRMENT

Please refer to *Nature Weaving*, under the adaptation for Orthopedic Impairment, page 76.

Deaf and Hard of Hearing

Using the turtle shape, demonstrate the over and under movement of the paper strips. See the Sign Language Guide (page 24) for these terms. Follow core activity.

Visual Impairment

You can try teaching weaving to students who are blind by using corrugated paper and fine sandpaper strips (or even fabric, such as corduroy). Students can more easily alternate strips in correct sequence if they can tactilely discriminate between "over" and "under" (i.e., the sandpaper can be "over," the corrugated paper becomes "under").

For the students with some visual acuity, make sure you use highly contrasting colors to make visual discrimination clearer — bright fluorescent paper would do the trick. Note: see how the black turtle shown here has greater visual impact than those woven with softer colors. Students with visual impairment do better with brighter contrasts.

Gifted

Students should be encouraged to cut a variety of paper strip sizes. Smaller strips should produce more intricate designs. Students might also want to use magazines and newspapers for strips — don't overlook the cartoon section of the newspaper. Perhaps these students can incorporate unexpected materials, such as malleable copper wire, twine, or even strips cut from student's old, recycled clothing — that certainly makes the weaving more personal.

Autistic Spectrum Disorder and Asperger's Syndrome

If the weaving concept of over-and-under (and vice versa) is the goal, teacher may have success by marking alternating slits with "x" and "o"(also known as "warp" and "weft"). This helps to identify which strips are woven over, and which will be woven under. However, there is always the possibility that some of your students are on the end of the Autistic Spectrum where weaving could quickly turn into an exercise in frustration. If that is the case, don't force it (the notion of not forcing students, in general, is very sound advice). Students with Asperger's Syndrome can follow core lesson.

What to do? Why not use the making of a turtle as a goal for now? Here's a way to make a turtle that is very simple... all you'll need is paper plates. Teacher may assist student in folding the paper plate in half briskly so that the outside ridge shows. Staple closed. Students can apply color (media of choice) to "turtle shell" (the patterning of shell is optional). Teacher will precut turtle heads (not unlike snakes — see *Snake in the Grass*, page 98). Staple turtle head to the shell. Students can draw the turtle's eyes (both sides) — plus a happy turtle smile! Hint: Three small slits made on the sides of the turtle would allow two strips of contrasting color to be woven in!

By: Karly Jardin

Kristy Sharpless

WHAT'S THE SCOOP?

MATERIALS

- Oaktag
- Scissors
- Glue
- Markers (scented)

TEACHER PREPARATION

Precut triangles for cone shapes and circles for ice cream scoops.

DIRECTIONS

What is your favorite ice cream flavor? Ask students to name as many flavors as they can — think about the multiple choices at the ice cream store.

Provide students with appropriate materials.

Allow them to create their own ice cream combinations — single and double deckers, super scoops, whatever!

Add jimmies (sprinkles), cherries, or whatever the heart desires.

Teachers note: paper ice cream has zero calories, no matter how many scoops!

SUGGESTIONS FOR FURTHER DEVELOPMENT

This activity would at first appear to be more suited to the younger child but don't be fooled. This subject has broad appeal for all ages. Ice cream cones are ideal subjects for graphic art design projects. For instance, a fold-out, flip-down ice cream cone would work beautifully.

ADAPTATIONS

INTELLECTUAL DISABILITY

Assist in making circles in brightly colored or fluorescent markers or crayons on paper. Paper plates may be used to trace the circle representing scoops — or they can be decorated directly. Cut two or three large triangles for cones out of corrugated paper, then cut the circles that students have drawn on paper. You staple circles together vertically and attach cones (triangles) at bottom. Multi-scooped cones can be hung with string through top scoop.

You can bring actual cones (no ice cream necessary) to class. Present precut flat paper triangles — point out the relationship between the real cone and the paper triangle. Students can color the cones on a screenboard (an adaptive device used primarily for students who are blind, see page 124) that may be employed to create texture that is similar to a real cone. Scented markers are suggested for ice cream scoops' colors. Help students staple cone and scoop together, paste on colored paper, and sign names. Display.

EMOTIONAL DISTURBANCE

Pair students as "business partners" in an ice cream store. The assignments will be creating a store front, making a sign, designing a counter, etc. They will need to use large mural-sized paper for each part of assignment.

All the students will be asked to create ice cream flavors with original names that encourage use of imagination. Encourage students to use their own names; i.e., Terry's

Tiger Stripe Fudge, Wendy's Wonderful Watermelon Swirl, Tasha's Terrific Mint Chip. Flavors can be illustrated in a way that best suits their part of the project. Display all store parts together.

Learning Disabilities

Please refer to some of the ice cream flavor descriptions stated under Emotional Disturbance and write them — plus a few more — on 3 x 5 cards to distribute (without student names). Demonstrate how to illustrate the flavor based on the descriptive names; i.e., chocolate swirl mint would suggest brown swirly patterns. When all scoops are completed, cut cone shapes and mount scoops on brown paper. Discuss the similarities and differences between flavors and the patterns created. Ask students to discuss their own personal likes and dislikes. It should provide a deliciously uplifting experience! In terms of learning value, the concept of bottom to top is reinforced, as are geometric shapes for younger students.

Orthopedic Impairment

Teacher will install an "Instant Ice Cream Parlor" by simply mounting white paper on an accessible classroom (or hallway) wall. Student will print the ice cream scoops — using a variety of printing tools (See Adaptive Aids, page 122) Bingo markers can applied in a circular manner. Depending on the range of mobility, scented markers may be employed. The brush itself may be used as a printing tool by gently pressing paint onto paper in a back and forth motion. Sponges, corks, and clay can be used for printing as well.

The triangular shape representing a cone is encouraged... but if larger motion is better, a bowl for an ice cream sundae is perfectly reasonable. A bit of glitter glue applied here and there — symbolic of sprinkles — will top it all off!

Deaf and Hard of Hearing

Describe steps of lesson, using samples to illustrate. Present any relevant reference material that you can bring to this lesson: photos, even food containers such as ice cream cartons, ice cream cone boxes, etc. Students, once the idea is conveyed, can directly follow core lesson.

Visual Impairment

Let your students use precut circle scoops, cone shapes and vertically sized paper (see student art). The logical stacking of the scoops in a vertical order is organizationally helpful. Use fruit scented markers for ice cream. Cones (triangles) can be colored for texture on screenboards. Remember, lightweight paper works best. With this approach, the multilayered cones will be mindfully glued to paper (glue sticks are recommended). Allow time for each student to discuss their ice cream choices. Display!

Gifted

Students can make a flip book, containing a bite-by-bite sequence describing the inevitable fate of all ice cream cones. Starting with a drawing of the full cone, students will show scoops and cone being eaten page by page. Students can think about facial expression of the person eating the ice cream cone. Since this is a basic animation project, students may want to use the style of cartoon characterization. The results are likely to be engaging!

Autistic Spectrum Disorder and Asperger's Syndrome

This is a fine opportunity to reinforce concepts of shapes. Furthermore, the idea of precut circle overlapping the next circle is in itself a challenge! In this case, it is suggested that the teacher follow the adaptation for visual impairment to complete this lesson (screenboard optional).

WINDOWS

MATERIALS

- Two sheets of construction paper, 11 x 18 inches (use light color for background, black for house) — one set for each student.

- Scissors

- Paste

- Crayons

- Fabric scraps

- Magazines

- Watercolors (optional)

TEACHER PREPARATION

Some children will need house and window openings precut. To simplify cutting of windows, fold paper and snip into fold vertically — then again along the fold in between. Repeat.

DIRECTIONS

Spend some time discussing how houses have their own styles and shapes.

Ask students to draw the outline of their house to the edge of their paper, using a bright crayon.

Cut out windows (see teacher prep) and house shape. Glue down on background paper.

Students create objects and faces for window, and compose area around the house. What time of day is it? What's the weather? What season is it?

Add fabric curtains or other details.

SUGGESTIONS FOR FURTHER DEVELOPMENT

Magazines can be used to provide faces and objects for windows. The houses can be anything from simple squares with triangle roofs to Victorian style castles, depending on student levels. This lesson can be expanded to a whole "village" of larger houses, to be displayed as a group project.

ADAPTATIONS

INTELLECTUAL DISABILITY

Precut simple house shape from white paper and cut spaces for at least two windows. The students will decorate the house with fluorescent (or brightly colored) crayons or paints. Colored tissue or colored acetate can be glued into windows with your assistance. Your "mobile homes" can be hung in the real classroom windows to catch the light and visually stimulate students.

Students who might have difficulty in cutting out windows may want to use squares and rectangles. These will represent windows and doors. Decorate and paste them down. Remind students of where doors and windows belong and why.

EMOTIONAL DISTURBANCE

As house form develops, get students further involved through suggestions of themes for windows--such as your friends, your family and your pets, people you know, etc. Emotions can be represented by faces in various windows, i.e., happy face, sad face, angry face, and so on. Word of caution: Some students may have extremely unstable housing situations, ranging from living in shelters, to what amounts to homelessness. Please approach this lesson with extra sensitivity. It's not the worst idea in the world to acknowledge that "some of us are in transition-which means we are in-between our usual homes and other arrangements." Ask students to illustrate their favorite house shape and follow lesson. Allow no disrespectful behavior towards students who fit into the aforementioned category, since news travels fast in the majority of schools.

Learning Disabilities

This activity centers on the relationship between the houses' exterior shapes to each other and to the houses' interiors. Students need to think about the functional placement of windows and doors. Eye-hand coordination and the concept of closure will be exercised through drawing and cutting window shapes. Then follow core lesson.

Orthopedic Impairment

Students can practice their scissors skills (see Adaptive Aids, page 122) by cutting squares for windows and rectangles for doors. If you have wallpaper samples, these make great window dressings; lace doilies make great curtains as well. People, plants, and animals can be added to windows, but this may require a helping hand.

Deaf and Hard of Hearing

Show students a sample of the finished product first. Demonstrate methods for cutting windows out of house front. NOTE: A "dialogue" can be created between the faces in the windows by using "talking balloons." This step is highly recommended (talking balloons may be precut.)

Visual Impairment

Guide students who are blind to a real window and door so that they can use their hands to explore the overall shapes and perimeters. Students with severe visual impairments often have difficulty in understanding the dimensions of a specific area. Another introduction to the activity is to present student with a dollhouse or other 3-D model of a house. This assists in mentally picturing the whole concept.

Window and door decoration can be done with paper squares on the screenboard. If you have embossed wallpaper samples, cut for window curtains and add them – or use fabric scraps instead.

A house-shaped drawing may be made on the larger paper, using "friendly" crayons (if there is availability of "construction paper crayons" please use them with screenboard art.) The addition of second layer of paper is optional (as stated in core lesson).

Gifted

This can be a gateway lesson to the study of historic architectural styles. Have students research and select a specific style for their houses. Make sure that all details agree with that style, e.g., a Southern mansion should have appropriate columns, porticos, etc. The understanding of specific architectural styles and their regions — as well as era in which they existed — is excellent for students who are gifted. The windows and doors are the elements that should attract visual attention.

Autistic Spectrum Disorder and Asperger's Syndrome

Precut house shapes with a pointed roof. Use visual cues... it is excellent if a communication board is available with a picture of a house (See Adaptive Aids, page 122). Present students with squares and rectangles for doors and windows. Help student to decide where the parts belong. Be clear on what shapes represent! This is very important. Verbal prompting...as well as hand-over hand technique... should ensure solid results. Remind students to apply components to paper house with the glue side down! Vocabulary skills will be reinforced if each student (who has language skills) can declare with their best voice "My house is _____" and finish the sentence. Be sure students' names are prominently displayed on each house!

WORKING WET WITH WATERCOLORS

MATERIALS

- White paper
- Brushes
- Paper towels
- Sponges
- Eyedropper (optional)
- Watercolor paintboxes
- Watercolor cups or containers
- Tissue paper
- Kosher salt (optional)

TEACHER PREPARATION

Since this activity depends on keeping the paper wet, have all supplies on hand to begin the lesson. A bucket of clean water might be more convenient than running to a sink repeatedly. Also, you might want to cut sponges into various shapes and sizes to use for added design details.

Before diving into their work, students should be instructed on the proper use of materials. First, load plenty of water on your brush to dip into the paints. Use individual colors and mix the colors inside the open lid. Each time you change colors, dip lightly in water and wipe brush on paper towel. (The paper towel is your "paint rag;" using it frequently will keep water clean.) Paint boxes should be left clean for future use. Paper towel corners can help clean between colors.

DIRECTIONS

With painting materials in front of them, students begin by wetting the paper, using a water-filled sponge (help assess the proper amount of water). Use broad arm movements.

Experiment. Wet paper will respond to the touch of the paintbrush with bursts of patterns.

Blot with the tissue, dab the sponge, and sprinkle the salt on the wet paint (see Suggestions for Further Development).

When a harmony of visual patterns and textures has been reached, the work is complete!

SUGGESTIONS FOR FURTHER DEVELOPMENT

Watercolor is a medium that lends itself to experimentation and spontaneity. Here are two techniques you could try for interesting effects:

Watercolor and Kosher salt: Kosher salt is recommended because it is coarser than regular table salt and will create a more grainy texture. Using watercolor paper, wet down area to be painted. Apply color heavily. Throw in pinches of salt where texture is desired. Let dry thoroughly. Brush off salt.

Eyedropper Painting: Create a splashy pattern by filling eyedropper with water mixed with watercolor. Wet paper and drop paint on it. Watercolor paper and rice paper work very well because of their absorbency.

ADAPTATIONS

INTELLECTUAL DISABILITY

Try creating "paint splatter patterns." Fill the brush with plenty of paint. Guide student's hands as you both flick paint onto the paper. When student appears able to work independently, move away. Change colors as desired; repeat until paper is covered with bursts of color. This activity is suitable for students because of its use of both kinesthetic movement and the visually stimulating results.

EMOTIONAL DISTURBANCE

You may want students to build a composition based on their fantasy and imagination. Take a good-sized brush and load with paint. Squeeze the end of the brush over the wet paper so that a blob of paint falls on it — this form will be manipulated with the brush. Ask students to create a picture based on what the paint splatter suggests to them. Add painted areas to help "grow" the paint blob into a composition. It may be abstract, nonobjective, or representational. Remind students that there *really* is no right or wrong visual appearance to their work — just try to use the whole page. Adjust areas of color to individual taste. Talk about work in an open group discussion when completed. Encourage students to remark on their classmates' art. No negative comments are acceptable — that will result in losing the right of participation. Determine time allowed before the discussion begins.

Often, watercolor painting has a calming effect. There is something about the experience that typically absorbs students and has a positive effect on behavior.

LearNING DISabLeD

The side of a sponge and paint brushes are needed. Ask students to leave room on all sides for a border. Demonstrate by painting a little scene on the wet paper — it should work well on a moist paper. Tell students to think about their own scenes — real or imaginary.

When images are completed, brush a selected color of paint onto the corner of the sponge. Create a border by printing the paper with the sponge.

In using this approach, you are asking students to plan ahead and to create their own spatial boundary, which lends a clear framework to the activity and further addresses closure skills.

OrthopedICally ImpaIred

If students do not have the physical movement required to dip sponge into water and wet their papers, you will need to help by keeping paper wet for them. However, the motion of dipping and squeezing sponges and wiping the paper is an excellent movement exercise. If students are willing to try it, encourage them.

For another worthwhile movement experience, you can create a rolling "paint printer." In advance of lesson, glue bits of sponges and yarn on a paper cardboard roll (paper towel or tinfoil dispenser type). Students will cover their paper with paint either by sponging colored water on or by painting directly with brush. Now roll or press the roller on the wet surface. The result is an interesting printed surface. (See Adaptive Aids, page 122).

Deaf anD HarD OF HearING

Students should enjoy doing the activity as outlined in the core. For a variation that will encourage class interaction, students can do "monoprints" of each others' work. Students should do contour paintings (line painting) of any subject desired. While wet, students will carefully place a blank paper on top of a "buddy's" work. Slowly remove, "pulling" from the corner of the top of the paper. A print will appear! Students should then develop the watercolor print with their own details.

Make sure you demonstrate this activity first — and aid in pulling prints later as needed.

Practice the watercolor monoprint technique prior to the introduction of this Adaptation — the degree of absorption of selected paper needs to be tested beforehand.

VIsual ImpaIrment

Students with visual impairment should enjoy fluorescent paints, which are water soluble and quite compatible with watercolors (See Adaptive Aids, page 122). A natural subject for "working wet" is undersea life: the fluorescent colors can be used to represent that iridescence of sea creatures.

Students who are blind need to use their unengaged hands to feel what part of their papers have been wet with paint. When they do direct watercolor you may want to skip wetting the whole paper. Watch out for students who are blind in reworking the same areas — they need to rotate their papers. Avoid over-rubbing with brush; it "pills" paper into brush and creates holes in paper. Guide each student's hand so he or she knows where cup and paints are located. Stabilize water cup with rolled masking tape at the bottom.

Blindness is not incompatible with the sensory experience of painting. As students become familiar with the medium, they tend to refine the balance of their compositions, based on where they feel water on the page. Although water, not color, seems to be the element on which the experience is built, students may inquire: "teacher, where is yellow? I want to paint the sun." If you can acquire Braille labels for each color, that would indeed be ideal!

GIFTeD

Students should be encouraged to use as many available objects as they can think of to create unusual patterns in the wet paint — rags, folded paper, corks, erasers, spools, etc.

You might also want to challenge imaginations by setting up a given theme, such as telling students to paint portholes into their compositions and then describe (in paint) what they see through them. This theme can also include diving bells, aquarium, a hole in the frozen lake, and so forth. Note: some students may want to use permanent markers to refine the depiction of these subject(s). Be prepared!

AUTISTIC SPECTRUM DISORDER anD ASPErger's SYNDROME

Students on the autistic spectrum should particularly enjoy this lesson. Not only will they be painting, they'll be painting wet! Reminder: this is an activity for which smocks — or recycled shirts — should be worn. The core activity may be followed, but close teacher monitoring is still needed. The recommendation is as follows: black and brown watercolor paint squares should be removed if possible. Students tend to over-use them... to the detriment of their paintings. Keep this in mind. Perhaps because this activity bears a close resemblance to water play, teacher will also double as lifeguard! Best wishes for smooth sailing!

YOU'RE A DOLL!

MATERIALS

- Yarn
- Colored pencils
- Heavyweight paper or oaktag, 9 by 12 or 11 by 14 inches
- Fabric glue (or white glue)
- Markers
- Scissors
- Buttons, lace, ribbon, fabric, doilies, etc.

TEACHER PREPARATION

Gather sewing notions and goodies to add textural interest — sequins, fabric scraps, ribbon, jewelry, etc. You may want to precut doll forms — or demonstrate how to cut out a full body (about the size of a paper doll or action figure).

DIRECTIONS

This is actually a full figure self-portrait, so discuss individual physical characteristics. Is your hair curly or straight? Are you tall or short? Do you have a distinguishing characteristic?

As students describe themselves, be prepared for negative self images. This may be avoided by asking for a "best self" — or point out positive characteristics, i.e. your big bright smile!

Give students paper to design a doll that is based on their features, their favorite outfits, or "fantasy" ones. Encourage students to use the whole paper for dolls' contours.

Apply color.

Cut out doll.

Add lace, trim, and other details.

SUGGESTIONS FOR FURTHER DEVELOPMENT

A cutout wardrobe can be developed for dolls, which will require some accuracy in fitting. For group projects, students can create a 3-D indoor and outdoor environment for figures out of cardboard or shoe boxes (i.e., parks, neighborhoods). Another idea: Mount several dolls in a row on length of paper to create a "chorus line!"

ADAPTATIONS

INTELLECTUAL DISABILITY

Students on the lower end of the intellectually disabled spectrum are likely to have a better experience with precut people shapes (See Adaptive Aids, page 122). Students can add facial features and clothing (with teacher support). Students can be helped in gluing a variety of fabric scraps to their dolls. Fabric offers an association with students' own clothing — an everyday tactile experience that should have meaning for students.

This lesson will reinforce body awareness. In a physically demonstrative way, ask students to help identify arms, legs, faces, and so forth. You can state, for example, "This is your hand." Show students corresponding parts on the precut dolls. Of course, how you approach this lesson depends entirely on your understanding of student levels.

Explaining facial features is often a lesson in itself. Thus, to tackle this entire lesson you need to break into steps: (1) face, (2) body, front, (3) body, back. Gluing should be done in hand-over-hand method.

EMOTIONAL DISTURBANCE

Discuss "body language" — what body postures say about moods and attitudes. Have students assume different poses that "say" proud, cheerful, relaxed, tense, and so forth.

Students will use the exercise to make dolls to express a particular mood. When dolls are completed, students should guess what each other's poses were intended to be.

NOTE: Some students may object to making "dolls," saying that they're too babyish, too silly, etc. If you think your students might be put off by the word "doll," then call them "cutout figures" or anything else that will be better received.

LEARNING DISABILITIES

Stress body parts relationships. "The arm is connected to the body by the shoulder," etc. Do warm-up exercises with instructions like "touch your right leg with your right hand"... then reverse the directions. Since many students may be dyslexic, this introduction helps with attention issues. In order to further understand body movement, you may want students to design dolls with moving parts, using paper fasteners for joints. There's something a little magical in articulated figures.

ORTHOPEDIC IMPAIRMENT

Self-image can be difficult for students with physical impairments. Take your cues from the students — if they want to create an alterego self, support their ideas. Realistic self-interpretation should also be respected. Adaptive Aids (page 122) help with cutting as needed.

DEAF OR HARD OF HEARING

Dolls may be used to "speak" for the students in informal dramatizations. The movement of dolls can be a "mime" type performance, or have a message written on the reverse side. Dolls can be mounted on popsicle sticks for this activity...thus transforming them into puppets!

VISUAL IMPAIRMENT

Body shape of precut dolls (See Adaptive Aids, page 122) should be compared to real anatomical information. Placement of facial features will require assistance. The textures of fabric, buttons, etc., should be incorporated into this lesson for sensory experience.

GIFTED

Use dolls as an anatomy lesson. Give students a choice: Show dolls as "x-rayed," revealing anatomy (skeletal, muscular, etc.) with accuracy, or allow students try to improve upon the design of the human form by inventing new or"replacement parts."

A different approach would be to use dolls for career development. Students create dolls as they might see themselves in the future. Give attention to details, e.g., what would you carry? A briefcase? A tool box? A cello case? What would you wear? And so forth. The answers may be surprising!

AUTISTIC SPECTRUM DISORDER AND ASPERGER'S SYNDROME

It is often problematic for students on the autistic spectrum to comprehend their own physical bodies as they exist in space. Put another way, students may not be aware of where their own bodies end and where the space around them begins. Students are sometimes given weighted vests, often by way of physical therapists, to help with body awareness issues. It is a form of sensory integration.

For this reason, the lesson of full body tracing would be concrete and logistically helpful (Please refer to *Faces and Traces*, page 48). Just the same, students would enjoy "doll" puppets after completing this activity. (See Deaf and Hard of Hearing adaptation for tips...). With these suggested adaptations, the goals are body awareness — and increasing communication skills respectively...both extremely important in the education of students with autism.

manual aids: get a grip...

To begin, all sorts of adaptive aids can find regular use for students with orthopedic impairments. Students who have manual grip issues with picking up and holding on to art tools, such as brushes, pencils and so forth may find things improve with simple solutions. The time-honored foam hair curler pictured here "fattens" the width and is easier to remove from the table once it is added to the pencil and similar objects. You might also note that a variety of brush and printing tools with more accessible handles are commercially available and effective as well.

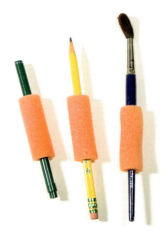

An object as simple as a foam hair curler is effective for limited grasp. Of course, there are adaptives available throughout occupational therapy sources, usually associated with rehabilitation centers.

Note the bulbous handled brush. It is available commercially. Also, a textural tool that can be used for painting and printing appears at right.

Other assorted objects may be incorporated into art lessons while allowing "handy" grip. In the photo at right, we have a common kitchen sink item that has a wide handle and multiple foam strips at the working end....that would transform into an intriguing paint brush, would it not? The cigar holder next to it provides a makeshift handle as a crayon holder. Another bright red wooden-handled brush sits next to scented markers which are actually quite helpful for sensory (olfactory) stimulation, particularly for students with advanced visual impairment (colors and smells form associations). A pair of scissors with a safety tip represents the huge variety of scissors of all kinds that may be purchased by catalog or online.

A common kitchen sink item can yield wonderful results when paint is in the picture. Students without use of arms can draw on an uplifted surface using the cigar holder —
see Mouth and Foot Painters pages 153-154.

Print it with Bingo markers! They are easy to hold and apply. Print, stamp or paint; Bingo markers are a favorite with all students. Empty shoe polish bottles with foam applicators can be filled with poster paint. What a fun novelty to try with students!

BINGO! Bingo markers are great for grip. Empty bottles of shoe polish also make handy painting devices.

Who doesn't love crayons? Today, there are so many choices! Crayons are available with a flat side that prevents them from rolling. Crayon "stumps" offer students better grip, and more control.

communication

Here is an extremely important part of learning for students on the Autistic spectrum.

Known as visual support, the communication boards shown here help students with autism organize their days, among other things.

Visual Support Devices

Thanks to the availability of computer science, many software programs are available to help students communicate. There are all sorts of excellent programs to meet student needs.

AUDITORY SUPPORT

Audio books for individuals who are blind make information available equitably. Museums provide accessibility — both physically (as in ramps) and educationally. Some have touch replicas for visitors who are blind.

visual aids

Earlier we discussed that scented markers can be useful for students who have severe visual impairment, since the scents are often matched with actual food...yellow may smell like bananas, etc. The scented dough, shown here, is excellent for similar reasons...and adds 3-D dimensionality to the learning!

Many people are surprised to learn how students who are blind can learn to draw. We often forget that the idea of the picture literally appears in our "mind's eye." Those watchful brown, blue, green or hazel eyes we have are, in fact, a means of transporting visual information. If an individual cannot see, other tactile information is still being absorbed. And, as pointed out, scent or "sense memory" is believed to be the most powerful of our six senses — and to last the longest. You might not be old enough to be a grandmother yourself...yet, chances are, you would likely be able to identify the exact aroma of your grandmother's kitchen, with your eyes blindfolded and with earplugs in both ears!

Students with residual vision will benefit from bright color use. It stimulates the eye... and student interest. "Bright is right" — try to incorporate shiny craft foil in your art lessons.

Image made on screenboard.

The texture of light sandpaper introduces a new, different feeling. A collage might be in order!

Do you know how students who are blind learn to draw? The answer is the screenboard. It's easy to make. All you need is a piece of cardboard cut to the same size as a precut screen (the kind you find in screened windows and doors). Attach screen to board with duct tape. Place lightweight paper on top of screen. Use soft "construction" crayons — or crayons that are not hard.

Similar to Braille, this paper can offer tactile guidance.

visual & tactile materials

The importance of sensory experiences cannot be emphasized enough! Students learn through all senses — touch, sight, taste, smell — all bring messages to the brain. As humans, the deepest memory we have is sense memory.

Scented markers stimulate the senses. These are truly helpful to students who are blind, allowing student associations between scent and color. Yellow may smell like bananas; blue may smell like blueberries; etc.

Glitter and bright shiny things — love them!

In the same way that scented markers are useful for students who have severe visual impairment, scented dough is an excellent choice...and adds 3-D dimensionality to the learning!

Precut figures and faces help with identifying the relationship of body parts to one another.

There are many forms of clay — play foam is one of them. Happy birthday, dinosaur...enjoy your cake!

This is a good example of the "hand-over-hand" method that provides support for students who require assistance.

ALTERNATIVE DEVICES

Paintbrushes can be affixed to specialized headgear, or you can simply get creative with a baseball hat!

Please visit pages 153-154 for painters from the Mouth and Foot Painting Association.

Pogo paint poles — this sure looks fun! Is it possible to learn — and to love it. Many great teachers believe that theory exactly!

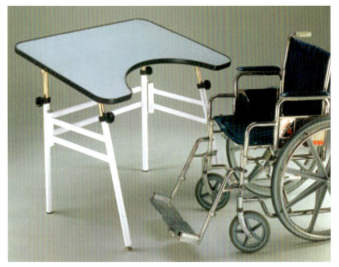

With students who are orthopedically impaired, properly scaled equipment is key.

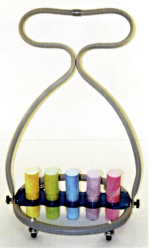

Different ways to express ourselves... this equipment is quite clever!

SECTION FOUR
The Art Classroom: What Every Teacher Should Know

The hope is that you teach art in a room that has been designated for that very purpose... and it's your art room. Your situation may be otherwise; the most common alternative is what we commonly refer to as Art a la Cart! (More about this under supplies and storage.)

Many of us have (or will have) spent at least a good portion of teaching art in the classrooms of other teachers. We will assume that you have reached professional understandings with your teaching colleagues about the comfort levels you both hold in terms of "messy" art activities, as well as other boundary issues. A little diplomacy goes a long way. In a space that is not your own, the circumstances can vary greatly. For this reason, the following art/classroom suggestions will be general in nature. Here are a few pointers:

Lighting is a factor to be noted. Lower light can be comforting to some students in the autistic spectrum...children can be really sensitive to light and sound. On the other hand, students who are visually impaired usually require brighter light to see (with the exception of Albinism, which typically involves photophobia, a profound sensitivity to light). Students who are hard of hearing can't often hear your voice or other sounds, so lights can be used for communication. As a teacher, flicking the lights for attention is critically important. Also, for students who lip-read, be sure you are facing them in a facially revealing light.

Although unlikely, exposure to bright, harsh, rapidly flickering light may trigger a seizure, particularly in students with epilepsy. See First Aid for Seizures (page 131) for more information. As for lighting issues overall, use your best judgment.

It appears that something quite wonderful is happening here. As we say in my art world, "One. Two. Three...INSTANT ART SHOW!"

TOOLS, EQUIPMENT, AND STORAGE

What I will tell you is fairly simple — keep the sharp tools out of student reach, locked up if possible. If you teach in a progressive, independent school, it may be fine to leave all (safe) materials within student reach; only if you know your students well. In a perfect world, colors would be labeled in Braille for all students who are blind — and students with orthopedic impairments could easily activate a button to have out-of-reach materials delivered by robotic arms, on demand. Back in the real world, we do the best we can — and keep looking for new innovations. Yes, some programs have great art supplies and offer art stations for their students during their scheduled art periods — which fosters independence — beautiful! Unfortunately, this is not the case in every school. If we are anything, art teachers are an adaptable species. We become more mindful with the growth of our experiences.

STUDENT FURNITURE

Placement is always a consideration for the art classroom dynamics — assuming desks are not bolted down in rows, as in the days of the old schoolhouse. If you are teaching students with emotional disturbances, you've probably figured out who should (or should not) be seated together. A preventative seating chart can make your decision seem more neutral, without causing additional disruptions. However, as time goes on, this seating arrangement might be adjusted, since dynamics change. We want students to learn positive interaction.

Do you require a "timeout" space? If so, the suggestion is to name it more creatively. How about Think Tank, Peace Corner, Time-to-Regroup Studio? It's just less inflammatory. We usually think in terms of the teacher stating, "Okay Anthony, it seems like you need some time out." Perhaps you can offer students a signal to use when *they* start to feel a meltdown coming. If the student displays and continues disruptive behavior, there should be a clear procedure in place. Consequences must be clear and consistent.

The same behavioral expectations apply to all students, including those with emotional disturbances...no "free pass" to a disrespectful student with a diagnosis. On that same subject, students with emotional disturbances will often do battle with the furniture...kicking chairs, shoving desks, etc. We know this is an expression of anger — or a way of seeking attention. It's still not acceptable. Be prepared to deal with all sorts of behaviors... even if your position is in a school with fewer incidents than expected, because we are dealing with human behavior after all. Stand with composure and redirect the student if possible — with room for self-remediation. Sometimes it seems as though we have to play "good cop/bad cop" at the same time! It's part of teaching — rise to your "higher self!"

Accommodations for students with orthopedic impairments are clearly needed. Special furniture is designed with this in mind. Your school is supposed to provide it, under federal law (See Adaptive Aids, p. 122). Yet there are some inventive art teachers who come up with original ideas. If you are one of them...safety first. Wheelchair access — and room for students using leg braces and other medical aids to negotiate space — is a logical consideration at all times.

Students who need to position their desks closer to the teacher include those with visual impairments and students who are hard of hearing. It's pretty standard to see a desk that sits right next to the teacher's desk...and it's not usually a reward for good behavior. Rather, it's often "reserved" for a student who is highly distracted — maybe with a diagnosis of Attention Deficit Hyperactive Disorder (see Learning Disabilities, p. 16). The student is unlikely to feel personally offended by this move... it's a widely accepted way for the teacher to help keep the student on track. The desk may have an agreed upon occupancy period...or simply be based on how each class unfolds.

An important reminder about the art room furniture...you can certainly move it around in accordance to different activities. However, there are instances in which one should NOT move the furniture before the class arrives without giving fair warning! The first consideration is for your students who are blind — the reasons should be obvious to the teacher. If a desk is moved spontaneously, rap your knuckles on the desktop and announce it. The other consideration in room rearrangement concerns students with intellectual disabilities. Many students with special needs, including the autistic spectrum, are comforted by a predictable environment. When a known, safe space suddenly changes, it can upset and confuse students. Please keep this in mind when you are overwhelmed by an urge to "redesign" your art room, along with the temptation to shout "surprise" to the students upon their arrival...and then expect them to be thrilled. *Au contraire.*

SUPPLIES AND STORAGE

Some art teachers have magnificent storage space — along with a great sense of organization. Others have only a small art room — with a few sagging shelves — and are thankful for it. If you've been in art education long enough, chances are your circumstances have gone from the sublime to the ridiculous...in-between and back again. Have you ever been assigned to two or three (or more) schools per week? Or perhaps you've heard the legends of other art teachers with curious spaces in which they delivered their programs. I met a teacher who taught daily (in a warm climate) under a big old oak tree (shelter provided when necessary). Art classes held in school cafeterias are not uncommon — nor is the auditorium stage (between rehearsals and concerts). Church annex basements, closets, dirt floors (enclosed by makeshift walls) boiler rooms...or...here's the irony — in a space originally identified for (what else?) *supply storage!* So you will forgive me if I don't provide a formula for you to store supplies. Let's just assume, for now, that you have adequate supplies and your own ways to handle their use. If your school district has an open policy on ordering — even storage equipment — catalogs like Dick Blick, online or otherwise, should have all you need.

Much like special education itself, there is no one-size-fits-all answer. Art teachers do require a budget for art supplies... the rest is negotiable. Some can teach until retirement with one oversized government-issue cabinet used for all art supplies, in the same art room. Among the best art teachers on the planet, there are likely to be those who work out of roll-away luggage. Did you ever see the trunk of an art teacher's car...never mind a minivan? Still others have a state-of-the-art computer lab installed in their ballroom-sized, fully-equipped art rooms. What then, you ask, is important? All students are served by you...equitably. You do the best as is *reasonable.* If untenable circumstances obstruct quality, let it be know to those in position to help you — get support and advocate! Should you have a proper art room? Of course you should. If you don't get one, would it stop you from teaching art? Doubtful...but keep negotiating. The bottom line is always your students...the authenticity and quality of the art experience you bring them.

SAFETY IN THE ART ROOM: WHEREVER YOU TEACH, THE RULE IS SAFETY FIRST!

Please take the list of Classroom Do's and Don'ts (next page) seriously. These tips apply to all students. It should be pointed out that many students with various health issues and conditions are particularly sensitive to toxins and predisposed to hazards. In order to understand exposure, realize that there are three basic ways harmful substances enter the body: ingestion, absorption (through the skin), and inhalation. Young students are typically more vulnerable because of their body weight, which is principally much less than that of an adult. For this reason, their tolerance of toxins is much less than that of a full grown adult.

Being aware of health conditions asks that you pay attention. If you open a bottle of poster paint and it smells strange, do not use it. Art products have their own shelf life... and "the nose knows!" Another art room tip is about the use of colored chalk. Sure, you can use it, but avoid those big clouds of chalk dust, which are highly irritating, particularly for students with asthma, bronchial issues, and allergies. The solution is to dip the end of the chalk into a water cup. The result will appear more "painterly" and have a rich surface. The use of dry chalk is not recommended. Refer to Dos and Don'ts for the basics.

Note to teachers: Dr. Michael McCann is an authority on art and safety. He has written several books on this topic.

While we are on the topic of safety, please see First Aid for Seizures, page 131.

WALLS, AND THE IMPORTANCE OF ART HISTORY AND ART APPRECIATION

There's an old saying...*The moment anyone enters the school in which you teach, it should be immediately known that an art teacher dwells there.* We all know what that means...and it's a good thing. The walls in the entrance are likely filled with student art. It's a positive message — one that at once brings a sense of life and energy! Cover as many walls as you can with your students' art.

Also, be inclusive, please. Students of all abilities deserve recognition. It's hard to measure just how much pride the display of student art means to the student — but we know it matters. And, if possible, please don't save it all for Parent's Night...or the end-of-the-year show. It's amazing how much those who see the art enjoy it — whether staff, visitors, or the students themselves. Additionally, an official exhibit of student work outside of school, in places such as arts and crafts stores, frame shops, art centers, and bookstores can really increase self-confidence for students — while promoting your school district in particular and advocating art in general.

For you art room, your students' art would naturally be featured. Just remember to rotate the selected images — and to discuss them! Whether or not your school's location is in close proximity to an art museum, the use of art posters is highly recommended (museum outreach programs may be of assistance). Use posters for reference...or "curate" them in any way you see fit. Remember, in our Art Activities section, many topics are supported by immediate reference, even though many images can be found on the internet.

Personally, I am a book lover and admit it openly. To keep art books and children's books in your curriculum will no doubt support your program — and keep books in children's lives. This benefits everyone, enforcing visual language and literature through art. Open a book and discover a whole new world. Who could argue it? One more thing...books are sensory. Some books even offer interactive experiences which are very engaging for special needs students.

It is important to point out to students that these images are reproductions. It doesn't mean they are "fake," just that the actual work of art is somewhere else, and the picture doesn't always tell the whole story. You can drive this concept home by showing a photographic image or art you've made (or own), then show your students "the real thing." If they can touch the object, great. But make sure to emphasize that even though art in museums cannot usually be touched (explain why), there is a big difference between a photograph of a painting or sculpture, then seeing the actual art. This is yet another sensory experience. The surfaces of paintings (think Impressionist brushstrokes and/or impasto) create a very tactile respone — even it it is delivered visually. Scale is another concept that is not accurately captured by art reproductions. They are useful and important anyway!

If you are within a reasonable distance of a museum, go! Let the education department or special visitors department know you are coming, so they can properly accommodate you. More about that is found in the next section, *Special Museum of Art*.

CLASSROOM ART MATERIALS: DOs AND DON'Ts

NOT RECOMMENDED FOR ART CLASSROOM USE	SAFER ALTERNATIVES
Permanent markers (may contain powerful solvents)	Watercolor markers, water-based markers
Rubber cement, epoxy resins, or other solvent-based glues	White glue or gluesticks
Dry tempera powders	Liquid poster paint or solid poster paint blocks
Oil-based paints, enamel paints	Acrylic paints and other water-based paints
Turpentine	Materials requiring soap and water cleanup, e.g. acrylics
Batik and commercial dyes, permanent vat dyes	Natural vegetable dyes; also water-based fabric paints; fabric crayons
Oil-based, solvent-based printing inks	Water-based printing inks
Chalk and pastel dust	Wet technique or oil pastels or crayons
Aerosol spray	Brush on technique using acrylic gloss medium (teacher supervised)
Instant papier-mâché mixes	Flour and water
Unmarked glazes or lead glazes	Paint clay with poster paint or acrylics, seal with acrylic gloss medium
Unvented or improperly vented kiln	Air-dry clay work (kiln must be correctly installed with exhaust hood for safe use

Stay away from solvent-based supplies...opt for a water-based alternative!

First Aid for Seizures

Generally, when a student has a scraped knee or sprained ankle, there is ample time to take him or her to the nurse for care. But seizures happen so suddenly that you must handle the matter on the spot. The way that the seizure is dealt with will not only affect that student, but the other students in the class as well. A reassuring teacher will calm the class; a panicked teacher will further upset them. The first step in dealing with seizures is learning about them and what to do when they occur.

The most dramatic seizure is the *grand mal* (generalized tonic-clonic). The student may become stiff and start to fall. Jerking movements will begin. Skin may turn pale or take on a bluish complexion because of reduced breathing. Saliva may escape from the mouth. Here's what you can do:

- Without leaving student, notify nurse or office (another student can do it...you might want to designate a student or two at the beginning of the semester so they know what to do if the situation arises).
- Ease the student to the floor. Do not try to restrain the student. The seizure must run its course.
- Do not force any objects into his or her mouth.
- Clear the area of sharp objects which could injure the student.
- Place something soft and flat under his or her head, like a folded sweater. Turn the student onto his or her side to release saliva.
- Loosen any tight clothing. Remove glasses.
- You cannot stop the seizure. It should end in a few minutes.

Hopefully you contacted the school nurse who knows that a seizure is taking place. If the seizure follows the usual course and the student gains consciousness, there is no harm. Rarely, one seizure follows another without the student gaining consciousness; this indicates the need for emergency medical assistance.

After the seizure, the student will be disoriented and confused. Do not offer anything to eat or drink unless the student is fully awake. After it is all over, the student will probably want to rest for a while. Allow the nurse to advise.

There are other seizures. The *petit mal* (generalized absence seizure) is most common in children and usually lasts less than a minute. The child may stare blankly and appear to be daydreaming. Finally, the complex partial seizure (temporal lobe, psychomotor) may include complex behaviors. The student may walk around aimlessly, make unusual chewing sounds, and act generally confused. This seizure may last anywhere from a minute to several hours.

There is nothing that you can do for petit mal seizures. You may want to reassure the student's classmates that everything is all right, however. In the complex partial seizure, the child *may* respond to calm and gently spoken directions. Do not try to restrain; move harmful objects out of the way. Notify the school nurse.

Of all the seizures, the grand mal seizure can be the most frightening for children. Among other things, the loss of consciousness distinguishes this seizure from the others. *A prepared and informed teacher can make all the difference*!

SAFETY IN THE ART CLASSROOM

A considerable amount of attention has been given to the safe use of art materials. Books, articles, lectures, and symposiums have become available to artists and teachers on this vital subject. Studio artists and hobbyists have been able to make adjustments in their materials usage as a result. Usually the changes are very simple. It is often a matter of receiving basic information and developing a sense of safety awareness. Once consciousness about health is attained, it almost works automatically. This section will guide you in the direction of safety in an uncomplicated way.

It is most important that you become informed about health and safety when you work with students. Young children and special students constitute part of what is known as a "high-risk" group. Because children and even older students are still growing, their body metabolism is more rapid than that of an adult, so they are more likely to absorb material quickly through exposure. Their immature defense systems and lower body weight also make them more physically vulnerable to hazards.

When special students are exposed to suspicious or unsafe materials, the effects can be even more serious than for other students their age. Many special students have health complications that could be worsened by potentially hazardous substances. Health conditions that may include respiratory ailments, allergies, and even physical or organic dysfunction are of particular concern; you would certainly want to avoid any possible threat to their health.

With a little effort, your art classroom can be reasonably hazard-free. There are very safe, available substitutes for materials containing unhealthy ingredients.

Young students do not have to perform advanced technical processes, and there is no need to expose them. For example, glazing, soldering, enameling, and so on are not recommended for high risk students. In fact, why not post the "Dos and Don'ts" on your art room wall? It's a perfect reminder that protects everyone.

SECTION 5
SPECIAL MUSEUM OF ART

The most gratifying experiences for all students to learn and make art is *with* art...so what could be more authentic than to visit the place where art lives...the museum! Fun fact: the word museum has the word muse in it. The derivation of the word is *"the place of the muse"... "a place of inspiration!"* Consider the source material — the original art — as the solid basis of art education.

Museums are set up to receive visitors of all ages. They operate in compliance with federal guidelines, which require ramps, parking, barrier-free space, and numerous other features which make the museum accessible to all. Along with physical accommodations, museums provide programs and resources for adults and students with disabilities.

The Philadelphia Museum of Art is one such example of robust and excellent programs. The materials and art work come out of a program called Form in Art. The examples you see here were designed specifically for individuals with severe visual impairment.

Touchable interpretation of *Still Life with Apples and a Glass of Wine* by Paul Cézanne, was designed by The Philadelphia Museum of Art's Director of Accessible Programs, Mr. Street Thoma.

Ceramic Face by student in classes for adults with severe visual impairments at The Philadelphia Museum of Art

Adult student who is blind created this interpretation of her instructor. Very cool!

When you schedule a visit to a museum, it should be made clear to the contact person what the needs of your students will be, so that the museum can best accommodate your group. You may be working with the education division, an office of accessibility or both. Students really enjoy museum visits...and the visit(s) will encourage students to build a lifelong engagement with art!

INSPIRED WORKS BY STUDENTS WHO VISITED ART & SCIENCE MUSEUMS

SECTION SIX
ART HEROES IN ART HISTORY: TRIUMPH OF THE HUMAN SPIRIT!

Many of the most well-known artists had disabilities...as do many lesser-known artists. It is important for our students to know that art has its heroes, too! You'll be surprised to learn just how these artists worked with their disabilities!

It is a source for encouragement, inspiration and pride...and serves us all.

Frida Kahlo: Orthopedic Impairment

Vincent van Gogh: Emotional Disturbance

Henri Matisse: Orthopedic Impairment

Paul Cezanne: Emotional Disturbance

Horace Pippin: Orthopedic Impairment

Edgar Degas: Visual Impairment

Pierre-Auguste Renoir: Orthopedic Impairment

Claude Monet: Visual Impairment

Henri Toulouse-Lautrec: Orthopedic Impairment

Edvard Munch: Emotional Disturbance

Francisco Goya: Deaf; Emotional Disturbance

Chuck Close: Orthopedic Impairment; Learning Disability, Prosopagnosia

Robert Rauschenberg: Learning Disabiltiy

Dennis Francesconi: Orthopedic Impairment

Simona Azori: Orthopedic Impairment

Carol B. Saylor: Deaf/Visual Impairment

Stephen Wiltshire: Autism Spectrum Disorder

If you think you know these artists, read on...

Chuck Close at work on *John*, 1992. © Chuck Close, courtesy Pace Gallery

Photo of Matisse in his studio, © 2014 Succession H. Matisse, Artists Rights Society (ARS), New York

Self-Portrait Dedicated to Leon Trotsky, 1937. Oil on masonite, 30 x 24 in. Courtesy of the National Museum of Women in the Arts, Washington, D.C. Gift of The Honorable Clare Boothe Luce. © 2014 Banco de México Diego D.F. / Artists Rights Society (ARS), New York

"IF IT Were NOT FOR THe ACCIDENT, I WOULD HAVe never BEEN A PAINTER." –FRIDA KAHLO

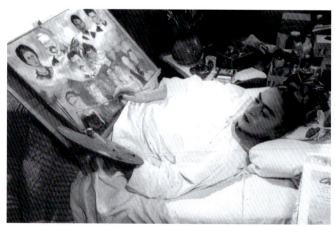

The Granger Collection, New York.

FRIDA KAHLO

Frida Kahlo (1907–1954) Mexican.
Orthopedic Impairment. Depression.

Frida Kahlo is recognized as an extraordinary painter in the history of art. As a child, Frida contracted polio at the age of six, which left her with a limp — and her classmates teased her. Frida, grew into an intelligent woman with a rebellious spirit who was, generally speaking, not easily intimidated. However, in late adolescence, her spine and pelvis were severely damaged in a nearly fatal injury in an explosive bus collision, from which she miraculously survived. This accident would cause her lifelong physical pain and multiple surgeries. She is best known for her intense self-portraits, many done when she was recuperating in bed. They are often filled with the lush tropical vegetation of her beloved Mexico. Many would describe the exacting expression of her style as surrealistic, which she denied. Towards the end of her prolific years as a painter — and after two marriages to infamous Mexican muralist Diego Rivera — Frida experienced depression, along with her declining health. In her time, Frida Kahlo showed herself to be a true original — a brilliant artist. She remains forever a symbol of hope, strength, and determination. In spite of her challenging circumstances, Frida loved life...as it is said in Spanish, *"Viva La Vida!"*

ACTIVITY

Self-Portrait Dedicated to Leon Trotsky, 1937

Frida creates a full figure-sized **self-portrait** in which she almost looks like a finely dressed little doll—which is not the way she typically paints herself. She holds a **special letter** she has written to a friend—signed, "with all my love." Students might enjoy creating a **portrait** of themselves in their "dressy best," leaving room for a letter they will insert into the picture, written to a friend, or artist, like Frida—or to Vincent (following page), who loved to write letters!

Supplies: pencil, pen, paper for writing; choice of watercolor, crayon or colored pencils.

BONUS: A Mexican/Spanish art tradition to consider: **Miracle Paintings,** which offer hand-written thanks for answered blessings. Writing usually appears at the bottom, with the specific event painted above the lettering. Frida collected these miniature **retablos**, painted on tin or copper (also wood or paper board).

VINCENT VAN GOGH

Vincent van Gogh (1853–1890) Dutch.
**Emotional Disturbance. Severe depression and anxiety.
Manic with seizure episodes. Interpersonal social difficulties**.

*"THE WAY TO KNOW LIFE IS TO LOVE
MANY THINGS." –VINCENT VAN GOGH*

Vincent van Gogh might just be the most popular Post-Impressionist painter of all time. He seems to evoke an emotional response from both children and adults alike! His combustible friendship with his talented and unstable friend Paul Gauguin is well known...a day when they painted together in Arles in the south of France, ended badly, with Vincent mutilating his own ear. Gauguin and van Gogh, in spite of their differences, actually learned from one another. The dark paintings van Gogh previously produced in the Netherlands (think *The Potato Eaters*) gave rise to a brighter palette when he moved to Paris. It was there he joined his art dealer brother, Theo, who represented Impressionists... and Vincent. The fact is that van Gogh sold only one painting in his short life, the last two years of which he was hospitalized for his severe emotional disturbances, but he was driven to paint masterpieces that are now worth billions to museums and collectors. His contribution to modern art is through his bold, colorful, decorative style...which is also highly expressive. Vincent van Gogh advanced the use of thick paint application beyond that which was used by the Impressionists and developed new ideas about art — which would be realized through the many generation to come.

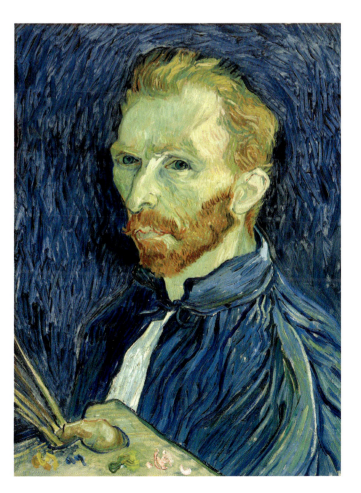

ACTIVITY

Vincent loved the act of painting, and would build up the surfaces of his paintings — much like a baker who slathers icing on a cake! You can see the movement of his brushstrokes in his art work. In this self-portrait, he proudly holds his brushes and palette — and wears a painter's smock. His technique is always distinctive, as is this self-portrait... an active surface that stimulates the eye. Sometimes he uses an outline. Students can have their choice of subject in addition to portraiture: landscapes (*The Starry Night*), still life (*Sunflowers*), or even a personal space (*Bedroom in Arles*). Students may want to work from reproductions or simply use their own imaginations. The selected subject will be drawn with pencil on canvas paper (or canvas board if possible). Along with these supplies, paintbrushes and acrylic paints, paper towels, and water containers are recommended. In the spirit of Vincent, students will paint with thick brushstrokes (impasto) — using strong colors — and build the surface. The results will be powerful and eye-pleasing...and they don't have to be perfect. Some students may employ outlines around contours of their subjects. (Refer to Adaptive Aids on p.122 if supplies suggested here are not suitable — also, if acrylics are not available, substitute with poster paint.) Remember that paintings with a tactile surface invite sensory engagement!

Self-Portrait, 1889. Oil on canvas, 22½ x 17¼ in. (57.2 x 43.8 cm); National Gallery of Art, Washington, D.C. Collection of Mr. and Mrs. John Hay Whitney, 1998.74.5

Henri Matisse

Henri Matisse (1869–1954) French.
Orthopedic Impairment.

First, it was a serious attack of appendicitis that introduced Henri Matisse to the idea of art. While Matisse was in his sick bed, his mother gave him color paints to help entertain him during his recovery. "*I knew this was my life,*" said Matisse, when he opened the box. "*I threw myself into (art) like a beast that plunges towards the things it loves.*" Matisse spent his many decades dedicated to color...mainly painting, but sculpture too. The inventive Matisse would receive great honor as one of the most original artists of the twentieth century — comparable to Picasso. With many famous paintings completed — and when Matisse was older — cancer was diagnosed. His following surgeries weakened him. Only then, in his bed, once again... and then, too, in his wheelchair, did he discover his beloved paper compositions. "*Painting with scissors,*" he called this new form of art, to which he dedicated approximately the next fifteen years. He said it also reminded him of sculpture by "*carving color.*" The cutouts, as they are called, delighted him for the rest of his life. He died at age 84 having invited millions to enter his brilliant and uplifting world!

Beasts of the Sea, 1950. Paper collage on canvas, 116⁵⁄₁₆ x 60⅝ in. (295.5 x 154 cm). National Gallery of Art, Washington, D.C. Ailsa Mellon Bruce Fund. © 2014 Succession H. Matisse / Artists Rights Society (ARS), New York

Photo of Matisse in his studio, © 2014 Succession H. Matisse, Artists Rights Society (ARS), New York

activity

Beasts of the Sea appears to be assembled by gluing the ends of various sized papers on to one another to create an overlapping paper column. The teacher may find that offering length of scroll sized paper will ensure steadier results. **Supplies** needed: colored construction paper, photocopy "brights," appropriate scissors and glue (glue sticks are best). Students may pick a theme, such as undersea life, enchanted forest, pet, or simply use freely cut shapes (see Matisse's image above) and paper scraps. Depending on your students, either glue the shapes and symbols that represent ideas *directly* on the length of paper, or create individual "pages" that will have the cut paper shapes glued upon them...then *assemble* on vertical scroll. Use highly contrasting colors and try to "*draw with scissors.*" When all are completed, display. Students discuss their **visual stories**. It's all about imagining!

"creativity takes courage"
–Henri Matisse

Paul Cézanne

Paul Cézanne (1839–1906) French.
Emotional Disturbance. Anti-social, paranoid, mood disorder.

Paul Cézanne's importance in the history of art is immeasurable. He was a Post-Impressionist who showed in the first Impressionist exhibition in 1874 with an earth-toned painting called *The House of the Hanged Man*. A kind, instructive Impressionist painter named Camille Pissarro would take Cézanne — a badly misguided young man from Aix-en-Provence — under his wing. Cézanne was sorely in need of a mentor and friend. His earlier years were spent beneath the rule of a strict, repressive father who gave little support to his son. Cézanne's early paintings reflect his frame of mind — they were, for the most part, murky struggles with paint and subject — attempts to imitate masters of past and present without success, some with disturbing psychological undertones. Yet Cézanne was not insensitive to poetry, music, and literature. Soon, he was off to Paris, where the paternal Pissarro recognized Cézanne's talents and encouraged him to paint outdoors. This was an ideal match, for if there was one motif Cézanne loved, it was nature.

Boy in a Red Waistcoat, 1888-1890. Oil on canvas, 35¼ x 28½ in. (89.5 x 72.4 cm). Collection of Mr. and Mrs. Paul Mellon, in Honor of the 50th Anniversary of the National Gallery of Art, Washington, D.C.

> "THE PAINTER UNFOLDS THAT WHICH HAS NOT BEEN SEEN."
> —PAUL CÉZANNE

ACTIVITY

The young model in **Boy in Red Waistcoat** is in a traditional pose... we've seen it since the Renaissance. Yet, it is extremely modern. Why? The way Cézanne painted the boy and his background to look rock solid. The folds of the curtain almost seemed carved out of the cloth. It is both familiar and unfamiliar. Here's an interesting idea to try: students will **create people** out of marble, wood, textile... free choice is acceptable: animal, vegetable, or mineral! Of course, we're talking about *images* of all these elements that are found (where else?) in magazines. **Supplies** for this activity are magazines, particularly architectural or decorator types. Discontinued wallpaper books may have faux textures. You will also need drawing paper, colored pencils, scissors, glue sticks, fine-point markers (optional). Students will need a figure reference...perhaps students can take turns modeling in a pose similar to the one shown in the Cézanne image. Otherwise, a simple example of the body can be provided or drawn on board by the teacher (for those who need pre-cut body forms, see Adaptive Aids, page 122). Students will select elements and glue on body form — some might want to draw a recognizable face. Cut out figures and display. Discuss — ask why particular selections were made. Now, let's see what you're made of!

As it would turn out, this socially difficult, suspicious, intense Cézanne would come to be *"the father of us all,"* as declared by Picasso—and to be acknowledged as **The Father of Cubism**—thus bridging Post-Impressionism to early modern art. His many paintings of Mt. Sainte-Victoire, as well as many other subjects, reveal extraordinary paint application that indeed anticipates cubism. How significant was his achievement? The surly Cézanne became a colossal artistic giant after all!

Horace Pippin

Horace Pippin (1888–1946) American.
Orthopedic Impairment; depression.

"The picture just comes to my mind, and I tell my heart to go ahead..."

–Horace Pippin

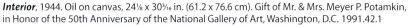

Interior, 1944. Oil on canvas, 24⅛ x 30³⁄₁₆ in. (61.2 x 76.6 cm). Gift of Mr. & Mrs. Meyer P. Potamkin, in Honor of the 50th Anniversary of the National Gallery of Art, Washington, D.C. 1991.42.1

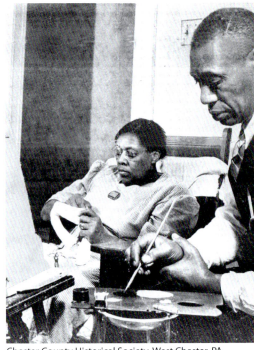

Chester County Historical Society, West Chester, PA

Horace Pippin was born in West Chester, Pennsylvania and grew up in poverty in Goshen, New York. Pippin showed an early interest in art and won an art contest, receiving a prize of crayons, watercolors, and brushes, thus confirming his loving commitment to art. Unfortunately, he had to leave school at 14 to help support his family. Life changed dramatically when World War I began — Pippin enlisted in the 369th Infantry, which was an all black unit. He soon found himself in heavy combat, surrounded by the horrific, unthinkable acts of war. Pippin held his own, until machine gun fire shattered his right shoulder and arm — ironically, on his final mission. He was discharged with a steel plate installed in his shoulder, while sustaining an essentially paralyzed right arm. Back home, he was trying to recover the use of his arm through painting while feeling depressed and discouraged. Both the ugliness of war, as well as the racial prejudice that remained in America, saddened him. But he painted seriously, employing his left arm to support the injured right arm —he even used amazing wood-scorching techniques with a burning poker to achieve visual textures. His themes were of genre scenes, domestic life, landscapes, portraits, trench warfare, social injustice, and religious subjects...his interests were taken from life itself. His art had an immediate appeal and attracted the attention of collectors and museums — even celebrities. The images are honest, direct and appealing. Pippin enjoyed a well-deserved, wide artistic recognition during his lifetime, which is rare for any artist, particularly for an African-American of his era. Pippin was considered by many to be a folk artist, having "*only his heart*" for his artistic training.

activity

The art of Horace Pippin offers students encouragement—if you create with your best efforts, your "heart," the results cannot be "wrong." Many pictures Pippin painted were done from **memory**. They are so straightforward. We are reminded of not only what the image illustrates, but the feelings or mood it conveys. The following topics are offered for students' consideration:

• A cozy room I like to remember (with me in it).

• The park I used to play in (or still do).

• The time I went to a carnival (or circus...or zoo).

• My favorite holiday or seasonal memory (including birthdays).

Supplies needed are: drawing paper, crayons, watercolors, and brushes...*the same materials that young Horace Pippin won as an art prize*! (You may want to incorporate the crayon resist technique.) Also include water containers and paper towels. Pencils may be used. Encourage students to think about the best colors to represent their picture and its mood. Try to put in swatches of color, like quilts or rugs, as Horace did. Think of your scene as a page from a visual story. When completed, display and share your memories!

EDGar DeGas

Edgar Degas (1834–1917) French.
Visual Impairment.

"PeOpLe CaLL me THe Painter OF Dancers, BUT I
reaLLy WISH TO Capture THe movement ITSeLF."
—EDGar DeGaS

Monsieur Edgar Degas was born in Paris, in which he took pride. He came from a respectable family, with a Creole mother. They had financial stability, but later lost it. Degas kept the habits of his background — which were aligned with his artistic interests. He frequented the horse races at Deauville, the opera, and, of course, the ballet. He was an active member of the Impressionists, but while they upheld the joys of painting outdoors (*en plein aire*), Degas did not particularly care for the effects of sunlight and landscape...it seemed as though the closest he came to trees was in the

Four Dancers, c. 1899. Oil on canvas, 59½ x 70¹⁵⁄₁₆ in. (151.1 x 180.2 cm).
Chester Dale Collection, National Gallery of Art, Washington, D.C. 1963.10.122

personal grooming. He was fascinated by all sorts of working movement. While in his thirties, Degas was diagnosed with an eye disease of the retina that profoundly affected his vision. It was progressive, and had other complications... one day he would likely be blind. As a result, he changed his art technique. Perhaps his early choices of subject and place may have been driven by his sensitive eyesight. At the point when his vision worsened,

painted stage scenery (see *Four Dancers*). Actually, bright sunlight bothered his eyes, so a controlled environment was more suitable. Degas's tastes were grounded in the past — in classical, linear traditions. He loved drawing and painting young dancers in their studios and on stage as well as female shop keepers, women doing chores, and moments of

Degas turned from oil painting to the more frequent use of pastels. As a medium, pastels are softer, easier to control, and offer deep color saturation. His work in pastel is visually stunning and a direct outcome of his growing loss of vision. He died at the age of 83, and was buried in Montmartre Cemetery in Paris, the city of his birth.

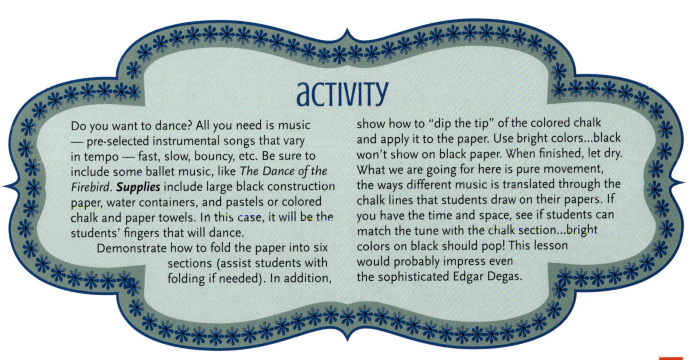

ACTIVITY

Do you want to dance? All you need is music — pre-selected instrumental songs that vary in tempo — fast, slow, bouncy, etc. Be sure to include some ballet music, like *The Dance of the Firebird*. **Supplies** include large black construction paper, water containers, and pastels or colored chalk and paper towels. In this case, it will be the students' fingers that will dance.

Demonstrate how to fold the paper into six sections (assist students with folding if needed). In addition, show how to "dip the tip" of the colored chalk and apply it to the paper. Use bright colors...black won't show on black paper. When finished, let dry. What we are going for here is pure movement, the ways different music is translated through the chalk lines that students draw on their papers. If you have the time and space, see if students can match the tune with the chalk section...bright colors on black should pop! This lesson would probably impress even the sophisticated Edgar Degas.

Pierre-Auguste Renoir

Pierre-Auguste Renoir (1841–1919) French.
Orthopedic Impairment; Rheumatoid Arthritis.

Oarsmen at Chatou, 1889; Oil on canvas, 22½ x 17¼ in. (57.2 x 43.8 cm);
National Gallery of Art. Collection of Mr. and Mrs. John Hay Whitney,
1998.74.5

Renoir was quite the Impressionist. He and Claude Monet painted together and became lifelong friends. While it is true that Renoir is best known for his joyful group portraits, figures, and wonderful portraits of children, everything about people seemed to interest him. It is said that *"Renoir came to painting as a duck goes to water."* Renoir loved little trips to scenic spots along the river Seine, which flowed out of Paris. Boat rentals and leisurely weekends were novel at the time — they were among the outcomes of the recent Industrial Revolution. Also, there was the new train system out of Paris to deliver enthusiasts to these delightful spots. Renoir could paint so naturally, outdoor paintings like this one at Chatou remind us not only of his mastery... they define Impressionism! Painting outdoors (*en plein aire*), capturing the light in multicolor dabs of paint and the pleasure of the day. It was now easier to paint outdoors. Why? The invention of the portable paint tube! And, of course, photography was invented around the time of Impressionism. The capturing of the moment...with scenes that remind us of the snapshots that would later appear.

Renoir was in his late thirties when this scene was painted. He never stopped painting, even when an aggressive type of Rheumatoid Arthritis made itself known to him at the age of 50, and progressed throughout the next 25 years. He moved south to Cagnes, to live and work in *Les Collettes* — his studio home. When he lost mobility, he painted from brushes that were placed into his curled hand, with wood supports along his arm to further aid him. Renoir painted from his wheelchair until the day he died at age 78. During his life, he produced over 4,000 paintings. Among the greatest masters of Impressionism,

ACTIVITY

Weather permitting, students might enjoy an *en plein aire* experience. Do your students have sketchbooks (see **Sketchbooks**, page 94)? Here's the impressionistic goal...find the right spot, and take in the atmosphere! How does the temperature feel? What's going on in the sky... with clouds, sun, or a passing hot air balloon (if you're lucky)...anything else? What sort of earth or grass do you see?

Are you near a stream or river...or pond? Really look around you. What sort of mood is nature in right now. Supplies suggested are colored pencils if you want to play it safe...watercolors if you're feeling liberated. When students feel "one with the fleeting moment"...begin! This is a contemplative exercise as well as an art activity. It should be conducive to cooperation. Time it according to your schedule — we want to complete most — ideally all of it — in one session. Follow-up in the art room to the **visual impression of the scene** might be a descriptive written narrative on the next sketchbook page — or a poem. This may be a fine way to turn an awareness experience into "togetherness." Didn't the Impressionists paint with one another? They not only shared ideas...they shared paint! It's just good form among friends.

his technique was not impaired by reduced physical mobility. Renoir was once asked by a rude reporter, "How can you paint with those hands?" Renoir replied, (roughly translated), "Ah, but I don't paint with my hands. I paint with my desire (to paint)."

"IF A PAINTER WORKS DIRECTLY FROM NATURE, HE ULTIMATELY LOOKS FOR NOTHING BUT MOMENTARY EFFECTS."
–Pierre-Auguste Renoir

claude monet

Claude Monet (1840–1926) French.
Visual Impairment.

Japanese Footbridge, 1899. Oil on canvas, 32 x 40 in. (81.3 x 101.6 cm). National Gallery of Art. Gift of Victoria Nebeker Coberly, in memory of her son John W. Mudd, and Walter H. and Leonore Annenberg. 1992.9.1

Claude Monet is regarded as a founder of Impresssionism, for he was its most consistent and steadfast leader. He supported the movement's principles: painting nature, weather effects, *en plein aire*, the capturing of the spontaneous moment, a heightened palette of eye-pleasing colors, and truth, meaning lack of artifice. Monet grew up in Le Havre, a northern seaport, so he understood water. No one can paint water like Monet — or landscape, for that matter. There are three major forces in the Monet legacy — one is his commitment to paint directly from nature under changing atmospheric conditions; next, his admiration and absorption of Japanese art and, last, in a culmination of both interests, Giverny, the garden studio he designed. He lived there for the second half of his life, planting flowers, cultivating ponds, and receiving profound inspiration for his art — notably, *The Water Lily* series. Monet said of Giverny, "*My garden is my most beautiful masterpiece.*" Monet was a strong man of hearty constitution who lived to 86. However, at age 65 he noticed a change in his vision. His perception of color was changing—colors were losing their intensity. There was also a shift to yellow tones which, combined with purple, made things muddy. His eyes were symptomatic of cataracts, which lend yellow to other colors — even vibrant reds seem dull. Also, he saw a strange fogginess that, as an Impressionist, bemused him, but that was brief, for he was not happy with his confusing vision. After 1915, his paintings could be taken for abstractions. Monet went to an ophthalmologist and tried eyedrops — to no avail. At age 82, Monet had cataract surgery on one eye and was quite frustrated, since he had the large *Water Lily* cycle to complete. He did not allow his eyes proper healing time, and went back to work, later receiving corrective lenses. Monet

"Landscape Does Not exist in its own right, since its appearance always changes." –claude monet

was inconvenienced by the distortions and sensitivities he experienced. His eyes were unreliable...he had to read color labels...and he refused surgery on his other eye. In spite of the effects of his cataracts, Monet managed to complete the huge commission of twelve vast canvases to be installed for the Prime Minister at the Musée de l'Orangerie. He did not live to see the unveiling in 1927. This installation is considered the Sistine Chapel of Impressionism. It is breathtaking and magnificent....and has no equal.

activity

Claude Monet loved Japanese prints. He was not alone. Degas, van Gogh, Gauguin, and Toulouse-Lautrec were similarly impressed with Japanese art. What was particular to Monet's fondness with Japanese art is the fact that Japanese printmakers worked in series. This was how Monet worked...in his many serial studies of the same subject at different times of the day...haystacks, poplars, even cathedrals. But it was even more than that particular fact... Monet's famous studio home at Giverny — the design, the plantings, the landscape, the lily ponds...reflect the artistic sensibilities of Japan. The Japanese footbridge Monet installed is a favorite theme. Japanese master Hiroshige produced a series called *The Fifty-three Stations of Tokaido Road*. It is a series of stunning prints that illustrate a journey. Many footbridges appear in the series, some crowded, some rainy with few figures, and so forth. Since we have one of Monet's numerous interpretations of his own Japanese Footbridge to consider, it's a good time to think about bridges. One suggestion is to take Monet's lead and illustrate the bridge as students might imagine it at three different times of day, using defining colors. Supplies needed are drawing paper, colored pencils and fine tipped markers. You might want to precut the paper in half lengthwise. Students can fold paper into three even sections. Ask students to think about time of day, weather, and any people who might be crossing the bridge. Consider what might be under the bridge as well. Use examples from Hiroshige if possible.

When all three sections are complete, unfold stories that might be implied by student's "series!"

HENRI DE TOULOUSE-LAUTREC

Henri de Toulouse-Lautrec (1864–1901) French.
Orthopedic Impairment.

Jane Avril, 1889; Five-color lithograph on thin wove paper, 22¹/₁₆ x 14¹⁵/₁₆ in. (56 x 38 cm); National Gallery of Art, Washington, D.C. Rosenwald Collection, 1953.6.137

Henri de Toulouse-Lautrec was a Post-Impressionist and extraordinary printmaker, painter, draftsman — and infamous wit! He was a true aristocrat, descended from the houses of Toulouse and Lautrec. Born in a magnificent chateau de Malrome at Albi, he left as a young man to live the life Bohemian in the Montmartre quarter of Paris. At that time, the spectacular Moulin Rouge opened. Toulouse-Lautrec would not only become a regular patron, he would immortalize the singers, dancers, and performers... who are recognizable to this day! Among the cast of characters are La Goulue — credited with making the Can-Can famous; The Rubber Man (her dance partner); Loie Fuller (avant-garde scarf dancer); and of course, the lovely singer, Jane Avril. Such was the talent at Moulin Rouge, who would appear in the bold, cleverly designed posters that served as advertisements. Imagine them plastered all over Paris!

As an adolescent of 13, Henri fractured his right thigh bone — within the next year, he fractured the left. The bones never healed fully. Since his mother and father were first cousins — not uncommon in aristocratic families — his medical problem was thought to be genetic. As a result,

Henri developed an adult male torso, while his legs stopped growing. He was very bright, well-educated, and enjoyed the company of his fellow artists, writers, and actors. Just the same, he endured ignorant remarks made by others about his short stature. Unfortunately, he heavily indulged in alcohol and died at the age of 36. So Toulouse-Lautrec is appreciated for his short but prolific career, in which he produced over 700 paintings as well as thousands of drawings, watercolors, prints, and posters. His use of line was skilled and fluid. Like his companions, he was influenced by Japanese composition and cropped angles. He is remembered for his silhouettes, wry depictions of theatrical nightlife, and his observations of the circus atmosphere at the turn of the twentieth century.

ACTIVITY

Oh, the nightlife of Paris at the turn of the 20th century! Toulouse-Lautrec took us behind the scenes...but brought out its stars, too! Let's imagine that we are commissioned to advertise fictional or real actors, singers, trapeze artists, jugglers, or high-wire acts!

Supplies would be large sized drawing paper, practice paper, pencils, poster paint (tempera), and assorted brushes. Provide images or use the internet to stimulate the imagination (think Cirque de Soleil) — then have students sketch their favorites. Refer to the imaginative way Toulouse-Lautrec "framed" and placed importance on his subjects...consult other Art Nouveau artists as well. Ready? Apply your design and "featured act." Make it big: **posters** need to be seen quickly, and from a distance. Think in terms of **dramatic postures**. Does it register when you back away? Students can draw first with pencil, then brush on strong colors. Expansive flat areas have strong impact, but some details are needed. How about the lettering that students use? Keep it consistent with the overall composition. *C'est fantastique!*

TOULOUSE-LAUTREC OBSERVES: "BIG CROWD TONIGHT." MOULIN ROUGE PROPRIETOR DECLARES: "TOO BIG! THANKS TO YOUR POSTER" –DIALOGUE FROM 1952 FILM, MOULIN ROUGE

EDVARD MUNCH

Edvard Munch (1863–1944) Norwegian.
Emotional Disturbance. Depression, anxiety, illness.

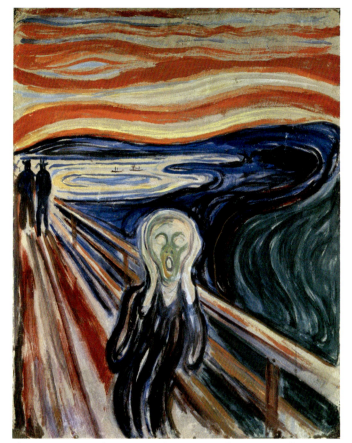

The Scream, 1893; Oil, tempera, and pastel on cardboard, 36 x 28⅔ in.;
Munch Museum, Oslo, Norway. Album/Oronoz/Album/SuperStock
© Munch Museum / The Munch-Ellingsen Group / Artists Rights Society
(ARS), New York, 2014.

Edvard Munch was a Symbolist painter and printmaker who,
like Vincent van Gogh, grew up in a northern region with an
intensely religious father. Unfortunately, as was prevalent
at the time, his family experienced considerable illness
and loss. This was deeply disturbing to the young Edvard,
whose own health was also poor, and the family subsisted
by meager means. It was not a cheerful situation. Edvard's
story is similar to others we've heard: he discovered his
talent in art which his father judged "an unholy trade."
He studied other disciplines, such as chemistry, physics,
and mathematics, but frequent illness interrupted his
attendance, and he dropped out and declared his wish
to become a painter. He then enrolled, in 1881, at the
Royal School of Art and Design. A "quick study," Edvard
mastered technique, experimenting with Naturalism
and Impressionism. Munch was attracted to the work of
Toulouse-Lautrec, Vincent van Gogh, and Paul Gauguin
who, besides being called a Post-Impressionist, was also
known as a Symbolist. The Symbolist doctrine was that,

" IN MY ART I ATTEMPT TO EXPLAIN LIFE AND ITS
MEANING TO MYSELF." –EDVARD MUNCH

unlike previous theories, truth in art can only be described
indirectly...this was in keeping with Expressionism, which
was developing in Germany. Symbolism was far more
introspective and psychological than any previous art
movement — and was a precursor of Surrealism. Sigmund
Freud and the birth of psychoanalysis made its entrance,
concurrently. Artists, poets, musicians, and writers were
fascinated with the role of the subconscious which,
theoretically, underscored all human behavior. This era could
not have been more compatible with Munch's goal for his
art: "the study of the soul, that is to say the study of my
own self." He would continue in this direction for the rest
of his life. However, the unprecedented attention received
by the image of *The Scream*, painted in 1893, and its epic
celebrity, would overshadow all the rest of his artistic work.
It is one of the most famous and most recognizable images
ever created. It is also the most parodied. By that measure,
it's right up there with the *Mona Lisa* and Michelangelo's
statue of *David*. *The Scream* is the last of a cycle of 22
paintings Munch produced for a Berlin exhibit with titles
like *Suffering, Love, Jealousy, Death, Menace*... mainly painful
emotions expressed, introspectively, through rings of color
and undulating line. When he painted *The Scream* his
state of mind was starkly revealed. By 1908, he required
hospitalization for emotional instability. Munch recovered,
returned to Norway and dedicated the artwork he had left to
Oslo (much of it had been stolen by the Nazis). He lived to
nearly 80 and, without doubt, stamped an indelible image of
The Scream on our universal consciousness. It's era-defying!

ACTIVITY

The Scream – what is it about this image?
Everyone has their own opinion. Many believe
Munch captured a perfect portrait of anxiety —
a personal "wit's end" moment of despair or
total "meltdown." Others see it as an icon for
the modern times in which we live: "The Age of
Anxiety." What do your students think it represents?
Interestingly, the blood-red sky may not be imaginary.
While Munch was painting *The Scream*, an enormous
volcano, Krakatoa, erupted in Indonesia. It turned
skies in Norway a blazing red-orange. Still, it's
effective for this painting.

Students will create an interpretation of *The Scream*
— the figure on the bridge, the two small figures
in the distance, and the rails of the bridge. With
the image for reference, **let's see what it takes to
change this mood**. (Expression, color choice, and
imagination.) Maybe a bouquet of flowers or
some pretty foliage would help. **Supplies** are
tempera paint or pastels paperboard, markers
(for following contours,) and pencils...these
were Munch's selections. It's time
to reinvent this most
famous image!

Francisco Goya

Francisco Goya (1746–1828) Spanish.
Deaf. Emotional Disturbance.

"fantasy...is the mother of the arts and the origin of marvel." –Francisco Goya

Modo de volar (A Way of Flying), published 1864; etching, aquatint, and drypoint, Harris 1964, no. 260, State III (1st ed.); National Gallery of Art, Washington, D.C. Rosenwald Collection, 1943.3.4717.m.

Goya was a major artist and printmaker, who transitions from the Old Masters, such as Rembrandt, to introduce the ideas for modern painting, as advanced by Edouard Manet. Goya was born in Spain to a Basque father...and under the family crest of his mother. As a young man, he lived with his family in Madrid, then he traveled to Rome, Italy to advance his skills. Before long, Goya caught the attention of royal Spanish court. At first, he painted designs for tapestries, usually of scenes of daily life, notably, *The Parasol* (1777). The royal court recognized his talent. By 1779 he was commissioned to paint portraits of a Duke and Duchess and others of high rank. He was soon made court painter to King Charles IV. Goya was financially retained to paint royal family portraiture. However, it was around this time that Goya developed a serious illness with an uncertain diagnosis. It left him deaf yet more introspective... he was still artistically productive. He began to expand his work to include the "common man" and recognized hardships. His style shifted a bit... he became more experimental. Still, he lived a prosperous life, and in1795, was named the director of the Royal Academy. Goya became interested in printmaking and created an etching series called *Los Caprichos* in 1799. while still producing official commissions. The 80 *Caprichos* prints eloquently expressed his observations of political greed, corruption, and repression. When France had invaded Spain in 1808, Goya was 62 and still remained a court painter under Napoleon. There was a bloody war, which drove him to paint his iconic scene of a firing squad executing an unarmed citizen, titled *The Third of May*. Soon, under Ferdinand VII, Spain won back its rule. Goya, in spite of his liberal views, was retained for his established artistic reputation. Goya, who had remained outwardly neutral

during the war, simply couldn't tolerate the absurd and hideous acts he saw. He then produced his commentary through a suite of imaginative engravings called *Los Proverbios Desparates* or Nonsense... *Follies* is perhaps the best description . The images represent nightmarish scenes that, for the most part, resemble a grotesque carnival of lost souls. His imagery grew markedly morbid. Goya bought a house, called *Quinta del Sordo* (Deaf Man's House) where he painted the "Black Paintings" most well-known of which is *Saturn Devouring his Son*, based on a Greco-Roman myth. The ferocity of this picture is daunting. It is said to represent Spain's self-destructive politics. At 75, Goya was depressed, alone, and isolated...which cannot be entirely disassociated with his deafness (isolation is consistently reported as the single most difficult aspect of the disability). In the end Goya, who died at age 82, not only led the way, artistically, to a whole new era...he gave us a moving, inventive and honest chronicle of his time. As it is said, "Without art, we have no record of civilization." *Gracias*, Señor Goya.

activity

A Way of Flying (modo de volar) is of one of 20 etchings Goya did between 1815 and 1823. He called the series *Los Caprichos*, which means *Follies*. Rather than social commentary, this picture almost seems, well, uplifting! First, there's the night — and it's mysterious. Then there's the idea of flying — or floating in the night sky. For this whimsical activity, let's **imagine that gravity on earth suddenly disappeared**. What then? Students can brainstorm how they might react, or deal with it. Marc Chagall is another artist who favored the creative dismissal of gravity — consult his work...you will find a few birds and angels too! Another source for reference is in your dreams...did you ever dream of flying? How did it feel? This lesson that takes its essence from Goya...flying and being weightless in space. Why not present those concepts to your students and suspend a specific outcome. Elements students will **illustrate** are purely of their own choice. Only one rule: you can't stand (or sit) on the ground in this gravity-free image! **Supplies**: construction paper (with enough dark blue or black for students who prefer night)...any other colors can "fly" in this magic place. Also, crayons, especially fluorescent, will work well. Can't wait to see what our students come up with!

CHUCK CLOSE

Chuck Close (born 1940) American.
Orthopedic Impairment. Learning Disability.
Prosopagnosia ("Face Blindness").

Fanny/Fingerpainting, 1985; Oil on canvas, 102 x 84 in.
National Gallery of Art, Washington, D.C. Gift of Lila Acheson Wallace, 1987.2.1. © Chuck Close, courtesy Pace Gallery.

Chuck Close is among the most recognized artists living today, principally for his mural-sized portraits of friends, family, fellow artists, and himself. Close's huge facial portraits appear with impact! The face fills the entire surface and could not appear to be any nearer to the viewer. To achieve these effects, Close uses a variety of processes: photography, printmaking, and painting. He would be the first to tell you that his work is process-driven...and although some images appear highly photorealistic, that's not a term he favors, since what is *not* real also interests him. Close is a world renowned, unconventional artist with a good life, but things weren't always that way. He was born in a working class, rural area of Monroe, Washington. As he succinctly puts it, "I have had a life with rocks in my shoes." Profound learning disabilities appeared in his childhood, along with neuromuscular difficulties. He was awkward and clumsy...many thought him lazy. He understandably had trouble at school. As someone with learning differences, an interest in art developed. Fast forward to 1961...Close earned a scholarship to Yale while attending the University of Washington. He received an M.F.A. from Yale and studied at the Academy of Fine Arts in Vienna on a Fulbright grant. In 1967, he moved to New York City, after a brief encounter with abstract art, and began his investigation of every imaginable medium to express his greatest interest: the portrait. His work is associated with the photographic image transferred to a grid, drafted onto a huge surface. It is a labor intensive process. But there's more to it...

" IF I HADN'T HAD exposure to art and music, something I could excel at, feel good about — I always said, 'IF I HADN'T GONE TO YALE, I could have gone to JAIL'." –CHUCK CLOSE

Fanny/Fingerpainting is an optical illusion. It was not made on a grid...it is composed entirely of fingerprints! Many of Close's portraits employ the building up of mosaic-like cells, much like Pointillism, which appears nonrepresentational when you stand inches from the picture. Only when you step back is the full image revealed. Close uses a similar optical concept...his work is a colorful, lively collection of small units that animate the eye. Step back, and you have a huge portrait! Close suggests that his attraction to portraiture is likely the result of his prosopagnosia, or face-blindness. This condition makes it difficult to remember a person's face. His portraits flatten facial features and somehow, this helps him to remember facial identities. Along with this condition, the artist had an arterial collapse of his spine in 1988, which he calls The Event, that caused paralysis of his legs, among other physical disturbances. He now straps brushes on to his wrists to paint. Yet regardless of The Event, prosopagnosia, and dyslexia, the inventive and intrepid Chuck Close hasn't missed a beat!

ACTIVITY

A Great, Big Face of Many Colors
Supplies: Kraft paper, cut into one-yard sections; scissors; drawing paper; markers; crayons; glue; and yardstick(s). Volunteers will draw grids on the paper. Measure to keep lines straight and equal. Depending on the size of the class, assign one grid paper for 5 to 6 students. Using one of Close's color portraits for inspiration, students can apply color to the blocks, one by one. When color application is complete, set aside. The next direction is simple: each student selects *one* facial feature...eye, nose, mouth/lips, ears and fills the *entire* drawing paper with the one greatly oversized feature selected. When these are completed, cut them out. Try to make sure there are roughly equal numbers of features (remember there are ultimately two eyes and two ears). Here's the part where it all comes together: students arrange features on the colored grid paper...this is a team effort. The results might look like a combination of Picasso (who many speculate had a learning disability) and Chuck Close. Try to align facial features in a somewhat realistic order. Glue to grid. Create a facial contour (with hair or cap, ears) that will help organize the features by drawing an outline — and do keep neck and shoulders in mind. Do students better understand Close's process... even without using the color blocks to define the face, like Close does?

ROBERT RAUSCHENBERG

Robert Rauschenberg (1925-2008) American.
Learning Disability; Dyslexia.

Estate, 1963; Oil and silkscreen ink on canvas. 96 x 70 in. (243.8 x 177.8 cm). Philadelphia Museum of Art. Art © Robert Rauschenberg Foundation / Licensed by VAGA, New York, NY.

Born in Port Arthur, Texas, Robert Rauschenberg would find his way into the artistic circles of 1950's New York. He was a part of many art undertakings, was quite active and widely-known...painter, sculptor, printmaker, lithographer, photo transfer enthusiast, performing artist, even window dresser. Although he participated in Abstract Expressionism, he is probably best known for his assemblages...or combines, as these works were called. He incorporated "found objects," an innovation that began with Marcel Duchamp, pioneer of the Dada movement. Rauschenberg also worked from a studio home in Captiva, Florida, where he continued experimenation with wall reliefs and sculptures from, among other materials, used boxes. He also tried his hand with commercial photo-transfer, placing himself somewhat in the Andy Warhol realm. Rauschenberg was a bit ahead of the Pop movement, but very grounded in the advancement of assemblage and collage. In 1951, Rauschenberg produced his White Paintings, Red Paintings... followed by the Black group. He used all sorts of material —wood, nails, newsprint, textiles were incorporated in his paintings. These were the forerunners to the combines, out of which collage and assemblage grew. The image of *Estate*,1963 combines silkscreen and ink on canvas.

"VALUE THE PROCESS" –ROBERT RAUSCHENBERG

We repeatedly hear of the positive outcome of providing art experience to those who learn differently. Robert Rauschenberg firmly believed that his dyslexia helped him create art. As a schoolboy, he doodled in the margins and had difficulty reading—a textbook indicator of Attention Deficit Disorder. Rauschenberg later joked that he enjoyed the printmaking process because it's reversed. For example, if you inscribe your name into a printing plate, it will come out backwards. If you read in reverse, it will look good to you! In the time when he grew up, no one knew about such things. Today, however, in the Disabilities Studies Quarterly, a full article appeared, written by Ken Gobbo, entitled *Dyslexia and Creativity: The Education and work of Robert Rauschenberg*. It's an excellent piece on many levels. The writer states that it was most likely the way Rauschenberg's brain processed information and allowed him to see possibilities in the environment that a "non-dyslexic" would not recognize. The combines, for instance, are powerfully expressive in ways that convey meanings both pictorially and texturally. Further, they are highly sensory. By this account, it is little wonder that the artist was able to engage in a vast array of media successfully. In his life, Rauschenberg received national awards for work in his belief in the learning disability and creativity. His success in the art world enabled him to create his own charitable venue. In 1990, he created the Robert Rauschenberg Foundation. Along with this he supported The Lab School in Washington D.C., a school that teaches students with learning disabilities through an art-based curriculum. Rauschenberg has underwriten scholarships for The Power of Art conferences held there, designed for art teachers of students with learning disabilities. He was an artist who certainly helped to put a positive spin on "different!"

ACTIVITY

Estate sends a message that your students could receive and discuss. The subject is urban. This is a specific city...how do we know? There's a clue (lower left). Goal: create a **collage of a metropolitan city**. **Supplies** are drawing paper, appropriate magazines, construction paper, scissors, fabric scraps and other safe scratchy and smooth textures, glue and — only if you wish — paint and brushes. First let's find words to describe this interpretation of New York City — what makes it look the way it does? Once students are properly inspired, begin! The city the student creates may be based on actual experience or a perceived idea. For additional reference: Romare Bearden, notably *The Dove*...this is NY's Harlem. Bearden is a fantastic collage artist. Incorporate him whenever you can! (Perhaps *Estate* could be compared to *The Dove*...) Are we there yet? When completed, discuss the kind of city you built and its energy. If time permits, talk about choices of materials, their use and importance. Display... and look both ways!

Dennis Francesconi

Dennis Francesconi (born 1963) American. **Orthopedic Impairment**.

"ANYTHING IS POSSIBLE, AS LONG AS YOU'RE WILLING TO TRY." –DENNIS FRANCESCONI

Serene Bay. © Dennis Francesconi. By the courtesy of the Association of Mouth and Foot Painting Artists Worldwide. www.vdmfk.com

attended college and earned an Associate in Arts Degree. While in college, he started sketching and quickly moved on to watercolors. This time, he held a brush between his teeth. By 1993, he submitted his work for submission AMFPA — the Association of Mouth and Foot Painting Artists. Intially, he was accepted as a Student Member, and in five years, he rose to the ranks as Full Member. Dennis went on to sell his work as an exhibiting artist internationally. He attracted media attention, which allowed him to share his art and story with larger audiences. His artistic talent extended to illustration, greeting cards, and product

Unlike the other artists whose names appear in the Art Heroes section, Dennis Francesconi and the artists who follow him probably will be new to you. It's a pleasure to introduce them. Dennis, who would probably describe himself as an active guy with a loving wife — would have to add his identity as an artist. At the age of 17, in 1980, Dennis' life changed dramatically. He had a water-skiing accident that left him paralyzed. As a quadriplegic, he had facial mobility and the willingness to write with a pencil in his mouth. Dennis then

designs. In 2008, he was honored by the state of California for his work. Dennis believes in reaching out to others, and he is generous of mind and spirit. His work is best described as iconic and representational. His paintings reveal craftsmanship and compositional clarity and are thematically diverse, often with a specific focus, such as a castle or a beautiful flower. His artistic vision is crystal-clear. There is nothing to indicate any disability whatsoever in his sharp, well-defined art.

ACTIVITY

To honor Dennis Francesconi, would the teacher be prepared to try an exercise in **mouth painting** with the students? *Supplies*: paper, masking tape, watercolors. Make sure ends of brushes are clean! Also important is the where the paper is placed. It must be accessible! If you don't have easels or drawing boards, taping paper (at the right height), perhaps on the wall, is your best bet. Note to teacher: You may want to try this yourself first. Please do not conduct this exercise if you don't feel comfortable with it! If you are ready, begin. Rule: NO hands. Students' first encounter with mouth painting always brings unprecedented responses. Again, this is more of an exercise. Students may want to use just one color. You might secure the water containers with rolled masking tape under containers on desks... include paper towels. The subject is free choice. Use teacher judgment with "running time" of this experience. Once you're finished and cleaned up (hands permitted), discuss this special painting. Dennis is remarkable...he made it look easy!

simona atzori

Simona Atzori (born 1974) Italian.
Orthopedic Impairment.

Self-Portrait. © Simona Atzoria. By the courtesy of the Association of Mouth and Foot Painting Artists Worldwide. www.vdmfk.com

Simona was born in 1974 without arms. Attempts made to fit the young Simona with prosthetic arms failed. She protested, feeling that they were impractical and weighed her down, so they were summarily rejected. Simona, an artist and a dancer, uses her feet to write, sketch, and perform daily tasks, such as driving, drinking cappuccino, putting on earrings, using the computer, texting...everything! This determined young girl started painting with her feet at age four. She had the support of her mother and artist Mario Barzon. In 1983, she was awarded a scholarship from the Mouth and Foot Painting Artists of the World. Another defining moment came when she was given audience with Pope John Paul II, at which time she presented him with the portrait she painted of him. At the age of six, she began to dance. She now had two loves...art and dance. Simona was able to study both in a Visual Arts program at the University of Western Ontario, Canada, where she graduated with honors in 2001. She paints and draws with the same emotional qualities of her dance style; her drawings are detailed and dramatic. Simona became associated with the Pescara Dance Festival, which she endowed with the *Atzori Award*. In 2006, she performed during the Opening Ceremony of the Paralympic Games in Turin, Italy. Simona is now a mother and is as radiant, capable and talented as ever. She continues to perform and to exhibit her art all over the world.

activity

Simona uses her feet as hands to make art so naturally, at first you do a double-take! *Are those her toes she's holding the pencil with*...you wonder? Exactly! So you might guess where this activity is leading. That's right, take off your shoes and socks and get ready to **draw with your feet**! It's really different from what you're used to, but you may find a new way to express yourself. ***Supplies*** are up to the teacher... crayons, watercolor or pencil—or try all three! Large drawing paper is placed on the floor. Students may want to sit on the floor... or create your drawing/painting while seated and aiming down to the paper. Experiment! Place the pencil/crayon/paintbrush between your big toe and second toe (yes, we'll allow your hands to help position the particular artist tool – even though Simona would not use this method.) Give it a go...it's new and daring! Again, free choice on subject. There's no hazard except maybe a foot cramp. The results should be great to discuss...what surprised you? Was it frustrating or fun? Would you do it again? Put on your socks and shoes...now, a Can-Can kick for Simona!

"why not?" –simona atzori

Simona is not sketching with her right hand — she is sketching with a pencil between her TOES! Eye-fooling, isn't it?

carol saylor

Carol Saylor (born 1937) American.
Deaf; blind.

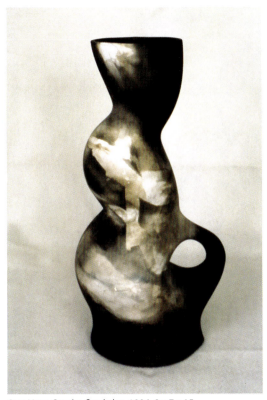

Cast Vase. Smoke-fired clay, 1996. 9 x 7 x 15.

Carol Saylor epitomizes "true grit." She is a painter, sculptor, ceramicist, and professional presenter. Life has struck her with one extraordinary challenge after another, which is manifest in her art. At the age of 39, she was raising five children, yet managed to graduate Magna Cum Laude from the Tyler School of Art. One rainy afternoon, she was told by an ophthalmologist that she was losing her sight. As a painter, this was indeed startling news. As her vision was diminishing, she began to teach. She was not only going blind, but deaf, too. Saylor continued to work in watercolor while she still had tunnel vision. As the two-dimensional medium grew more difficult, she turned to sculpture, for which she would gain considerable recognition. She exhibited widely and her work was acquired by museums and collectors. In her personal life, she has experienced heavy losses. Her two year old son died suddenly and without medical explanation; cancer claimed her husband; and then, some years later, she lost her daughter, who was the mother of three young children. Now, completely blind and using a guide dog, Saylor is increasingly deaf, but she cares for her grandchildren. The creation of art at this point helps with pure survival, although she probably wouldn't put it that way. Her life powers her art. Most of her recent work is clay... although she's had her hand in papier-mâché, plaster, wood, bronze, and resin sculpture. Her favorite patina is smoke-fired. Themes include the female form, which is conceptually suggested in the smoke-fired vase shown here. An original idea that the artist developed is somewhat abstract and novel: sculptural pieces that have an interior which the visitor is invited to experience tactilely. Saylor's work conveys the emotions of a lifetime — from sorrow to joy, gratitude, and hope. Saylor states, "I am grateful for the wonderful transition my brain has been able to make."

"I am a mind and a spirit... and my eyes have nothing to do with vision, just as my ears have nothing to do with listening." –carol saylor

Saylor, now 75, recently met Armand Mednick, 80, an artist and teacher who is also visually impaired. "It was love at first sight," says Armand. Photo by Ed Hille. Used with permission of the Philadelphia Inquirer, Copyright ©2014. All rights reserved.

STEPHEN WILTSHIRE

Stephen Wiltshire (Born 1974) British (born of West Indian parents). **Autism**.

"DO THE BEST YOU CAN AND NEVER STOP."
–STEPHEN WILTSHIRE

Have you heard about a brilliant artist whose phenomenal memory enables him to quickly remember entire cityscapes, often observed by helicopter...then draw them in exacting detail, including number of windows? Meet Stephen Wiltshire, who was diagnosed with autism at the age of three. His speech was delayed until he was five and said his first word: paper. At an early age, he began sketching landmark London bridges, among other subjects. By the age of nine, he learned to speak fully — and also received his first commission! It was from the late Prime Minister Edward Heath who wanted Stephen to draw the Salisbury Cathedral. It seems that his artistic career was launched! His next ambitious project at age ten was called *The London Alphabet* — a group of pictures that illustrated famous British landmarks in alphabetical sequence, from Albert Hall (a famous musical venue) to the London Zoo. Stephen's incredible talent was in popular demand. By the 1980s, Stephen acquired literary representation for a book he wrote — and enjoyed a visible artistic presence. He was recognized by the late Hugh Casson, former president of London's Royal Academy of Art, and placed under his mentorship...Stephen was identified as "possibly the best child artist in Britain." In short, Stephen Wiltshire was celebrated as an artistic genius!

The young man attended college, with a keen interest in drawing and painting. His career developed along with his excitement for capturing entire cities with his pen. As his level of public recognition grew, Stephen was invited on many helicopter rides, where he was able to mentally record the architecture of iconic cities around the world in very short amounts of time. His mind has been compared to a camera — he is able to record the finest of details when he returns to a studio space. His fame grew. Wiltshire has his own gallery in the Royal Opera Arcade — with Her Majesty the Queen's blessings. He seems to be drawing himself around the world, creating magnificent panoramic cityscapes. He's visited Tokyo, Rome, Frankfurt, Madrid, Dubai, Jerusalem, Sydney, Paris and Shanghai — to name a few! Stephen has a particular fondness for New York City. When he was only five years old, he drew his own imaginary apartment there. Later, in a *London Times* article, he was quoted as saying, "I'm going to live in New York someday. I've designed my penthouse on Park Avenue."

Top: **London Panorama**. 2008; Pen, ink, and pencil on paper, 13 feet. Courtesy of the artist.
Above: The artist at work on **Aerial View of Manhattan Skyline**, 2011.

Stephen did travel to New York City, where he sketched the legendary skyscrapers of Manhattan. Stephen created a 250-mile-long panoramic memory of New York which is on display on a giant billboard at JFK Airport. Stephen has referred to New York as his "spiritual home." Knowing this artist's love of buildings, monuments, and architecture, it is easy to understand his attraction to the great American metropolis. It is a vast and complex undertaking. One way the viewer can recognize a this particular city and others is that Stephen includes its monuments. Again, he excels in the depiction of all he sees and memorizes...and will often include people, cars, and taxis. All these elements lend scale and a vivacious touch. On many occasions, Stephen adds color — and presents night scenes as well. His work has made him an internationally famous artist.

Additional artists on the autistic spectrum who may be of interest are: Maria Iliou, who is also an advocate for Autism Spectrum Disorder, George Widener, Jessica Park, Christophe Pillault, Ping Ling Yeak,and many others (http://www.webdesignerdepot.com/2010/03/the-amazing-art-of-disabled-artists). Anyway, it's Art Spirit at work, again!

ACTIVITY

Famous Monuments and Landmarks Around the World: A Panorama

Here's an opportunity to learn some of the world's most famous architectural and historic landmarks. Stephen is described as an autistic savant, which places him in the rare classification of artistic genius. Students will create ink drawings using fine-tipped permanent black markers (Wiltshire uses a Staedtler pen). The teacher should provide images from books, magazines, and, of course, the internet. Some important icons are: Giza and the pyramids of Egypt in Africa; The Taj Mahal at Agra, India; Stonehenge in England; and the temples in Bali, Indonesia, "land of a thousand temples." In Europe, we have the Eiffel Tower to represent Paris, France; in England, there's the Clock Tower in London, affectionately known as Big Ben; in Rome, Italy, there still stands a symbol of the ancient city, the Colosseum; and in Greece we find the Parthenon. In Mexico you'll find another mighty pyramid — Chichen Itza on the Yucatan Peninsula. In North America, the Chrysler Building towers over New York City, and not very far away stands the Statue of Liberty — a national monument that represents a universal symbol of freedom and democracy. The teacher may add to or edit these suggestions.

Here's the tricky part (and Stephen's first word): paper. Ideally, the teacher would precut 5-6 foot lengths of white paper from a roll. This method assumes that the art room has the surfaces to accommodate the paper lengths. Confident students would divide into groups to discuss the placement of their choices, and then draw them directly on to the paper. To combine the various monuments and landmarks, students will consider compositional ideas for the sky and ground to create a unified whole and although this is a liberal interpretation of the concept of panorama, the finished piece will have a large scale, panoramic appearance! The finished product will take us around the world. Color may used at teacher's discretion. If watercolor is selected, the markers must the permanent non-toxic kind...or they will "bleed" the image. If other water sensitive markers are used, colored pencils or crayons are fine to use.

An alternative for students who might have a hard time with the previously mentioned approach: students will individually (or "buddy system" style) draw a straightforward image of their world landmarks on drawing paper. Pencils (first) and larger markers may work here. The teacher can then decide if students should cut out and glue their drawing on large paper or on a few display boards when finished. The end result will still take us through their visual accomplishments!

Top: Future Art Heroes at work! Above: Chuck Close at work on *John*, 1992. © Chuck Close, courtesy Pace Gallery

What do these Art Heroes have in common? They didn't let their conditions stop them. In fact, they "dance" with their disabilities! There are some artists with disabilities who may feel that their conditions are a creative gift, and don't particularly want to be known as brave. It is the observation of this author that life itself takes courage. We can't help but admire people who manage their lives with purpose and conviction, in the face of daunting circumstances. In Yiddish, this is called chutzpah, which is an attitude of indomitable determination. After watching my young students who were blind paint with success...how can that not impress me as an artist and teacher? To quote Simona Atzori (page 154), "Being able to solve problems depends on how you approach them." Practical, yes. Yet she and her art are dazzling. I do believe disability can fire up creativity...I still believe in courage...and in Art Spirit!

157

Glossary

albinism: A lack of pigmentation occurring primarily in skin, hair, and eyes. May include light sensitivity (photophobia). Often visual impairment accompanies albinism.

athetosis (athetoid): form of cerebral palsy marked by slow, involuntary movement.

audiologist: specialist who evaluates hearing disorders.

autism: referred to as autism spectrum disorder; Can include severe behavioral aberrations, most commonly marked by antisocial, communicative features.

behavioral therapy: a treatment that helps change potentially self-destructing behaviors. It is also called behavioral modification or cognitive behavioral therapy. Medical professionals use this type of therapy to replace bad habits with good ones.

bilateral: refers to two sides.

bipolar disorder (formerly manic-depressive disorder): characterized by mood swings of mania and depression.

blindisms: a set of behaviors that are often engaged by blind children, such as rocking back and forth, flicking fingers in front of eyes, rubbing hands in eyes, looking into lights, etc.

body parts: refers to arms, legs, head, and torso and their relationships to one another.

brain damage: congenital or acquired injury or disease that impairs a part of the brain causing learning disability, intellectual disability, or neurological dysfunction.

cerebral palsy: a central nervous system disorder often marked by erratic movement, awkward stumbling gait, and slurred speech.

closure (visual closure): a contour that is defined by an unbroken line, defining a shape by completing an outline.

cognitive: an intellectual thought process yielding awareness and knowledge.

concepts: characteristics that describe an idea, an abstract idea, or theme. Concepts include big/little, in/out, up/down.

congenital: a characteristic or condition existing since birth.

contracted muscles: shortened muscles, reducing body movement.

desensitize: a process in which materials or methods are gradually introduced to those who may have an aversion to them. As acceptance begins, quantity and exposure time are increased. This technique is useful in art with tactually defensive students. Other treatment of tactile defensiveness may be behavioral therapy.

developmental level: stage at which certain skills would normally be present or acquired.

directionality: orientation of the body to space around it; awareness of left/right, up/down, diagonals, etc.

discrimination: the ability to recognize differences and act upon that knowledge, as in sorting out information or materials.

Down Syndrome (formerly Mongolism): a chromosomal abnormality that includes retardation. Recognizable physical characteristics include a definite slant to the eyes, rounded features, and childlike appearance into adulthood.

dyslexia: lack of ability to read. Often characterized by "reversals." Printed page may appear as a scramble of incoherent data. A common learning disability.

ecolalia: a speech aberration in which "parroting" takes place. Ecolalic patterns are often a verbal "playback" of the words and spoken phrases of others.

eye-hand coordination: movement of the hand as directed by the eye and brain.

field loss: reduced visual range due to injury or disease, i.e., tunnel vision

fine motor: small movements with hands.

gross motor: refers to larger movements of the body.

hand-over-hand: technique in which teacher places his or her hand over the student's hand to teach a skill manually.

homebound: refers to a situation where students are unable to attend school due to short- or long-term illness or injury. Homebound teachers visit students in their homes or in the hospital placements to instruct them during their absence from school.

hyperactive: excess of energy; restless, easily distracted, i.e., unable to sit still.

hypoactive: absence of energy; lethargic, listless, very quiet.

inclusion: the practice of placing exceptional students in the nondisabled classes.

individualized education program (IEP): an educational plan, designed by teachers and other related professionals, recommending services and programs to meet students' special needs.

kinesthetic (kinesthetic sense): the sensory experience of the body's movement; physical awareness of the body's position in space.

laterality: awareness of one side of the body in relationship to space around it; a directional sense.

light perception: discrimination between light and dark.

"left-brain": theory that holds the left brain responsible for reading and verbal tasks.

legally blind: by definition, 20/200 vision or less in the better eye with glasses or lenses; a severe field loss, such as tunnel vision.

midline: the imaginary middle line of the body that defines the right and left halves.

multiply handicapped: a combination of two or more disabilities, often involving intellectual disability, physical, and/or motor dysfunction.

multisensory: unvolving several or all senses.

neurological: of or referring to the nervous system.

occupational therapist: specialist in providing activities designed to improve skills and movement.

olfactory: sense of smell.

paralysis: loss of function and/or movement of a part of the body, often involving sensation. Hemiplegia refers to paralysis affecting one side; paraplegia refers to paralysis below the waist; quadriplegia is a paralysis of both arms and legs.

parts-whole relationship: understanding the connections between a given part to the whole volume.

perceptual disability: impairment in the ability to accurately process and interpret written, auditory, sensorial, or visual information.

perseverate: difficulty in shifting from one activity to the next; repetition of language, action, or visual image.

physical therapist: rehabilitative specialist who provides exercises and techniques to improve health, skills, and physical abilities.

pincer grasp: grasp utilizing the thumb and index finger, i.e., the small finger movement needed to pick up a bead.

palmer grasp: grasp that does not utilize the thumb; objects are "raked in," using four fingers in a palm-down motion.

prosthesis: an artificial part used to replace an anatomical loss or amputation.

range of motion: extent to which a limb can move in all directions.

reversals: perceiving, reading, and writing words and letters backwards. For example, "was" appears as "saw;" b as d." A trait that is common to individuals diagnosed with dyslexia.

"right brain": the theory that the right side of the brain is the creative side, responsible for art and spatial comprehension.

rote learning: memorization through repetition, not dependent on intellectual process.

schizophrenia: serious personality disorder usually characterized by a psychotic break with reality.

seizure: also epilectic convulsion— an attack involving a series of contractions of the muscles. Grand mal (clonic-tonic) is a violent, jerking disturbance where muscular control and consiousness are lost. Petit mal may involve some twitching or loss of awareness, but is not usually violent in nature.

sensorial, sensory: of or pertaining to the senses.

sequencing: placement of materials, events, or information in logical progressive order.

sheltered workshop: an employment setting for individuals whose disabilities prevent them from entering the job mainstream. Workshop participants are usually paid modest salaries. Work often involves simple tasks.

spastic (spasticity): contracted, restricted, and stiff muscular movement.

stimmies: teacher slang for self-stimulatory behaviors, such as rocking, finger flicking in front of eyes.

tactile defensiveness: strong aversion to textures, materials, or even human touch. In art, common aversions include clay and paste.

verbal cueing (also prompting): helping students to perform an activity through teacher's talking, giving directions, and offering praise for correct responses. Reinforcement and repetition are often required.